UNTIL HE COMES

AMIR TSARFATI
& BARRY STAGNER

HARVEST PROPHECY
An Imprint of Harvest House Publishers

Unless otherwise indicated, all Scripture verses are taken from the New King James Version.® Copyright © 1982 by Thomas Nelson. Used with permission. All rights reserved.

Verses marked KJV are taken from the King James Version of the Bible.

Cover design by Bryce Williamson

Cover images © artplus / Getty Images

Interior design by KUHN Design Group

For bulk, special sales, or ministry purchases, please call 1-800-547-8979.
Email: CustomerService@hhpbooks.com

This logo is a federally registered trademark of the Hawkins Children's LLC. Harvest House Publishers, Inc., is the exclusive licensee of this trademark.

Until He Comes
Copyright © 2025 by Amir Tsarfati and Barry Stagner
Published by Harvest House Publishers
Eugene, Oregon 97408
www.harvesthousepublishers.com

ISBN 978-0-7369-9201-5 (pbk)
ISBN 978-0-7369-9202-2 (eBook)

Library of Congress Control Number: 2024952805

No part of this book may be used or reproduced in any manner for the purpose of training artificial intelligence technologies or systems.

All rights reserved. No part of this publication may be reproduced, stored in a retrieval system, or transmitted in any form or by any means—electronic, mechanical, digital, photocopy, recording, or any other—except for brief quotations in printed reviews, without the prior permission of the publisher.

Printed in the United States of America

25 26 27 28 29 30 31 32 33 / BP / 10 9 8 7 6 5 4 3 2 1

To the remnant, the true followers of Christ who live with boldness, patience, endurance, and conviction. Stand for the King, stand by His people, Israel, and stand strong in your faith, never forgetting that for those who fight the good fight there is a crown of righteousness laid up for you in heaven.

AMIR

To my sister Jan: You fought the good fight and finished the race. Well done, little sister. Love you!

BARRY

*The law of the L*ORD *is perfect, converting the soul;*
*the testimony of the L*ORD *is sure, making wise the simple;*
*the statutes of the L*ORD *are right, rejoicing the heart;*
*the commandment of the L*ORD *is pure, enlightening the eyes;*
*the fear of the L*ORD *is clean, enduring forever;*
*the judgments of the L*ORD *are true and righteous altogether.*
More to be desired are they than gold,
yea, than much fine gold;
sweeter also than honey and the honeycomb.
Moreover by them Your servant is warned,
and in keeping them there is great reward.

PSALM 19:7-11

ARE YOU LIVING WITH EAGER ANTICIPATION?

There are many reasons God included prophecies in the Bible. One of the more significant ones is that He does not want the future to be a mystery to us. He wants us to know that the chaos and wickedness so prevalent in the world around us won't last forever. There is coming a day when He will make all things right—a day when the Lord and Savior Jesus Christ will reign over all the earth.

The prophecies found in the Old and New Testaments are meant to encourage us to look ahead to the future. They're meant to fill us with anticipation and hope. By hope, we don't mean, "We hope this will happen." Rather, we point to the hope spoken of in 1 Peter 1:3-4: "According to His abundant mercy [God] has begotten us again to a living hope through the resurrection of Jesus Christ from the dead, to an inheritance incorruptible and undefiled and that does not fade away, reserved in heaven for you."

This hope is a *living* hope that is *guaranteed* by Christ's resurrection. Because He rose from the dead, we will too. We have an inheritance waiting in heaven for us. The hope we've been given is secure and eternal!

As we survey the hundreds of prophecies in Scripture, we become aware of an interesting fact: For every prophecy about Christ's first coming, there are eight about His second coming.

What does that tell us about the importance of Christ's return? Clearly, God wants the promise of the second coming to have a prominent place in our minds and hearts. These prophecies were given to make us a people who live in fervent and ongoing anticipation.

Philippians 3:20 says "our citizenship is in heaven, from which we also eagerly wait for the Savior, the Lord Jesus Christ." That's the spirit in which we have written this book—to stir up your eagerness for Christ's return.

As you read these daily devotions, may you find yourself saying, with the apostle John, "Even so, come, Lord Jesus!" (Revelation 22:20).

Amir and Barry

DAY 1

JESUS IN THE OLD TESTAMENT

There are many takeaways from the familiar encounter of the dejected disciples who walked with the resurrected Lord on the road to Emmaus the very day He rose from the dead. But there is one that stands above them all.

> Beginning at Moses and all the Prophets, He expounded to them in all the Scriptures the things concerning Himself (Luke 24:27).

What the two men expected from Jesus was popular among the Jews of their day. They were waiting for a Messiah who would deliver them from Roman domination.

The disciples who were on the road to Emmaus completely missed the majesty of what had just transpired because they were not looking for a Messiah who would die for their sins, but for a Messiah who would free them from Rome. They overlooked prophecies like the one in Isaiah 53:5: "He was wounded for our transgressions, He was bruised for our iniquities; the chastisement for our peace was upon Him, and by His stripes we are healed."

In times such as these, when governments are oppressing and restricting God's people, we need to be careful about falling into the same mistake as these two disciples by overlooking Jesus' first coming. The truth is that what we needed most has already happened:

> You, who once were alienated and enemies in your mind by wicked works, yet now He has reconciled in the body of His flesh through death, to present you holy, and blameless, and above reproach in His sight (Colossians 1:21-22).

Let's not overlook the wonder of Jesus' first coming and focus only on His second. Yes, He is coming again. Yes, we are coming with Him. Yes, He will rule and reign in righteousness. Yes, we will rule and reign with Him. But these things are true only because He first came as a Lamb, slain for you and me according to God's plans from before the foundation of the world (Ephesians 1:4).

DAY 2

GOD SPEAKS THROUGH MIRACLES

Other than the Lord Jesus Himself, few things in Scripture teach us more about the nature and character of God than that of His relationship with the nation of Israel. Through Israel, we have learned the Lord is our provider, protector, redeemer, enabler, deliverer.

As Romans 11:25-27 says,

> I do not desire, brethren, that you should be ignorant of this mystery, lest you should be wise in your own opinion, that blindness in part has happened to Israel until the fullness of the Gentiles has come in. And so all Israel will be saved, as it is written: "The Deliverer will come out of Zion, and He will turn away ungodliness from Jacob; for this is My covenant with them, when I take away their sins."

Many teach that the church has replaced Israel, and this is nothing more than the proverbial "cut off your nose to spite your face" mistake. In other words, if God cast off those whom He made unconditional and eternal promises to, then we are all in trouble. If He cast off Israel, then He could do the same with the church.

Many who do not believe that modern Israel is biblical Israel also believe that God chooses to save some and not others, and those whom He chooses to save cannot be lost because they are eternally secure. Yet they deny this very thing when it comes to the nation of Israel. If God doesn't change, then how can their belief that God has cast off modern Israel be true?

So take heart! Learn from Israel that God is faithful to His promises, and not even nearly 2,000 years outside of their national homeland can separate them from His unconditional and everlasting promises. That means we can know, with certainty, that when we blow it—and we all do—that God will remain faithful to us, for He cannot deny Himself.

You won't find a greater proof of this than the miracle of the regathered nation of Israel, in which God brought His people back into their national homeland.

DAY 3

THE TRUMPET OF THE RAPTURE

There is a lot of confusion surrounding the "last trumpet" Paul mentioned in 1 Corinthians 15:52. Note what 1 Thessalonians 4:16-18 says about "the trumpet of God":

> The Lord Himself will descend from heaven with a shout, with the voice of an archangel, and with the trumpet of God. And the dead in Christ will rise first. Then we who are alive and remain shall be caught up together with them in the clouds to meet the Lord in the air. And thus we shall always be with the Lord. Therefore comfort one another with these words.

Early Christians referred to the death of the body as sleep, based on their belief in the future bodily resurrection of the dead in Christ. Like sleep, the grave was temporary, and thus, they likened it to sleep.

The confusion over the last trumpet often results from mixing up the trumpet judgments of Revelation with the "voice of an archangel, and with the trumpet of God" that signals the end of the church age, as stated in 1 Thessalonians 4:16.

If the last trumpet in 1 Corinthians 15:52 is the same as the last of the seven trumpets in Revelation, then there is a problem with finding comfort in the words of Paul. There is also a problem that arises with other scriptures, such as Revelation 3:10: "Because you have kept My command to persevere, I also will keep you from the hour of trial which shall come upon the whole world, to test those who dwell on the earth."

The Lord doesn't say, "I'll keep you from the bowl judgments during the last part of the tribulation." Rather, He says He will keep you from the whole of the tribulation, the hour of trial coming on the whole world.

So, dear saints, take comfort in the fact that the unknown day and hour when the dead in Christ and those alive in Christ will meet Him in the air—to be with the Him forever—might be today!

DAY 4

THE CHURCH IN THE TRIBULATION?

While it is increasingly popular for Bible prophecy teachers to say that the church will go through the great tribulation, there is one point often overlooked that ends the debate. That point is found in Daniel 9:24:

> Seventy weeks are determined for your people and for your holy city, to finish the transgression, to make an end of sins, to make reconciliation for iniquity, to bring in everlasting righteousness, to seal up vision and prophecy, and to anoint the Most Holy.

The 70 weeks of Daniel are divided into three sections: 7 weeks and 62 weeks are connected, and the seventieth week is separate from the other 69. The first set of 7 years represents the time it took Nehemiah to rebuild and restore Jerusalem, or 49 years. The 62 weeks continue and take us up to the time of Jesus' triumphal entry into Jerusalem, shortly after which the Messiah was "cut off," meaning killed, but not for Himself, but for others (verse 26).

Here is the obvious and overlooked point: The church was not present on the earth during the first 69 weeks "determined" (meaning "carved out") for Daniel's people and the holy city, so why would the church be present during the seventieth week?

Consider what 2 Thessalonians 2:7-8 says: "The mystery of lawlessness is already at work; only He who now restrains will do so until He is taken out of the way. And then the lawless one will be revealed, whom the Lord will consume with the breath of His mouth and destroy with the brightness of His coming."

If the Antichrist cannot rise to power until the Holy Spirit's work through the church is removed, how can the church be present on the earth during any part of the seventieth week of Daniel? The answer is that we will not be here, but will be with Jesus in the Father's house until He returns to the earth, and we with Him!

DAY 5

THESE ARE DARK DAYS

Imagine that you have received a legitimate notification that you've inherited a large fortune. The notifying entity informs you that the time necessary to transfer the funds to you will take three to four weeks. Think about how this would affect your view of any current financial woes you happen to have.

Obviously, such a scenario rarely happens. However, as a Christian, what *has* happened to you is way more important than financial freedom. You have received notification from the King of heaven that a pain- and problem-free existence is in your future! Your feet will walk streets of gold, your eyes will behold ultimate beauty, your ears will hear unimaginable things, and most of all, you will see the King of kings and Lord of lords face to face!

As 1 John 3:2 says, "Beloved, now we are children of God; and it has not yet been revealed what we shall be, but we know that when He is revealed, we shall be like Him, for we shall see Him as He is."

This notification we have received is not spam, nor are there any catches or hidden fees. This is a promise from God, who cannot lie (Titus 1:2), that someday we will see Him as He is. As John 14:1-3 says,

> Let not your heart be troubled; you believe in God, believe also in Me. In My Father's house are many mansions; if it were not so, I would have told you. I go to prepare a place for you. And if I go and prepare a place for you, I will come again and receive you to Myself; that where I am, there you may be also.

Whether through death or the rapture, our future is nothing like our present. When we are absent from the body, we are present with the Lord (2 Corinthians 5:8). And until our future becomes our present and permanent experience, we would do well to remember that He who promised is faithful, and a bright future lies ahead for us through Him.

DAY 6

BE OF GOOD CHEER

Jesus, having told His disciples of the nearness of His death and His promise to return, said this: "These things I have spoken to you, that in Me you may have peace. In the world you will have tribulation; but be of good cheer, I have overcome the world" (John 16:33).

The Bible constantly points our thinking to the future to encourage us in the midst of the trials and tribulations of this life. Scripture never seeks to lessen the hard realities of life, but reminds us that life is more of a battleground than a playground.

It is easy to get tired of warfare in the present evil day and to want a time of peace. This is the very reason the Bible points our thinking ahead, to when peace comes and the Prince of Peace rules this war-weary world. Until then, we will have tribulations and trials. Yet, as Jesus told the disciples, in these things we can "be of good cheer," for He has overcome the world.

Here is what's interesting about this statement. Jesus was in the world when He said these words, but He had not yet overcome the world through the cross. This is a common practice in Scripture—to speak of the future as though it has already come to pass. For example, consider these words found in the great messianic chapter, Isaiah 53:

> He was wounded for our transgressions, He was bruised for our iniquities; the chastisement for our peace was upon Him, and by His stripes we are healed (verse 5).

Things that would happen 700 years later were written of as though they had already come to pass. He "was" wounded, He "was" bruised, the chastisement for our peace "was" upon Him. The reason for the literary practice is that this was God's plan from before the foundation of the world (Ephesians 1:4).

So remember: If God has promised or ordained something, nothing can stop it, and it is as good as done!

DAY 7

LEARN FROM THE FIG TREE, PART 1

While the subject is debated by some, the fact that national Israel is represented by the fig tree multiple times in Scripture is clear. Joel 1:7, Hosea 9:10, and Jeremiah 24 are a few examples. In Matthew 24:32, we read, "Now learn this parable from the fig tree: When its branch has already become tender and puts forth leaves, you know that summer is near."

Arbor-culturally, for the fig tree to put forth leaves was an indication of a change of seasons, and when the branch was tender, symbolizing new growth, and leaves sprouted, that meant summer was near, and the late harvest season (fall) was in the near future. The fig tree was also the last of the spring fruit trees to bud, so when it put forth leaves, people knew a seasonal change to summer was near.

When Jesus first came, the four spring feasts of Israel were fulfilled—Passover, the Feast of Unleavened Bread, the Feast of Firstfuits, and Pentecost. Summer would then arrive, and there would be no fulfillment of the fall feasts until after the fig tree became tender and put forth leaves, or until Israel became a nation again.

In Matthew 24:34, Jesus said, "Assuredly, I say to you, this generation will by no means pass away till all these things take place." That means that the fulfillment of the Feast of Trumpets, Yom Kippur (the Day of Atonement), and Sukkot (the Feast of Tabernacles) will happen within a single generation of the rebirth of the nation of Israel.

From 1882 to 1903, approximately 35,000 Jews immigrated to Israel, joining the pre-existing Jewish population, which, in 1880, numbered 26,000. Since then, 3,340,000 Jews have made Aliyah (ascent) to Israel, with millions now having been born in Israel. Thousands more have made Aliyah even in the midst of war.

Why is this continuing even during war and ever-worsening antisemitism? Because God is bringing His people back into the land for His name's sake (Ezekiel 36:22), and to prepare them for what is coming.

DAY 8

LEARN FROM THE FIG TREE, PART 2

In Zechariah 12:10, God said, "I will pour on the house of David and on the inhabitants of Jerusalem the Spirit of grace and supplication; then they will look on Me whom they pierced. Yes, they will mourn for Him as one mourns for his only son, and grieve for Him as one grieves for a firstborn."

The House of David and the inhabitants of Jerusalem are the same group of people, and they are not Muslims, nor Arabs, nor Palestinians. They are Jews. This promise will happen at the fulfillment of the Feast of Trumpets, the second coming, as the one-third of the Jews who have survived the great and terrible Day of the Lord will look upon the returning Christ Jesus as the Holy One of Israel, their Savior.

At the time of this writing, May 14, 1948, was more than 76 years ago, and while we do not know what the length of a "generation" is, we know the 76 years is a lot closer to the end of it than the beginning. As Matthew 24:36 says, "Of that day and hour no one knows, not even the angels of heaven, but My Father only."

The unknown day and hour can only be referring to the rapture of the church and not the second coming. The second coming is 42 30-day months, or 1,260 days after the abomination of desolation, which will occur at the midpoint of the tribulation. The rapture can occur at any moment, which is why the day or hour cannot be known.

Today, the Jews are back in the land, the nation is now approaching 80 years old, and the world is gathering against Israel, just as the Bible foretold. So let's keep our eyes lifted up and be listening for the sound of the trumpet and watching for His glorious appearing.

DAY 9

DON'T SEEK TO BE THE MAJORITY

At one time or another, we have all felt, to some degree, what Elijah did when he was running for his life from the wicked Jezebel, who had sworn to kill him. After a 40-day journey, he arrived at Mount Horeb and hid in a cave, and had this encounter with the Lord:

> There he went into a cave, and spent the night in that place; and behold, the word of the LORD came to him, and He said to him, "What are you doing here, Elijah?" So he said, "I have been very zealous for the LORD God of hosts; for the children of Israel have forsaken Your covenant, torn down Your altars, and killed Your prophets with the sword. I alone am left; and they seek to take my life" (1 Kings 19:9-10).

Elijah was then told by the Lord, "Yet I have reserved seven thousand in Israel, all whose knees have not bowed to Baal, and every mouth that has not kissed him" (1 Kings 19:18).

While we will never be the majority in this world, as citizens of heaven living on Earth, it should be noticeable that we are from somewhere else. If that is true about people from one country who transplant themselves into another, how much more should that be true of us?

We are not of this world, and there is, by comparison, a small remnant of us. This should affect us two ways: We should feel out of place here, like a resident alien, and others should be able to know "we're not from around here." If you are the only Christian at work, at school, or even in your own family, remember, you are not alone. There are others like you. Don't change to become part of the majority; remember, you're a sojourner and pilgrim. This world is not your home, and most importantly, remember that someday, we will all be going home.

DAY 10

FINISH THE RACE

The apostle Paul loved using metaphors to describe the Christian life. Among his favorites were a soldier, a boxer, and a runner. His use of each would be specific to a point he was making, but they each carried with them a common theme: commitment. The soldier must be committed to the battle, the boxer to their training, and the athlete to preparations for the race.

There is one way, however, that a runner is different: "Since we are surrounded by so great a cloud of witnesses, let us lay aside every weight, and the sin which so easily ensnares us, and let us run with endurance the race that is set before us" (Hebrews 12:1).

While the boxer and soldier may have weight training included in their preparations, the runner does not. Extra weight slows a runner, and the same is true for the spiritual application in Hebrews 12:1. Running a race with the weight of sin saps our endurance. The race that was once a joy becomes a burden when we become ensnared by other things. The Greek word translated "ensnares" means "to stand still."

In 1 Corinthians 9:24, the apostle Paul wrote, "Do you not know that those who run in a race all run, but one receives the prize? Run in such a way that you may obtain it."

Paul is not implying that if you break the rules, you will lose your salvation. But your endurance can come to a standstill if you burden yourself with weights and sins.

As we near the end of the race, the enemy will put many hurdles and obstacles in our way, and running through or jumping over them requires that we lay aside the things that hinder our ability to run.

We have all seen a long-distance runner who saves an extra kick for the end of the race, and we are at that stage in ours. So let's lay aside the endurance-robbing distractions of this life and run strong as we near the finish line and the imperishable crown that awaits us!

DAY 11

DON'T BE LUKEWARM, PART 1

While there is much debate among Bible scholars about whether or not the letters to seven churches in Revelation 2–3 present a timeline of church history, the historic parallels are undeniable. The seventh and final letter has some very interesting parallels to what is happening in our day.

> To the angel of the church of the Laodiceans write, "These things says the Amen, the Faithful and True Witness, the Beginning of the creation of God: 'I know your works, that you are neither cold nor hot. I could wish you were cold or hot. So then, because you are lukewarm, and neither cold nor hot, I will vomit you out of My mouth'" (Revelation 3:14-16).

The name *Laodicean* is a compound of two words that, when combined, mean "rule of the people." In other words, in the last days, the church will be ruled by the people. This is confirmed by 2 Timothy 4:3-5:

> The time will come when they will not endure sound doctrine, but according to their own desires, because they have itching ears, they will heap up for themselves teachers; and they will turn their ears away from the truth, and be turned aside to fables. But you be watchful in all things, endure afflictions, do the work of an evangelist, fulfill your ministry.

In the last days, people will defect from sound doctrine and replace it with teachings they want to hear. This tells us that many of the church's doctrines will be ruled by or decided on by the people.

In these times, when sound doctrine is not endured and people are lining up to listen to teachers who will tell them what they want to hear, Paul says to Timothy—and us—"Be watchful in all things." In other words, don't fall for this. Be consistent in your teaching, even though doing so will cause afflictions. Be careful about who and what you listen to. God has forewarned that not all that sounds good is good or even true.

DAY 12

DON'T BE LUKEWARM, PART 2

Notice what those in the early church committed to: "They continued steadfastly in the apostles' doctrine and fellowship, in the breaking of bread, and in prayers" (Acts 2:42).

But people will defect from doctrine in the last days. Instead of the apostles' teachings ("doctrine" means "teaching"), popular thought and cultural acceptance will define much of what is taught in the church, including fables that use biblical language yet have no biblical foundation. It is important to remember that the Bible has always demanded that people choose between truth and fables.

Jesus told the people in the church in Laodicea that their spiritual status was lukewarm, a condition the Lord described as sickening to Him. We recognize that hot water is good for cleansing and purifying, and cold water is refreshing. But lukewarm water is neither. This is the consequence of not enduring in sound doctrine—losing the ability to purify, cleanse, and refresh a dark and dying world.

In these days of full-scale defection from truth by false teachers, we must remain watchmen and fulfill our ministries of being evangelists, knowing that doing so requires us to endure afflictions. The time has come when false apostles and deceitful workers are presenting a message disguised as the light but is actually a message of darkness. We are seeing a prophetic, large-scale rejection of sound doctrine, which is being replaced with a message that cannot purify, cleanse, and refresh, but can only nauseate.

Joshua told the people of Israel,

> If it seems evil to you to serve the Lord, choose for yourselves this day whom you will serve, whether the gods which your fathers served that were on the other side of the River, or the gods of the Amorites, in whose land you dwell. But as for me and my house, we will serve the Lord (Joshua 24:15).

No matter what is happening in the church today, we must choose this day whom we will serve and not falter between fact and fable. We must decide to be for and not against the Lord by standing on and for His unchanging Word!

DAY 13

A DOT IN ETERNITY

While it is true that we all have our individual struggles and battles against our flesh as believers, it is also true that some battles are more common among us than others. Seeking first the kingdom of God and His righteousness is among them. One of the greatest battles against our flesh is for contentment.

Paul wrote, "Now godliness with contentment is great gain. For we brought nothing into this world, and it is certain we can carry nothing out. And having food and clothing, with these we shall be content" (1 Timothy 6:6-8).

The Greek word translated "contentment" means a perfect condition of life in which no aid or support is needed. We can better understand this type of contentment by considering what Paul wrote to the Philippians:

> Not that I speak in regard to need, for I have learned in whatever state I am, to be content: I know how to be abased, and I know how to abound. Everywhere and in all things I have learned both to be full and to be hungry, both to abound and to suffer need. I can do all things through Christ who strengthens me (Philippians 4:11-13).

This tells us that the contentment the Bible speaks of is more about attitude than circumstance. Contrary to what the Word of Faith movement teaches, it is not God's will that every Christian be wealthy. If this were true, why would the Spirit inspire Paul to tell us to be content with what we already have? Or why would Paul, a great man of faith, know what it is like to be abased, hungry, and suffer need?

Advertisers spend billions to convince us that we can't be content without their products, and that having the things of this world is the key to contentment. The Bible says differently—contentment doesn't come through things or circumstances, but rather, through godliness. Don't fall for the world's deceptions. Godliness with contentment is great gain.

DAY 14

THE JOY OF THE LORD IS OUR STRENGTH

While in the shadow of a pagan temple in Caesarea Philippi, Jesus asked the disciples a question: "Who do men say that I, the Son of Man, am?" (Matthew 16:13). This question was followed by a high point, and then immediately a low point, in Peter's years of traveling with Jesus during His earthly ministry.

> They said, "Some say John the Baptist, some Elijah, and others Jeremiah or one of the prophets." He said to them, "But who do you say that I am?" Simon Peter answered and said, "You are the Christ, the Son of the living God." Jesus answered and said to him, "Blessed are you, Simon Bar-Jonah, for flesh and blood has not revealed this to you, but My Father who is in heaven. And I also say to you that you are Peter, and on this rock I will build My church, and the gates of Hades shall not prevail against it" (Matthew 16:14-18).

In the very next exchange in Matthew 16, Peter was rebuked by the Lord for saying He shouldn't be crucified (verses 22-23). In one setting, Peter went from being told He had a revelation from the Father to being called Satan by the Son of God, which would certainly be a humbling moment for Peter.

Jesus then turned to the whole group and told them, "If you want to come after Me, then you must take up your cross and deny yourself" (see verse 24). If we read this in the context of the Lord's previous words to Peter—about being mindful of the things of men and not the things of God (verse 23)—we can understand the meaning of this statement more clearly.

In Matthew 6:33, we are commanded, "Seek first the kingdom of God and His righteousness, and all these things shall be added to you." While we may not have all the things some people do, no one will ever regret having sought first the kingdom of God. Doing this will have benefits that reach far beyond the things of this world and life.

DAY 15

KNOWN FOR OUR LOVE

In John 13:35, Jesus said, "By this all will know that you are My disciples, if you have love for one another."

What do the people on social media platforms know about us? That we are Jesus' disciples, or what we think of certain political candidates or policies? It is not that some of the issues that have distracted and divided the church are unimportant. But they cannot be allowed to take the place of sharing the gospel and loving each other as Christ loved the church. Whether you are from Israel or the United States, or any country that has free and legitimate election processes, the Christian voice needs to be heard. But again, these matters fall a distant second to the saving of the human soul.

That's why we should take Philippians 2:1-4 to heart:

> If there is any consolation in Christ, if any comfort of love, if any fellowship of the Spirit, if any affection and mercy, fulfill my joy by being like-minded, having the same love, being of one accord, of one mind. Let nothing be done through selfish ambition or conceit, but in lowliness of mind let each esteem others better than himself. Let each of you look out not only for his own interests, but also for the interests of others.

You may have heard about an acronym that we would do well to live by—it is JOY: Jesus, Others, You.

We live in a time when you could almost say, "Do whatever is the opposite of what the world says to do, and your life will be rich and full." When you put others first, reach others with truth, and esteem others better than yourself, your life will be all that God has intended it to be. The world says to look out for number 1, don't worry about other people, and know how important you are. Such thinking has given us the world we live in today.

God's way is always better and always leads to blessings!

DAY 16

WHAT WE MUST HOLD ON TO

As we await the glorious appearing of our great God and Savior Jesus Christ (Titus 2:13), there are a myriad of indications that the hour is late and the time of our redemption is near. We can certainly see indications that the church age is drawing to a close through all that Israel is experiencing.

There are also signs within the church that things are wrapping up, and sadly, those signs are negative. The Bible does not say there will be a huge revival or a global great awakening prior to the rapture. In fact, it says the opposite will happen.

> The time will come when they will not endure sound doctrine, but according to their own desires, because they have itching ears, they will heap up for themselves teachers; and they will turn their ears away from the truth, and be turned aside to fables (2 Timothy 4:3-4).
>
> [Know] this first: that scoffers will come in the last days, walking according to their own lusts, and saying, "Where is the promise of His coming? For since the fathers fell asleep, all things continue as they were from the beginning of creation" (2 Peter 3:3-4).

When people refuse to endure sound doctrine, there are consequences they will experience because they prefer to listen to teachers who will scratch their itching ears with teachings that aren't true. This will contribute to the scoffing that Peter says will be present in the last days. The Greek word translated as "scoffers" can also mean "mockers," and it is the same word that is used to describe false teachers.

To scoff or mock the teaching of the rapture of the church is to not endure sound doctrine. The rampant practice of mocking the rapture should remind us that time is running out, and the church age is rapidly coming to a close. Jesus is coming for us soon!

DAY 17

LIVING AND POWERFUL

The Bible is the best-selling book in the history of the world. Some 20 million Bibles are sold each year, with 1.66 million Bibles sold each month. That comes to 384,615 Bibles sold per week, and 54,945 Bibles sold every day.[1] United Bible Societies estimates five to seven billion copies have been printed in the last 1,500 years.

The Bible is also the only book that, when you finish it, you can immediately start again and not feel like you're reading the same old stuff or not learning anything new.

Hebrews 4:12 says this about the Bible: "The word of God is living and powerful, and sharper than any two-edged sword, piercing even to the division of soul and spirit, and of joints and marrow, and is a discerner of the thoughts and intents of the heart."

The Word of God is alive and filled with words of power that are relevant to generation after generation. It exposes man's thoughts and intents of the heart, and reveals man's desperate need for a Savior. The Bible not only reveals the human condition, it is also a revelation about the nature, character, and majesty of Almighty God.

The more we read the ultimate bestseller, the more we find out about God. It is the only book that can be read over and over and always seem new, even when you encounter age-old truths.

You may have heard the saying, "Seven days without reading the Bible makes one weak." This highlights another component of this matchless book: It is a source of strength and encouragement. It also answers the big questions of life: Where did we come from, what is the meaning of life, and is there life after death?

Don't let a week go by without taking advantage of the strength-enduing power of hiding God's Word in your heart. We cannot afford to be weakened in these last days—nor should we, especially when we have such a great source of strength.

DAY 18

IT IS GOD WHO FIGHTS FOR ISRAEL

Sadly, the vast majority of the church today sees the nation of Israel as nothing more than a political entity and not the fulfillment of prophecy. This requires a great deal of overlooking clear scriptures that make statements to the contrary.

One such passage is Ezekiel 36:22-24:

> Therefore say to the house of Israel, "Thus says the Lord GOD: 'I do not do this for your sake, O house of Israel, but for My holy name's sake, which you have profaned among the nations wherever you went. And I will sanctify My great name, which has been profaned among the nations, which you have profaned in their midst; and the nations shall know that I am the LORD,' says the Lord GOD, 'when I am hallowed in you before their eyes. For I will take you from among the nations, gather you out of all countries, and bring you into your own land.'"

Ezekiel 37 gives specific details about the gathering of God's chosen people back into their land. Chapters 38–39 record a battle that has no historic parallel and thus is in the future. Ezekiel 40–48 describes a temple that has yet to exist—the temple during the millennial reign of Christ on Earth. Chapter 48 says the 12 gates of the city will be named after the 12 tribes of Israel.

If God has cast off His chosen people, then why would the gates of the temple grounds from which Jesus will reign be named after the tribes of Israel? Why would He return to the Mount of Olives in Jerusalem, and why would our eternal home that descends from heaven be called the New Jerusalem?

None of what Ezekiel wrote was fulfilled at the time of Jesus. None of it was fulfilled for some 2,600 years, until May 14, 1948, when, as Isaiah 66:8 says, a nation was born in a day.

The nation of Israel is the most significant fulfillment of prophecy of modern times, and much more will soon follow!

DAY 19

CAN YOU HEAR HIS VOICE?

A pastor asked a church member what he thought the biggest problem in the church at large was: ignorance or apathy. The man replied, "I don't know, and I don't care."

That's not how it should be. Ephesians 5:8-10 says,

> You were once darkness, but now you are light in the Lord. Walk as children of light (for the fruit of the Spirit is in all goodness, righteousness, and truth), finding out what is acceptable to the Lord.

Our fictitious account about the pastor and church member makes a point, but the point is not fictitious at all. Many Christians today have little or no interest in finding out what is acceptable to the Lord.

Paul's words in Ephesians 5:8-10 reveal some lofty implications, including what is acceptable to the Lord. This information is accessible to us all. And there is a common resource through which we can attain this much-needed information. That source is the Word of God.

While it is true that God speaks to us directly as He answers our prayers and orders our steps, and that for some He speaks through dreams and visions, we have to recognize that all the things we think we hear from Him need to be confirmed by His Word, not by emotions or opinions. Matthew 6:33 says we're to "seek first the kingdom of God and His righteousness, and all these things shall be added to you."

How curious it is that we profess that God is omnipotent (all-powerful) and omniscient (all-knowing), and yet we don't always ask what His will is before making major decisions. This is choosing to live in ignorance and apathy. God's will and ways are always better and more personally beneficial to us.

God's ways are always best, and blessed are we when we walk in them.

DAY 20

THE WONDER OF HIS WORD

In Joshua 1:8-9, God said this to Joshua:

> This Book of the Law shall not depart from your mouth, but you shall meditate in it day and night, that you may observe to do according to all that is written in it. For then you will make your way prosperous, and then you will have good success. Have I not commanded you? Be strong and of good courage; do not be afraid, nor be dismayed, for the LORD your God is with you wherever you go.

In the same way the Lord was with Moses, so, too, would He be with Joshua. In this promise, the Lord gave Joshua the keys to a successful and prosperous life as Israel's leader: meditate on His word, and God would be with him wherever he went. This applies to us too.

Why settle for the opinions of family members or friends, or our feelings, when the Lord of all creation has promised good success and prosperity to those who do all that is written in His Word? That is not to say God cannot use others to speak to us. But even when that happens, we need to have His Word as a filter.

How sad it is for a believer to go through life not knowing or caring what the will of the Lord is. Nothing is more important than finding out what is acceptable to the Lord. Not knowing and not caring could be an indication of self-deception, as happened with the people in the church at Laodicea: "You say, 'I am rich, have become wealthy, and have need of nothing'—and do not know that you are wretched, miserable, poor, blind, and naked" (Revelation 3:17).

If you feel adrift on the sea of life, get into God's Word and find out what He has to say to you. His Word is more reliable than feelings and opinions, and the best thing about His Word is that all of it is true!

DAY 21

BE THE LIGHT

Paul's time in Corinth, as recorded in Acts 18, should serve as a reminder that the church has been called to infiltration, not isolation. Corinth was a pagan city steeped in sexual immorality. Yet God did not say, "Paul, get out of there—it's pagan." He said, "Paul, it's pagan, and that's right where I want to use you."

Acts 18:11-13 tells us what happened: Paul "continued there a year and six months, teaching the word of God among them. When Gallio was proconsul of Achaia, the Jews with one accord rose up against Paul and brought him to the judgment seat, saying, 'This fellow persuades men to worship God contrary to the law.'"

Whenever we try to reach a lost world, there will always be opposition. Jesus was criticized for being a friend of sinners, which was viewed as a negative by the religious elite. Yet sinners are the very ones God sends us to with the gospel. Paul wrote,

> I wrote to you in my epistle not to keep company with sexually immoral people. Yet I certainly did not mean with the sexually immoral people of this world, or with the covetous, or extortioners, or idolaters, since then you would need to go out of the world. But now I have written to you not to keep company with anyone named a brother, who is sexually immoral, or covetous, or an idolater, or a reviler, or a drunkard, or an extortioner—not even to eat with such a person (1 Corinthians 5:9-11).

It is interesting how often people in the church shun the ones they are supposed to reach and welcome the ones they are supposed to shun. We have been hearing of the wonderful work God is doing in places like Iran and Afghanistan, and we have all heard testimonies of people whom God picked up out of the gutters of life and saved and transformed them. The reason we hear such testimonies is that someone was willing to share the gospel with them.

Let that be our goal each day!

DAY 22

UNTIL HE COMES

Our world is growing more bizarre and evil by the day, and it would be easy to isolate ourselves from it and simply wait for the Lord to come and get us. Yet it was Jesus who said we are to "occupy till I come" (Luke 19:13 KJV). The other scenario we are watching unfold today is the "If you can't beat 'em, join 'em" kind of attitude, where the church is becoming more like the world.

God still says to us in these perilous times, "Do not be afraid…I have many people in this city" (Acts 18:9-10). In this statement to Paul, the Lord was implying there were many people He was going to save, and Paul should not view the city of Corinth as a potentially fruitless situation. The same is true for your city and neighborhood, or your workplace or school. God has you there for a reason.

Yet we live in a time during which our message is largely rejected by the masses. That does not mean God is no longer saving souls; nor does it mean there are no more people in your city He wants you to reach. As 2 Peter 3:9 says, "The Lord is not slack concerning His promise, as some count slackness, but is longsuffering toward us, not willing that any should perish but that all should come to repentance."

Remember, God will save many people during the tribulation, and He will save many more during the millennium. Yes, most will reject Him, and yes, masses will choose Satan over God at the end of the 1,000-year kingdom. But none of that changes the fact that God is still saving many even in the midst of perilous times and circumstances.

God wants to save people you encounter every day. And guess who He wants to use to reach them? You guessed it: That person who greets you in the mirror every day is the someone He has called to go out and preach the gospel.

DAY 23

BEWARE OF APOSTASY

When the Bible describes something about the future that is of a spiritual or moral nature, it is not only foretelling the existence of that spiritual or moral climate, but it implies the prevalence of that climate during that time.

Jesus said that when He is about to return, things will be as they were in "the days of Noah" (Matthew 24:37). In those days, the thoughts and intents of man's heart were "only evil continually" (Genesis 6:5). This was the predominant way of thinking in Noah's day, and that is true about our day too.

Second Timothy 4:3-4 says, "The time will come when they will not endure sound doctrine, but according to their own desires, because they have itching ears, they will heap up for themselves teachers; and they will turn their ears away from the truth, and be turned aside to fables."

A time will come when sound doctrine will be replaced with fables taught by teachers who have turned away from the truth, and that problem will be predominant in the church as well. We live in just such a time.

We need not look too hard or far to see that what is popular in the "church" today is not sound doctrine. Rather, people prefer whatever makes them feel good or touches their emotions. This includes words about prosperity and health through faith.

We hear many words in churches today about how to improve our lives rather than how to arrive in heaven in the afterlife. God seems to have become secondary, while the people in the seats have become the primary subject of the messages offered.

In Psalm 119:11, a psalmist who was diligent about following God wrote, "Your word I have hidden in my heart, that I might not sin against You."

If you never or seldom hear the Word, how can you hide it in your heart? Faith comes by hearing the Word of God. Be careful what, and therefore who, you listen to in these last days, because Jesus said false teachers will abound.

DAY 24

SHADOW OR SUBSTANCE?

While most would never recognize or even acknowledge it, most people love religion. Religion is defined as "a specific fundamental set of beliefs and practices generally agreed upon by a number of persons or sects," "usually involving devotional and ritual observances, and often containing a moral code governing the conduct of human affairs."[2]

People love religion because usually religion has requirements, and fulfilling requirements creates a sense of deservedness—that is, because I did this, I now deserve or have earned an associated reward. All people are religious to some degree, including atheists who say there is no God. They are adherents to a system of beliefs, and those beliefs dictate their definitions of right and wrong. Even if they say, "There is no right or wrong," that still implies that those who believe there is are in error, and this establishes their moral code.

The people of Israel are a prime example of love for a religious system. God had something far better in mind for them than a system of observances and rituals. God desired a relationship with them. In John 5:39, Jesus said, "You search the Scriptures, for in them you think you have eternal life; and these are they which testify of Me."

While the people of Israel had the advantage of having the "oracles of God" committed to their care (Romans 3:2), it wasn't this responsibility and their faithfulness to it that gained them favor with God. Nor did it make them deserve His blessings.

Many in the church have fallen into the same trap. They settle for shadows rather than the relationship God desires. This is an easy trap to fall into because man loves religion. People do good works because doing so makes them feel good. It makes them feel worthy of their own positive life experience or even eternal rewards.

Thankfully, the Bible makes it clear that salvation is not of works but is the gift of God (Ephesians 2:8-9) for as many as received Him (John 1:12)!

DAY 25

GOD'S CHOSEN PEOPLE

What did God mean when He told the Israelites, "You are a holy people to the Lord your God; the Lord your God has chosen you to be a people for Himself, a special treasure above all the peoples on the face of the earth" (Deuteronomy 7:6)?

The Lord was not trying to set up a religious system to make the people of Israel feel better about themselves. He loved them, He wanted a relationship with them, and He set His love on them. The same is true today for the church—in 1 Peter 2:9, we are called "chosen." Like with Israel, God is not looking to set up a religious system that creates followers who deserve heaven because of their efforts. Rather, God so loved the world He gave His only begotten Son to reestablish what was broken in the garden by sin—a relationship that could be restored only by the shedding of innocent blood (Leviticus 17:11).

Then in 2 Thessalonians 2:15, we read, "Therefore, brethren, stand fast and hold the traditions which you were taught, whether by word or our epistle."

There is value in our traditions, but we must guard against letting them become the source of our sense of worth or deservedness. We have our traditions, rituals, and even cultural observances that we practice, but as the church, we have been given only two ordinances that we are to maintain in every culture and age. They are communion and baptism, and both speak of Christ's death, which is the only means by which the broken relationship between man and God can be restored.

This is what separates the Christian faith from all other religions. The Christian faith is not centered on what *we* do to become pleasing to God, but rather, on what was done *for* us, which pleased God and imputed Christ's righteousness to us.

Salvation is a gift, and like all gifts, it is given, not earned. Thanks be to God for His matchless gift (2 Corinthians 9:15)!

DAY 26

OUR GREAT HIGH PRIEST

There is a movement in the church today known as the Hebrew Roots movement, in which "Torah observant Christians" seek to keep the law and observe the feast days and ordinances given exclusively to Israel. This is an exchange of substance for shadows, much like preferring a picture over the actual person in the picture.

Hebrews 9:11-12 says, "Christ came as High Priest of the good things to come, with the greater and more perfect tabernacle not made with hands, that is, not of this creation. Not with the blood of goats and calves, but with His own blood He entered the Most Holy Place once for all, having obtained eternal redemption."

The law was a minister of death; it condemned all as guilty under sin, and there was no provision for salvation within it. It pointed to man's need for a Savior who is Christ the Lord. For all who believe, Jesus Christ came to replace the rituals of religion with a personal relationship.

Here's what Galatians 2:20-21 says:

> I have been crucified with Christ; it is no longer I who live, but Christ lives in me; and the life which I now live in the flesh I live by faith in the Son of God, who loved me and gave Himself for me. I do not set aside the grace of God; for if righteousness comes through the law, then Christ died in vain.

Paul saw the work of Christ on the cross as personal and transformational. We would do well to think as he and John the apostle did, who called himself the disciple whom Jesus loved (John 13:23). Let's not settle for the shadows of religion when the substance of what we believe is an intimate relationship with Jesus Christ. He loves you and gave Himself for you. You are a disciple whom Jesus loves!

Don't settle for a relationship with a picture when the One who loves you wants to have a personal relationship with you.

EAGERLY AWAITING

Of the ten times we find the English word *eagerly* in the New Testament, six of those times it is used in relationship to the return of Christ. In all six instances, it is paired with the word *wait* or *waiting*, and it is actually the Greek word translated as "wait" that is in the manuscripts. The word is paired in English translations with *eagerly* because the Greek word for wait means "to expect fully."

Think about what all this means to our outlook and priorities in life. If you "expect fully" that Jesus could come for the church today, your life will be lived accordingly, and your attitude will be impacted greatly. If you "expect fully" that today you could receive a new body when Christ appears, the aches and pains of life will not be so consuming.

Imagine what life would be like if we lived every day fully expecting the rapture (which we should), and not thinking that it is someday in the future. How would that impact our interactions with other people? Who would we be desperate to share the Lord with, and what relationship would we seek to repair or restore? What activity would we repent of, or what wrong would we make right? Eagerly waiting for the glorious appearing of our great God and Savior Jesus Christ is far different than simply acknowledging that it will happen someday.

The rapture is coming. Second Peter 3:9 says,

> The Lord is not slack concerning His promise, as some count slackness, but is longsuffering toward us, not willing that any should perish but that all should come to repentance.

If the Lord doesn't meet us in the air today, there are reasons beyond our understanding for why that is the case. However, that means tomorrow the rapture is even more likely to happen. And thus, with each passing day, we should fully expect the rapture more and more. One day we will awaken, and it will be that day.

DAY 28

BORN OF THE SPIRIT

We live in a very label-conscious world. Clothing manufacturers print their names on or sew their labels on the outside of a garment so others can see your brand of clothes. Car emblems "label" the owner with a certain financial status or environmental conscience level. Computer users are labeled as either a PC or Mac person. Your political label assigns you to a category of people of a certain mindset regarding social, economic, and moral issues.

This practice has even made its way into the church, where there are denominational names and descriptive labels used to identify what kind of Christianity you follow.

However, just as there are visible outward expressions through skin tones, physical features, and dialects, there is only one race of people, and that is the human race (Acts 17:26). So, too, there is only one kind of Christian, and that is a born-again Christian. Jesus affirmed that in John 3:1-3:

> There was a man of the Pharisees named Nicodemus, a ruler of the Jews. This man came to Jesus by night and said to Him, "Rabbi, we know that You are a teacher come from God; for no one can do these signs that You do unless God is with him." Jesus answered and said to him, "Most assuredly, I say to you, unless one is born again, he cannot see the kingdom of God."

Consider all the "labels" Jesus brushes aside in this passage. Nicodemus is identified as a Pharisee, a label of his religious status. He is also a ruler, a label that indicates his social status. His ethnicity is identified as being "of the Jews." He even comes to Jesus and says that he recognizes Jesus is different than all other teachers, and that He has come from God, and that God is with Him.

Yet in spite of all these impressive credentials, Jesus says to Nicodemus, "You must be born again."

DAY 29

NATURAL OR SUPERNATURAL?

First Corinthians 2:14 says that "the natural man does not receive the things of the Spirit of God, for they are foolishness to him; nor can he know them, because they are spiritually discerned."

Some countries today enter a religious affiliation on birth certificates and driver's licenses. But the truth is, as Jesus said to Nicodemus in John 3, no one is saved by their first birth—no one is born a Christian. You must be born again. That's why Paul said the natural man cannot comprehend the things of God; they can be discerned only by those who are born of the Spirit. Paul also said this:

> Now I plead with you, brethren, by the name of our Lord Jesus Christ, that you all speak the same thing, and that there be no divisions among you, but that you be perfectly joined together in the same mind and in the same judgment. For it has been declared to me concerning you, my brethren, by those of Chloe's household, that there are contentions among you. Now I say this, that each of you says, "I am of Paul," or "I am of Apollos," or "I am of Cephas," or "I am of Christ." Is Christ divided? Was Paul crucified for you? Or were you baptized in the name of Paul? (1 Corinthians 1:10-13).

Paul warns the church against sectarianism by reminding us that there is only one church, of which Christ is the head. The one church is comprised of people of various social, ethnic, and financial statuses who share one common feature: They have been born again.

Some say baptism must be done this way or that; others declare their denomination has it right and all others are wrong. But the question is not whether you are Baptist, Presbyterian, Greek Orthodox, or Coptic, or any other human label. The question is, Are you born again? According to Jesus, who is still the head of the church, you must be, for those who are not cannot enter the kingdom of heaven.

DAY 30

THE PROPHETIC WORD

In a world hungry for information about the future or the past, it is amazing the lengths people will go, only to end up with unreliable and fabricated information. Yet there is a resource available to them that they could access for free online or by purchasing a copy of it. This resource has a 100-percent accuracy track record: the Bible.

> We have the prophetic word confirmed, which you do well to heed as a light that shines in a dark place, until the day dawns and the morning star rises in your hearts; knowing this first, that no prophecy of Scripture is of any private interpretation, for prophecy never came by the will of man, but holy men of God spoke as they were moved by the Holy Spirit (2 Peter 1:19-21).

One question often posed about spiritists and psychics is, How are they able to tell people details about the past or help police find a crime scene or a hidden grave? The answer is quite simple: The devil was present in the past and he can reveal information to those who tap into the realm of darkness so they can speak about the past with great specificity. Where the spiritists and psychics run into problems is with the future. Satan can make educated guesses about the future, but he cannot reveal details like God can.

The Bible, however, accurately names people, places, nations, and events hundreds or thousands of years in advance because the authors were writing under the inspiration of the Holy Spirit.

People today seek out spiritists for information they want to know. The Bible won't tell us sports scores or lotto numbers in advance—things we may wish we could know. But it will tell us everything we *need* to know about things that are far more important, including how to have a right relationship with God and spend eternity in heaven. How do we know that information is accurate and correct? We have the prophetic Word confirmed through fulfillment.

DAY 31

ALL THINGS WORK TOGETHER FOR GOOD, PART 1

It has frequently been said that the three primary rules of Bible interpretation are context, context, and context. Here's an example: "I can do all things through Christ who strengthens me" (Philippians 4:13).

Many take this to mean that because we know Christ, we can, by faith, do anything or have anything we set our mind to. The context, however, is this:

> Not that I speak in regard to need, for I have learned in whatever state I am, to be content: I know how to be abased, and I know how to abound. Everywhere and in all things I have learned both to be full and to be hungry, both to abound and to suffer need (Philippians 4:11-12).

Paul says, "Through Christ's strength, I can do poverty, and I can do riches. I can do fullness, and I can do hunger. And I can be abased [humiliated], and I can do abundance."

Context is also critical for another famed yet often misapplied passage: "We know that all things work together for good to those who love God, to those who are the called according to His purpose" (Romans 8:28).

Many love to quote this verse when hard times come. While they might mean well, the interpretation can be misleading. Context is established by reading the surrounding verses. Case in point: If you were to keep reading Romans 8, you would find this: "For Your sake we are killed all day long; we are accounted as sheep for the slaughter" (verse 36).

This tells us that the good in view in Romans 8:28 is the greater good. It is not saying that because something bad happened to us, something good will come from it to cancel out the bad. Rather, it is saying that ultimately, no matter what happens in life, there is good waiting for us in the end, when we are finally in the presence of the Lord.

DAY 32

ALL THINGS WORK TOGETHER FOR GOOD, PART 2

The pain that comes from the loss of a child or the untimely death of a spouse never goes away. They are lifelong pains and sorrows that may lessen over the years, but the pain never goes away completely in this life. That won't happen until later:

> God will wipe away every tear from their eyes; there shall be no more death, nor sorrow, nor crying. There shall be no more pain, for the former things have passed away (Revelation 21:4).

Someday, no more tears, death, or sorrow and a pain-free existence will be ours forever. Until then, Christ will strengthen us to do and endure all things. Thus, we must remember that no matter what comes our way, there is an ultimate good that awaits us in the future.

Until that time, consider role models like Joseph, who was betrayed and sold to Midianite slave traders by his brothers, lied about then imprisoned by Potiphar, forgotten by those he had helped while in prison, yet eventually found himself to be the second-most-powerful man in all of Egypt.

Later in life, with his brothers atoning before him, Joseph said this: "As for you, you meant evil against me; but God meant it for good, in order to bring it about as it is this day, to save many people alive" (Genesis 50:20).

After years of negative experiences, Joseph could now see that what was intended as evil against him led to the saving alive of many people because of the position he wound up in. But not all hard things in life lead to temporal good things. Yet for those who love God, all things will lead to ultimate good when we see the Lord as He is and we are like Him (1 John 3:2).

So when life brings events or circumstances that don't make sense or that hurt us deeply, remember, there is an ultimate good that awaits us all.

DAY 33

BE READY

The subject of Bible prophecy continues to be a hotly debated topic within the church. Some see the Bible's prophecies as already fulfilled, others see them as allegorical lessons, but the most accurate way to approach the study of Bible prophecy is to see prophecy as history written in advance. Consider these passages written by John:

> I was in the Spirit on the Lord's Day, and I heard behind me a loud voice, as of a trumpet, saying, "I am the Alpha and the Omega, the First and the Last," and, "What you see, write in a book and send it to the seven churches which are in Asia: to Ephesus, to Smyrna, to Pergamos, to Thyatira, to Sardis, to Philadelphia, and to Laodicea" (Revelation 1:10-11).

> After these things I looked, and behold, a door standing open in heaven. And the first voice which I heard was like a trumpet speaking with me, saying, "Come up here, and I will show you things which must take place after this." Immediately I was in the Spirit; and behold, a throne set in heaven, and One sat on the throne (Revelation 4:1-2).

What exactly happened with John is also a matter of debate. Was he transported into the future, or did he see visions of the future revealed through God's supernatural power? Either way, what's important is that John "saw" these things—they were literal events. The reason that is important is it tells us that the content of Revelation cannot *not* happen. John went to, or saw, history in advance.

The fig tree has put forth leaves (the Jews are a nation again), according to the Scriptures. People are buying and selling and going on with their lives as though judgment is not near or imminent, just as Jesus said (Matthew 24:37-38). Someday, one will be taken to heaven in a moment and the twinkling of an eye, and another will be left here on Earth to face the tribulation, just as it was written.

Are you ready for departure?

DAY 34

DO YOU HAVE A HEART FOR ISRAEL?

As we watch our world spiral downward into Nazi-era antisemitism, we need to recognize that the side effect of this will be and is a disdain, and eventually hatred, for those who support the nation of Israel. This will turn into a hatred of those who not only love the Jews but love the King of the Jews, Jesus of Nazareth. This brings Revelation 6:9-11 to mind:

> When He opened the fifth seal, I saw under the altar the souls of those who had been slain for the word of God and for the testimony which they held. And they cried with a loud voice, saying, "How long, O Lord, holy and true, until You judge and avenge our blood on those who dwell on the earth?" Then a white robe was given to each of them; and it was said to them that they should rest a little while longer, until both the number of their fellow servants and their brethren, who would be killed as they were, was completed.

As we watch the rise of global antisemitic thinking and behavior, we must remember that this is not a coincidence nor happenstance. Rather, it is the precursor to what John prophesied will happen during the tribulation. We also know that at the end of the tribulation, those who are still alive on the earth will be judged by Jesus based on their treatment of the Jews. As Genesis 12:3 says, "I will bless those who bless you, and I will curse him who curses you; and in you all the families of the earth shall be blessed."

This is not saying that loving Israel saves a person. But it does tell us what attitude the saved should have toward Israel. It is completely inconsistent to say you love the King of the Jews but despise the Jews of the King. So don't let the ignorant antisemites of our day bully you into silence. If God has not cast off Israel—and He hasn't—we shouldn't either.

DAY 35

JESUS PROVES THE BIBLE IS INSPIRED

One of the main assaults on the inspiration and infallibility of Scripture is that man wrote the Bible. Yet any student of Scripture knows this is not even remotely possible. Forty authors wrote the Bible over a span of 1,500 years, and, for the most part, they never met or talked to any of the others. The fact they wrote at different times from different places yet provided a consistent message is what makes human authorship a virtual impossibility.

One person alone proves the divine nature of the Bible, and that is Jesus Christ. One author said He would be born in Bethlehem (Micah 5:2). Another author said He would be called out of Egypt (Hosea 11:1). Another said He would ride into Jerusalem on a donkey (Zechariah 9:9), while still another said He would be killed (Daniel 9:26). Yet another wrote He would be despised and rejected by men, beaten with stripes yet stay silent, die among the wicked, and yet be buried with the rich (Isaiah 53). And the list goes on and on.

The person of Jesus of Nazareth proves the divine inspiration of the Bible! All the prophecies written by these various authors concerning Him came to pass, and there is no man or group of men who could have offered such specific insights into the future and given so many accurate details hundreds of years in advance unless God had inspired what they had written.

Psalm 1:1-3 says this about those who trust the Bible as God's Word:

> Blessed is the man who walks not in the counsel of the ungodly, nor stands in the path of sinners, nor sits in the seat of the scornful; but his delight is in the law of the LORD, and in His law he meditates day and night. He shall be like a tree planted by the rivers of water, that brings forth its fruit in its season, whose leaf also shall not wither; and whatever he does shall prosper.

This is as true today as when it was written by King David more than 3,400 years ago.

DAY 36

CHOOSE ETERNAL LIFE

God's righteous judgment is a stumbling block to many in our day. We live in a world in which many say that the behaviors and choices people make should be accepted by all. For someone to have any moral objection to a person's choices or behavior is deemed to be hatred and bigotry. Because of this, God is rejected by many.

This brings up a curious irony: Those who reject God do so by rendering judgment on Him for His moral standards over His own creation, and they ignore the fact that God has made a way for people to be saved: "As many as received Him, to them He gave the right to become children of God, to those who believe in His name: who were born, not of blood, nor of the will of the flesh, nor of the will of man, but of God (John 1:12-13).

Receiving Him and becoming children of God allows us to escape His judgment. This, however, does not mean God turns a blind eye to our errors. Nor does He compromise His righteous judicial nature by overlooking our transgressions and sins. Isaiah 53:5-6 explains who took that judgment for us:

> He was wounded for our transgressions, He was bruised for our iniquities; the chastisement for our peace was upon Him, and by His stripes we are healed. All we like sheep have gone astray; we have turned, every one, to his own way; and the LORD has laid on Him the iniquity of us all.

Judgment day is coming for everyone, and in this life, we must choose which judgment awaits us: the one where we stand before Jesus and have our works rewarded, or the one where we stand before the Maker of heaven and earth and have our actions judged against God's holy standards.

If you haven't made that choice yet, make it today. For the choice to believe God and have righteousness accounted to you is the only way to have your name written in the Lamb's Book of Life.

DAY 37

THE JEWS ARE THE KEY TO BIBLE PROPHECY

The whole of the last-days prophetic scenario centers on Israel and the Jews, both the people and the land God has given to them. This tells us that when we see antisemitism growing against the Jewish people and global calls for dividing the land God gave them, we know we are watching prophecy being fulfilled.

Zechariah 12:3 tells us, "It shall happen in that day that I will make Jerusalem a very heavy stone for all peoples; all who would heave it away will surely be cut in pieces, though all nations of the earth are gathered against it."

Then in verse 10, God says, "I will pour on the house of David and on the inhabitants of Jerusalem the Spirit of grace and supplication; then they will look on Me whom they pierced. Yes, they will mourn for Him as one mourns for his only son, and grieve for Him as one grieves for a firstborn."

There is a progression here that was once not possible. The Jews were outside their homeland, and there was no Jerusalem for the world to gather against. But now there is, and for the past 77 years, since the rebirth of Israel in 1948, the prophetic wheels have been moving toward the outpouring of God's Spirit on His people and the Lord fighting as He fights in the day of battle.

All of this tells us that it is more likely now than ever that the fulfillments of the destruction of Damascus, the Ezekiel War, the seventieth week of Daniel, and the words above from Zechariah are on the near horizon. And that means something else is very near:

> The Lord Himself will descend from heaven with a shout, with the voice of an archangel, and with the trumpet of God. And the dead in Christ will rise first. Then we who are alive and remain shall be caught up together with them in the clouds to meet the Lord in the air. And thus we shall always be with the Lord (1 Thessalonians 4:16-17).

DAY 38

IN THE MIDST OF THE STORM

All of us have faced trials and temptations, and one of the common questions most Christians have wrestled with at some point is, Why do bad things happen to God's people? Isaiah gives us a powerful reminder of this reality when he wrote, "'No weapon formed against you shall prosper, and every tongue which rises against you in judgment you shall condemn. This is the heritage of the servants of the Lord, and their righteousness is from Me,' says the LORD" (Isaiah 54:17).

Isaiah does not promise the absence of weapons fired against us, but the Lord does promise through the prophet that the weapons will not achieve their intended end—they will not prosper. We see this proven time and again throughout Israel's history with nations like Babylon:

> Thus says the LORD: After seventy years are completed at Babylon, I will visit you and perform My good word toward you, and cause you to return to this place. For I know the thoughts that I think toward you, says the LORD, thoughts of peace and not of evil, to give you a future and a hope. Then you will call upon Me and go and pray to Me, and I will listen to you. And you will seek Me and find Me, when you search for Me with all your heart. I will be found by you, says the LORD, and I will bring you back from your captivity; I will gather you from all the nations and from all the places where I have driven you, says the LORD, and I will bring you to the place from which I cause you to be carried away captive (Jeremiah 29:10-14).

None of us are exempt from the storms of life, and at times, it will seem like our attackers and oppressors have the upper hand. And yet we can know that the weapons formed against us—God's servants—will not prosper, says the Lord.

DAY 39

YOU ARE A NEW CREATION

If a list were to be compiled of "life verses" submitted by Christians from around the world, there are some passages that would surely make the top-ten list of favorites:

> If anyone is in Christ, he is a new creation; old things have passed away; behold, all things have become new (2 Corinthians 5:17).
>
> I have been crucified with Christ; it is no longer I who live, but Christ lives in me; and the life which I now live in the flesh I live by faith in the Son of God, who loved me and gave Himself for me (Galatians 2:20).
>
> I can do all things through Christ who strengthens me (Philippians 4:13).

This trio of pinnacle verses would almost certainly be among those on the list, as well as a myriad of others. There is one verse that isn't likely to be among the familiar favorites, but it captures the essence of all the passages that do. For those who see the famed passage of Philippians 4:13 as a banner to hang over their lives, they need to make sure they read verse 12, which sets the context for it: "I know how to be abased, and I know how to abound. Everywhere and in all things I have learned both to be full and to be hungry, both to abound and to suffer need" (Philippians 4:12).

If we read into Philippians 4:13 that we can successfully do anything we want or attempt through Christ, we are going to be disappointed. But if we view the verse from the perspective that we can face anything that comes our way through Christ strengthening us, we will experience the true meaning of the verse.

Here and now, we are called to walk by faith and not by sight. However, one day, we'll walk by sight and not by faith. We will see the Lord face to face as He is, and be with Him forever.

DAY 40

THE LAST HOUR

We have noted that Jesus as the Messiah of Israel is clearly presented in the Old Testament via passages such as Isaiah 53. It is also worthy of mention that while prophecies concerning the first coming of the Messiah abound, there are far more prophecies about His second coming in both testaments.

We find in Scripture direct statements about Christ's return, descriptions of the cultural and the spiritual climate on Earth when His return is near, and there is even an entire book in the New Testament in which Christ is unveiled in all His matchless glory, titled "The Revelation of Jesus Christ."

When Jesus' time on Earth was nearing its end, He told His disciples,

> Let not your heart be troubled; you believe in God, believe also in Me. In My Father's house are many mansions; if it were not so, I would have told you. I go to prepare a place for you. And if I go and prepare a place for you, I will come again and receive you to Myself; that where I am, there you may be also (John 14:1-3).

Not only did Jesus directly state He would return, He also stated in the Olivet Discourse the signs that would indicate His return was near. Among those signs are spiritual deception, complacency, and apathy: "As in the days before the flood, they were eating and drinking, marrying and giving in marriage, until the day that Noah entered the ark, and did not know until the flood came and took them all away, so also will the coming of the Son of Man be" (Matthew 24:38-39).

Matthew 24 tells us that an indifference to the signs that judgment is near will be birthed out of a season of prosperity, as implied by Jesus' words about people "eating and drinking, marrying and giving in marriage." In other words, the things of God will take second place in the last hours of the church age. Jesus is coming soon!

DAY 41

IT'S ALL ABOUT THE RESURRECTION

There are many events from the past that people would categorize as historically significant, some of them being negative like war or the assassinations of leaders. Others would note positive events, like the discovery of a medicine or cure to treat a disease, or mankind landing on the moon.

But there is one event that is unequalled in importance and impact, and that is the resurrection of Jesus of Nazareth from the dead.

> If the dead do not rise, then Christ is not risen. And if Christ is not risen, your faith is futile; you are still in your sins! Then also those who have fallen asleep in Christ have perished. If in this life only we have hope in Christ, we are of all men the most pitiable. But now Christ is risen from the dead, and has become the firstfruits of those who have fallen asleep. For since by man came death, by Man also came the resurrection of the dead. For as in Adam all die, even so in Christ all shall be made alive. But each one in his own order: Christ the firstfruits, afterward those who are Christ's at His coming (1 Corinthians 15:16-23).

Early Christians referred to death as sleep. They knew that because Christ rose from the dead, they would too. So they saw the death of the body as a temporary condition.

The resurrection of Jesus is not just another historical event, and the empty tomb assures us that we are not "still in [our] sins"! Paul went as far as to say that if the dead do not rise, the Christian life is a pitiful existence. Think about it: persecution, tribulation, rejection, ostracization, and for some, even death—all because you know Christ. And then after death nothing but a cessation of existence? If that were true, it would be a pitiable existence indeed.

But Christ has risen from the dead, and we will live forevermore through Him.

DAY 42

ISRAEL AND THE TRIBULATION

The seventieth week of Daniel, also known as the time of Jacob's trouble and the tribulation, is a decisive—if not the most decisive—argument for the pretribulation rapture of the church.

> Seventy weeks are determined for your people and for your holy city, to finish the transgression, to make an end of sins, to make reconciliation for iniquity, to bring in everlasting righteousness, to seal up vision and prophecy, and to anoint the Most Holy (Daniel 9:24).

There are six things that are prophesied to happen during the 70 seven-year periods spoken of here that are in relation to Daniel's people, the Jews, and the holy city, Jerusalem.

To "finish the transgression" means to bring Israel's apostasy to an end. To "make an end of sins" means to bring sin under final judgment. To "make reconciliation for iniquity" points to the cross of Christ. This will usher in "everlasting righteousness"—vision and prophecies concerning the Jews and Jerusalem will be fulfilled, and the Most Holy will be anointed as King and sit on David's throne.

The seventieth week of Daniel is a time during which God will deal with the nation of Israel, Daniel's people, and the city of Jerusalem, the holy city. It is specific to them as a time of affliction that causes the earnest seeking of the One whom they have long rejected. Notice that there is no mention of the presence of the church during the seventieth week of Daniel.

God is not done with the nation of Israel. He does not choose people and then cast them off forever or replace them with another group after having made unconditional and everlasting promises to them. The people of Israel are back in their national homeland, and that means the time of their affliction is near. The church, the bride of Christ, will be in the Father's house during that time, for the church does not have an appointment with God's wrath, and her reconciliation to the Father has already come to pass.

DAY 43

DEMONSTRATING OUR LOVE FOR JESUS

The restoration of Peter on the shores of the Sea of Galilee is one of the most poignant moments recorded in the New Testament. It reminds us of the grace of God and His desire to restore people even after they have made huge mistakes. Remember what Peter had done before the crucifixion?

> Jesus said to them, "All of you will be made to stumble because of Me this night, for it is written: 'I will strike the Shepherd, and the sheep will be scattered.' But after I have been raised, I will go before you to Galilee." Peter said to Him, "Even if all are made to stumble, yet I will not be." Jesus said to him, "Assuredly, I say to you that today, even this night, before the rooster crows twice, you will deny Me three times." But he spoke more vehemently, "If I have to die with You, I will not deny You!" And they all said likewise (Mark 14:27-31).

Peter's three denials were known of by the Lord when Peter was chosen to be one of the Twelve. The Lord knew of Peter's personality. He knew of Peter's pride.

Afterward, the Lord asked Peter three times if he loved Him. The first time, He dealt with Peter's pridefulness when He asked him, "Do you love Me more than these?" The second time Jesus simply asked, "Do you love Me?" (John 21:15-16). Then came the third exchange:

> "Simon, son of Jonah, do you love Me?" Peter was grieved because He said to him the third time, "Do you love Me?" And he said to Him, "Lord, You know all things; You know that I love You." Jesus said to him, "Feed My sheep" (verse 17).

Peter's denials led to Peter's brokenness, and Peter's brokenness led to Peter's usefulness. Don't ever let the devil deceive you into thinking the Lord doesn't want anything to do with you because you made a mistake. He knew all about us when He saved us, and nothing we do is a surprise to Him.

DAY 44

GOD DOESN'T NEED OUR HELP

We all have our favorite people in Scripture we look forward to meeting someday. Many would love to hear what it was like for David to look into the eyes of a nine-foot-tall-plus Goliath, or ask Daniel what it was like to spend the night with hungry lions. The line for those who want to chat with Paul will certainly be a long one too.

There are also some people in the Bible whom we identify with on a more personal level. Busy Martha would be one, doubting Thomas another. It seems likely that Peter will have a long line of those who would like to meet him simply because so many of us are like him. We have all tried to help out God at times, or to counsel Him as to how we think He should handle things.

While at Caesarea Philippi, Jesus asked His disciples who people thought He was, and after a few possible answers were offered, Peter said, "You are the Christ, the Son of the living God" (Matthew 16:16). Jesus then replied, "Blessed are you, Simon Bar-Jonah, for flesh and blood has not revealed this to you, but My Father who is in heaven" (verse 17).

Moments later, we read about Peter rebuking the Lord for saying "that He must go to Jerusalem, and suffer many things...and be killed, and be raised the third day." Jesus told Peter, "Get behind Me, Satan! You are an offense to Me, for you are not mindful of the things of God, but the things of men" (verses 21-23).

We have all done what Peter did, though in different contexts. We've all wondered why the Lord has allowed this or that, or hasn't done what we've been earnestly praying for. We've all told Him what we think He ought to do, even if only in our minds.

The one great truth about what happened with Peter was that the Lord was true to His word. In Matthew 16:18-19, He told Peter He was going to use him at the dawning of the church age, and He did—even after Peter had blown things in a major way. And what was true for Peter is also true for you!

DAY 45

IN THE BEGINNING...

The New Testament is replete with undeniable proofs of Jesus' deity—such as His ability to defy the laws of nature, to rebuke the forces of evil, to heal the sick, and to raise the dead. One of the most frequently overlooked proofs of His deity is His connection to the creation narrative in Genesis:

> He is the image of the invisible God, the firstborn over all creation. For by Him all things were created that are in heaven and that are on earth, visible and invisible, whether thrones or dominions or principalities or powers. All things were created through Him and for Him. And He is before all things, and in Him all things consist (Colossians 1:15-17).

The Bible frequently includes mentions of the creation story to remind us of the majestic power of our God. This helps us to keep our eyes lifted above the difficulties of life and on the One who is our hope. In the passage above, Paul tells us that Jesus is the physical manifestation of the invisible God and is the authority and rightful heir (which is what "firstborn" means) over all creation. This right is established by the fact that all things were created by, through, and for Him. Paul then points out the eternality of Jesus, a characteristic He shares with the Father and Holy Spirit, and concludes with the fact that "in Him" all things consist. The word "consist" means "to hold or band together."

As it pertains to you and me as individual members of the body of Christ, we would do well to remember that we are among the "all things" that He holds together. When life is hard and trials and tribulations come, when spiritual principalities and powers and earthly thrones and dominions seek to oppress and hurt us, we need to look to our source of help and lift our eyes above the momentary light afflictions of life and place them on the One who is a present help in our time of need—Jesus.

DAY 46

DECEPTION IS EVERYWHERE, PART 1

Many people have thought or said at one time or another, "I never thought I'd see the day…," then followed those words with some bizarre or mind-boggling incident or event. When it comes to our day, we could say, "I never thought I would see the day when doctors would support things they know aren't true." Or, "I never thought I would see the day when parents would allow five-year-olds to determine their gender and permit them to have surgery or take puberty blockers to keep their bodies from proving their feelings are wrong."

How are we to navigate our way through such times, when there are growing numbers of people who believe things that science has proven to be untrue? As 2 Thessalonians 2:7-12 says:

> The mystery of lawlessness is already at work; only He who now restrains will do so until He is taken out of the way. And then the lawless one will be revealed, whom the Lord will consume with the breath of His mouth and destroy with the brightness of His coming. The coming of the lawless one is according to the working of Satan, with all power, signs, and lying wonders, and with all unrighteous deception among those who perish, because they did not receive the love of the truth, that they might be saved. And for this reason God will send them strong delusion, that they should believe the lie, that they all may be condemned who did not believe the truth but had pleasure in unrighteousness.

The mystery of lawlessness has long been at work. To this point in time, it has been restrained by the power of the Holy Spirit and the presence of the true church on Earth. When the church is removed and the Holy Spirit no longer restrains the rise of the Antichrist to power, the whole world, having already been prepared to reject facts and truth, will fall for his signs and lying wonders and believe the lie that he is God.

Do not be deceived!

DAY 47

DECEPTION IS EVERYWHERE, PART 2

We live in a time when we could say, "I never thought I would see the day when…" That day is here. Matthew 24:12 describes our era this way: "Because lawlessness will abound, the love of many will grow cold."

The Greek verb translated "cold" is *psychō*. It means "to breathe," or figuratively, "a reduction in temperature." The implication is clear that when someone stops breathing, their body grows cold. Similarly, because of abounding lawlessness, natural love and affection will die. The English word *psycho* is a fitting description of our day, though the Greek term means something completely different.

The days in which we now live can be overwhelming, and in Psalm 27:13-14, King David gives us some Holy Spirit-inspired counsel as to how to handle them and not lose heart: "I would have lost heart, unless I had believed that I would see the goodness of the LORD in the land of the living. Wait on the LORD; be of good courage, and He shall strengthen your heart; wait, I say, on the LORD!"

David tells us to wait on the Lord. The Hebrew word translated "wait" can mean "to tarry," or even "expectant hope." The primary meaning of the word is "to bind together."

We're also given this instruction in Hebrews 10:24-25: "Let us consider one another in order to stir up love and good works, not forsaking the assembling of ourselves together, as is the manner of some, but exhorting one another, and so much the more as you see the Day approaching."

The closer we get to "the Day" that we are taken out of the way, the more we are going to need the fellowship of other believers. We can see the goodness of God in the land of the living even when things are becoming more and more psycho by the day.

Tell someone about Jesus today, and you will see the goodness of God at work.

DAY 48

FOLLOW JESUS TODAY

It has been said, "Prophecy is meant to prepare us, not to scare us." The question is, prepare us for what? In Old Testament times, many prophecies were given to prepare the world for the coming of the Messiah. Other prophecies warned of coming judgment, and still others spoke about the rebirth of the nation of Israel in the "latter days."

In New Testament times, prophecy plays a more singular role. While New Testament prophecies include details about the spiritual state of the church and the moral state of the world, both of those elements are stated in relation to the proximity of the coming great tribulation. Matthew 24:21 says, "Then there will be great tribulation, such as has not been since the beginning of the world until this time, no, nor ever shall be."

First Thessalonians 5:9, 2 Thessalonians 2:7-8, and Revelation 3:10 all remind us that the church will not go through the time of "tribulation, such as has not been since the beginning of the world." Why, then, is the church given so much information about a time it will never see? This is especially true about the book of Revelation, which provides one of the most detailed accounts of any period in human history. The answer is so we will know how to escape the tribulation, and so we will sense an urgency to tell others how to as well.

In Matthew 24:44, Jesus said, "Be ready, for the Son of Man is coming at an hour you do not expect."

Notice Jesus did not say "get" ready, but rather, "be" ready for the coming of the Son of Man, for He is coming unexpectedly. The truth is, when He is ready, we will be taken up at the speed of the twinkling of an eye (1 Corinthians 15:52), and it will be too late for us to get ready.

It is only through Jesus that we can escape the things that will come upon the whole world. If you are following Him today, rest assured that you are ready for His coming.

DAY 49

THE HEART OF WORSHIP

Most of us are familiar with the encounter Jesus had with a Samaritan woman at a well, where He had gone to get a drink of water. He asked the woman to assist Him, and the conversation quickly turned to the subject of worship. The woman said to Jesus, "Our fathers worshiped on this mountain, and you Jews say that in Jerusalem is the place where one ought to worship" (John 4:20).

Jesus replied to the Samaritan woman that worship was not about Mount Gerizim or Mount Zion (Jerusalem), or any mountain or location, for that matter. Nor was it about ethnicity or nationality. He said to her that worship was not about a place or specific people. Rather, worship is a spiritual encounter that cannot be limited to a time, place, or people. He then said to her:

> The hour is coming, and now is, when the true worshipers will worship the Father in spirit and truth; for the Father is seeking such to worship Him. God is Spirit, and those who worship Him must worship in spirit and truth (John 4:23-24).

Many within the church today say, "Worship must be this style of music," or "Worship has to be with these kinds of instruments." Others say, "Worship needs to be quiet and ethereal," and some claim, "Worship needs to be energetic with anthems of praise."

Yet as Jesus said to the woman (in paraphrase), "Worship isn't what man thinks it is; worship is what God says it is, and the hour has come that true worship must be a spiritual act based on truth."

Here is where man needs to relinquish control and recognize what true worship is. The Greek word translated "worship" literally means "to kiss the hand." It pictures bowing before a superior and kissing the hand in absolute obeisance. It also means to prostrate one's self and submit.

That means worship is a life surrendered to the will and Word of God. Are you worshipping Him today?

DAY 50

GOD IS IN CONTROL

While man's battle against his flesh (carnal desires) will have various manifestations, there is one battle that is common to many, and that is the desire to be in control. We even have adages and colloquialisms that reveal this as true, such as being the captain of your own ship, or the master of your destiny, or looking out for number one.

This desire for control has even infiltrated the church. There are many who teach that, by faith, you can control the flow of financial blessings to yourself or determine the status of your health in life. But the Bible says God is the determiner of such things:

> You shall remember the LORD your God, for it is He who gives you power to get wealth, that He may establish His covenant which He swore to your fathers, as it is this day (Deuteronomy 8:18).

Man likes to be in control and take credit for his accomplishments and accumulations. But ultimately, it is God who is in control of all things.

In Luke 4, when Jesus was in a synagogue, He read from Isaiah 61 and said the passage was concerning Himself and was fulfilled in their hearing (Luke 4:21). He went on to reveal to those in the synagogue that being a Jew did not give them exclusive rights to salvation, and therefore worship. And because of this, "all those" in the synagogue were filled with wrath and sought to throw Him off a cliff (verses 28-29).

Many people today don't like what the Bible has to say. And curiously, one of the main arguments made against the divine inspiration of Scripture is that man wrote it. However, we can rest assured that if man had written the Bible, it would not say so many negative things about man, and it certainly would approve of more fleshly behaviors.

The truth is, God is in control, and every word of God is true. You can be the captain of your own ship if you want, but things are better with God in control.

DAY 51

WISDOM FROM ABOVE

We live in a time when mankind thinks it has everything all figured out. The Bible's record of creation has been replaced with the "theory" of evolution. The Bible's moral code that has been the foundation for the laws of many countries for centuries is now considered antiquated and has been assigned a place in history as the way people "used to think." The Bible's claim that the way of salvation goes exclusively through Jesus Christ is now viewed as closed-minded and offensive. Man's wisdom has now been elevated above the Word of God.

But notice what the Bible has to say about man's wisdom:

> Who is wise and understanding among you? Let him show by good conduct that his works are done in the meekness of wisdom. But if you have bitter envy and self-seeking in your hearts, do not boast and lie against the truth. This wisdom does not descend from above, but is earthly, sensual, demonic. For where envy and self-seeking exist, confusion and every evil thing are there. But the wisdom that is from above is first pure, then peaceable, gentle, willing to yield, full of mercy and good fruits, without partiality and without hypocrisy (James 3:13-17).

The wisdom that comes from God is pure. In this passage, the word "pure" literally means "chaste, clean, or perfect." It can also mean "reverent, sacred, pure from every evil and carnality." In contrast, earthly wisdom is sensual and demonic, impure and imperfect, irreverent, filled with every evil and carnality.

Psalm 14:1 adds further perspective, saying, "The fool has said in his heart, 'There is no God.' They are corrupt, they have done abominable works, there is none who does good."

When people believe the pure wisdom that comes from above, they abandon their foolish beliefs and behaviors, including the claim, "There is no God." When the pure wisdom that comes from God is rejected or denied, foolish beliefs and behaviors will ensue. So in all the decisions you are faced with today, choose the wisdom from above.

DAY 52

THE DECEPTIVE PEACE

Among the multitude of indicators that we are nearing the end of the church age is the fact people are believing things that are not true. This is preparing the way for the man of sin who will deceive the world:

> The coming of the lawless one is according to the working of Satan, with all power, signs, and lying wonders, and with all unrighteous deception among those who perish, because they did not receive the love of the truth, that they might be saved. And for this reason God will send them strong delusion, that they should believe the lie, that they all may be condemned who did not believe the truth but had pleasure in unrighteousness (2 Thessalonians 2:9-12).

Notice how accurately these verses describe today. Unrighteous deception is rampant, the truth is largely rejected, lies are not only promoted but also legally protected, and unrighteous pleasures are the order of the day.

Isaiah, Jeremiah, Ezekiel, Daniel, Amos, Zechariah, and a host of New Testament authors have told us what is coming and what to look for when it is near. All of this is happening right now, including the fact people all over the world are unhappy with their governments and are hungry for change.

First Thessalonians 5:3 speaks of end-times delusion as well: "When they say, 'Peace and safety!' then sudden destruction comes upon them, as labor pains upon a pregnant woman. And they shall not escape."

In a world hungry for peace, at a time when deception and delusion are rampant, we can be assured the world is ready for the false peace that the Antichrist will offer. As Paul told the church in Rome, "The night is far spent, the day is at hand" (Romans 13:12). As Christians, we are waiting for the prolonged darkness to end and for a new day to dawn, when we are forever with the Lord!

DAY 53

ONCE AND FOR ALL

While there are many distinguishing features that separate Christianity from all other religions, there is one that stands above them all.

> When we were still without strength, in due time Christ died for the ungodly. For scarcely for a righteous man will one die; yet perhaps for a good man someone would even dare to die. But God demonstrates His own love toward us, in that while we were still sinners, Christ died for us (Romans 5:6-8).

Virtually all religious systems in the world require people to do what their belief system prescribes in order to benefit from those religions. Only the Christian faith bases the reward of eternal life entirely on what was done *for* us and not *by* us.

> "Sacrifice and offering, burnt offerings, and offerings for sin You did not desire, nor had pleasure in them" (which are offered according to the law), then He said, "Behold, I have come to do Your will, O God." He takes away the first that He may establish the second. By that will we have been sanctified through the offering of the body of Jesus Christ once for all (Hebrews 10:8-10).

What wonderful truth this is! Christ died for us while we were still sinners; He sanctified us through the offering of His body as the payment for our sins. And He did this once and for all. The works of sacrifices and offerings for sin were not the means by which salvation could be attained; only the offering of the body of Jesus would satisfy the justness of God on our behalf and make us holy (which is what it means to be sanctified).

What separates Christianity from all other religions is that it proves that God loves people more than works and rules. God proved that by saving us in spite of us. For that, we should live each day with hearts filled with thanksgiving for the matchless gift of His Son Jesus Christ!

DAY 54

THE WORLD IS READY

There are certain indicators we are all familiar with that tell us, with certainty, that something will happen in the near future. When a family begins boxing up all their belongings and stacking the boxes in one room, you know there is a move coming. When two weeks' worth of clothes are being crammed into suitcases and loaded into a car, you know that a vacation is ahead.

Jesus tells us of another indicator we should watch for:

> He spoke to them a parable: "Look at the fig tree, and all the trees. When they are already budding, you see and know for yourselves that summer is now near. So you also, when you see these things happening, know that the kingdom of God is near. Assuredly, I say to you, this generation will by no means pass away till all things take place. Heaven and earth will pass away, but My words will by no means pass away" (Luke 21:29-33).

Jesus makes it clear there are other prophetic precursors that tell us certain events are in the not-too-distant future. The prophets gave us clues as well. Today, we see a coalition of nations working together that were identified by Ezekiel more than 2,500 years ago. Three of them, Russia, Turkey, and Iran, all have troops on the northern border of Israel, the very direction from which the Bible says they will invade.

If we are seeing these nations gathered and poised to strike Israel from the north, and the protesting nations developing relationships with Israel (see Ezekiel 38:13), and we see things happening in Western Europe that will lead to the Antichrist's rise in power, then we know what is about to happen, even though we don't know the day or hour.

We're about to go on a trip to the Father's house in the twinkling of an eye! Remember, the only thing you can take on this trip is other people, so tell someone about Jesus today! Our new bodies and forever being with the Lord are coming soon!

DAY 55

BE ANXIOUS FOR NOTHING

It has been said that 90 percent of the things we worry about never happen. While that may be true, it is also true that the 90 percent still gets our attention much of the time and manifests itself in worry and anxiety.

We also recognize that when the Lord tells us to do something and we don't do it, or He tells us not to do something and we do it, these are the very definition of sin. But before we pack our bags and head out on a guilt trip because we do worry even when we're told not to, some clarity is in order about anxiety and worry.

In Philippians 4:6-7, Paul wrote,

> Be anxious for nothing, but in everything by prayer and supplication, with thanksgiving, let your requests be made known to God; and the peace of God, which surpasses all understanding, will guard your hearts and minds through Christ Jesus.

The word translated "anxious" comes from a Greek word that means "distraction." The phrase "be anxious" could also be read as, "Don't live in a constant state of anxiety." Living like this would obviously cause us to be distracted from the promises and plan of God for our lives as His children, which is exactly how the enemy wants us to live.

We must remember that we can always be thankful even for things we may not be thankful for. It is unlikely that people have ever prayed, "Thank You, Lord, that my child is sick," or "Thank You that my loved one was in an accident," or "Thank You that I lost my job." What we *can* do, however, in the midst of such situations, is pray, "Thank You, Lord, that You are sovereign and good. While I do not understand why this was allowed to happen, I have entrusted You with the well-being of my eternal soul, so I am going to trust You through this temporal time of trial and tribulation."

DAY 56

BELIEVING HIM

The apostle Peter tells us in 2 Peter 1:4 that we have received "exceedingly great and precious promises" through our faith and trust in Jesus Christ. We see some of those promises spoken by Jesus at the Last Supper, and we have to wonder if some of these were not in Peter's mind when he wrote what he did.

Consider that Jesus had just given the disciples some troubling news: One of them would betray Him, He was going away soon, and He told Peter that he would deny the Lord three times before the next morning when the rooster crowed. After making these facts known, the Lord began unveiling a series of "exceedingly great and precious promises," but prefaced these with a word of instruction: "Let not your heart be troubled; you believe in God, believe also in Me" (John 14:1).

The Greek word translated "let" could also be translated as "forbid" or "stop." The word "troubled" means "to agitate," "inward commotion," or "to take away calmness of mind." That tells us that the word "heart" here is figurative for thoughts, feelings, and emotions.

I am sure we have all had a well-meaning friend tell us, in times of troubling news, "Don't worry." That well-intended sage advice is of little help without some type of information that tells us how or why we don't need to worry.

After Judas left to betray Him, Jesus tells the remaining 11 disciples, "Stop letting your hearts be agitated and take away your calmness of mind." He then says, "You believe in God, believe also in Me." In other words, He told them, "The way you think about God the Father and remember His faithfulness, wisdom, provision, and power, think also about Me."

Believing is not simply cognitive recognition; it is believing Jesus is and does what Scripture says about Him, which keeps our hearts from being troubled even in troublesome times.

DAY 57

APPOINTED TIMES

Among all the realities of life, one of our least favorite things to do is wait. We often express our excitement about something by saying "I can't wait" for this or that. Preteens say they can't wait until they are 13. Thirteen-year-olds can't wait until they are 16. Sixteen-year-olds can't wait until they are 18. Many say each year they can't wait for Christmas, or they can't wait to go on vacation. While the expression is one of anticipation and excitement, the truth is that waiting is a part of life, including waiting for God's appointed times.

Isaiah 40:31 says, "Those who wait on the LORD shall renew their strength; they shall mount up with wings like eagles, they shall run and not be weary, they shall walk and not faint."

This famous verse reminds us that waiting on the Lord's appointed times for various things is not merely a part of life but can and should be times of renewed strength. For most of us, the positive aspect of waiting is elusive. This is due, in part, to not recognizing what waiting means in the biblical sense.

The word "wait" in Isaiah 40:31 means "to bind together." Solomon painted a good picture for us of what being bound together with the Lord looks like: "Though one may be overpowered by another, two can withstand him. And a threefold cord is not quickly broken" (Ecclesiastes 4:12).

"Wait," meaning to "bind together," implies what Solomon wrote of. We might understand it as a braid—intertwining ourselves to and with the Lord is how we renew our strength, mount up with eagles' wings, and run and not become weary, and walk and not faint.

Waiting is also a time that the devil loves to exploit by trying to invade our thoughts with his negativity. He will try to get us to think, *It won't happen*, or, *God is not going to come through*. So when you wait, intertwine yourself to the Lord and keep going. That will lead you to renewed strength.

DAY 58

KNOW THE TRUTH

Genesis 3:1 tells us, "Now the serpent was more cunning than any beast of the field which the Lord God had made. And he said to the woman, 'Has God indeed said, "You shall not eat of every tree of the garden"?'"

Nothing has had more of a negative impact on our world than the rejection of the word of God. Think about the outcome of this conversation: Satan questioned the word of God, Eve was deceived, she gave the forbidden fruit to her husband, and he ate. And we are still experiencing the consequences of this one sin.

As 1 John 1:8-10 says,

> If we say that we have no sin, we deceive ourselves, and the truth is not in us. If we confess our sins, He is faithful and just to forgive us our sins and to cleanse us from all unrighteousness. If we say that we have not sinned, we make Him a liar, and His word is not in us.

The word "confess" means to "see as" or "speak of" as the same. If we say that something is not a sin that God has declared to be sin, the truth is not in us. If we say that our actions are not sinful when the Bible says they are, we call Him a liar, and His Word is not in us.

What began in the garden continues to this day. Satan uses the same tactic he did with Eve, and he gets us to call into question the validity of His Word.

When you accept Christ as your Savior, you are also accepting the Word as truth. The two are inseparable. Jesus is the Word, the Word is truth, and therefore, Jesus is the way to the Father and eternal life. Denying the truth only leads to believing strong delusions like "There are other paths to heaven apart from Jesus Christ." Such deceptions are a clear sign of the last days!

DAY 59

THE DAYS OF DECEPTION

In Matthew 24:3, when the disciples asked Jesus about the signs of His coming and the end of the age, the first warning Jesus gave them was to "take heed," which means "to see and discern." Jesus then added "…that no one deceive you." In other words, don't let what you see fool you.

Paul wrote in 2 Thessalonians 2:9-12,

> The coming of the lawless one is according to the working of Satan, with all power, signs, and lying wonders, and with all unrighteous deception among those who perish, because they did not receive the love of the truth, that they might be saved. And for this reason God will send them strong delusion, that they should believe the lie, that they all may be condemned who did not believe the truth but had pleasure in unrighteousness.

The deception of the last days is revealed here as "lying wonders," meaning "phony miracles." And strong delusion sent from God will cause all who "did not receive the love of the truth" to "believe the lie" of the Antichrist and worship him during the tribulation.

Today, there are people who believe that gender is fluid and a choice, and they want to tell the rest of us how to manage our health. There are people who believe that a vast cloud of dust and gas exploded billions of years ago and, through a gradual series of evolutionary steps, became the universe we see today, and they are largely in control of our educational institutions. Even in the church there are people who promote signs and wonders that look nothing like they did in the Bible, and yet they claim these are manifestations of God's power.

These are the types of deceptions Jesus warned would happen when the time is near for Him to come for His church and raise up the dead in Christ. When things that are untrue are accepted as facts, this tells us Jesus is coming for us soon!

DAY 60

THE FREE GIFT

Among the many wonderful aspects of the Christian faith, one of the hardest for some people to accept is a truth that makes Christianity exceptional from other belief systems. That truth is the fact no one can earn or deserve the forgiveness of sin and the reward of heaven. Rather, our faith is based solely on the sacrifice of another on our behalf.

There is no one who is moral enough, no one who has done enough good works, no person who has ever been religiously observant enough to warrant God's forgiveness and His offer of an eternal, heavenly home.

> As it is written: "There is none righteous, no, not one; there is none who understands; there is none who seeks after God. They have all turned aside; they have together become unprofitable; there is none who does good, no, not one" (Romans 3:10-12).

While some people don't like to hear this, it is one of the most magnificent truths that has ever been revealed by God. What we could not do for ourselves through works, personal righteousness, or religious observance, God did for us "by sending His own Son in the likeness of sinful flesh" and dying on the cross (Romans 8:3).

Another part of this wonderful truth is that if God saved us while we were yet sinners, we can be assured He will not forsake us when we sin after we're saved.

> In Him you also trusted, after you heard the word of truth, the gospel of your salvation; in whom also, having believed, you were sealed with the Holy Spirit of promise, who is the guarantee of our inheritance until the redemption of the purchased possession, to the praise of His glory (Ephesians 1:13-14).

As born-again Christians, we have in us a guarantee of our future inheritance in the person of the Holy Spirit, and that means when we mess up, we don't give up. Instead, we get up and keep going.

DAY 61

DENY YOURSELF

After the Holy Spirit came upon the disciples on the day of Pentecost and Peter preached the first gospel sermon of the church age, he said this to the Jews in Jerusalem who questioned the sobriety of those who had been baptized in the Spirit:

> "Therefore let all the house of Israel know assuredly that God has made this Jesus, whom you crucified, both Lord and Christ." Now when they heard this, they were cut to the heart, and said to Peter and the rest of the apostles, "Men and brethren, what shall we do?" Then Peter said to them, "Repent, and let every one of you be baptized in the name of Jesus Christ for the remission of sins; and you shall receive the gift of the Holy Spirit. For the promise is to you and to your children, and to all who are afar off, as many as the Lord our God will call" (Acts 2:36-39).

While repentance certainly implies a change in our actions, the primary meaning of the word "repent" is "to think differently" or "to change your mind." To Peter's audience, it was clear they needed to change their minds about Jesus and be baptized as a point of identification with Him, resulting in their receiving the gift of the Holy Spirit. This sequence, Peter says, is true for as many as the Lord our God will call. As the Lord said, "If anyone desires to come after Me, let him deny himself, and take up his cross daily, and follow Me" (Luke 9:23).

This, too, is true for as many as the Lord our God will call. Maybe you have been taught that confessing to a priest, repeating certain phrases, or having your good works outweigh your bad are the means by which forgiveness is obtained and heaven is accessed. You need to deny such things, change your mind, and recognize that the only thing that can wash away your sins is the blood of Jesus.

DAY 62

SALVATION IS NOT BY AFFILIATION

It has been reported that there are some 4,200 religions in the world today, and most of them have subgroups within them, bringing the number up closer to 10,000. Why is it that man has such a love for religion?

Most have heard Karl Marx's famous statement, "Religion is the opium of the people." The full quote gives a bit more insight into his claim, which says, "Religion is the sigh of the oppressed creature, the heart of a heartless world, and the soul of soulless conditions. It is the opium of the people."[3]

People love religion for two reasons: First, it makes them a participant in receiving the proposed benefits and thus worthy or deserving of them; and second, being worthy of the promised benefits makes people feel better about themselves.

Marx was right to a degree. Masses of people follow the various religions of the world and gain a sense of satisfaction or worthiness from doing so. The problem is that religion does nothing to resolve man's biggest problems, which are sin and death. Romans 3:23 says, "All have sinned and fall short of the glory of God," and Romans 6:23 says, "The wages of sin is death, but the gift of God is eternal life in Christ Jesus our Lord."

Religion might make someone feel better, or even deserving of something positive, but religion can't do anything about man's sin problem.

Christian is not a religious affiliation assigned at birth. *Christian* is a title assigned at rebirth. It means to be Christlike. That can't be inherited through family tradition, and religion can't make you a Christian.

In His grace, God sent His Son to die for the sins of the world. And faith in His death, resurrection, and ascension saves us. Not religious rituals, not observing feast days, not keeping Sabbaths, not repeating phrases or prayers. We are saved by the blood of Jesus Christ and redeemed to the Father through His death.

DAY 63

FIGHTING THE GOOD FIGHT

We are in a battle with the forces of darkness over souls who are lost and perishing without Christ. These souls cannot come to saving faith apart from hearing the Word of God (Romans 10:17), and every one of us has been sent to the world to preach the gospel to every creature.

The battles many engage in with other Christians are like going up the down escalator—lots of activity but no progress in advancing God's kingdom. In fact, sometimes these battles over interpretation or tradition get so intense that Christian behavior is put on hold and the flesh rules the day. However, our call is to fight the enemy, not each other.

Titus 2:11-14 says,

> The grace of God that brings salvation has appeared to all men, teaching us that, denying ungodliness and worldly lusts, we should live soberly, righteously, and godly in the present age, looking for the blessed hope and glorious appearing of our great God and Savior Jesus Christ, who gave Himself for us, that He might redeem us from every lawless deed and purify for Himself His own special people, zealous for good works.

Our calling as followers of Christ is to live soberly, righteously, and godly while looking for the blessed hope of the glorious appearing of our great God and Savior, Christ the Lord.

Doing that is going to be a fight at times, and that fight is twofold: Satan will fight against us getting started, and after we get started, he will fight against us continuing. He will use our flesh in his efforts to do both. Busyness and weariness are two excuses he likes to exploit so that we justify in our minds that tomorrow is a better day to begin. However, busy and tired people who answer God's call are more likely to experience divine empowerment than those who wait, then move ahead in their own strength.

DAY 64

WAITING ON GOD'S TIMING

One of the hardest aspects of the Christian life is when the answer to our prayer is either no or wait. Sometimes it seems that God's timing is out of sync with our petition or need, and yet while He is the One who instituted time, He dwells outside of time and moves according to His timing and purposes.

Peter mentioned this very fact in his second epistle:

> Knowing this first: that scoffers will come in the last days, walking according to their own lusts, and saying, "Where is the promise of His coming? For since the fathers fell asleep, all things continue as they were from the beginning of creation" (2 Peter 3:3-4).

In other words, a time will come when people will doubt the return of Christ because it hasn't happened yet, and from a human perspective, it has been a long time since He gave the promise of His return.

Doubt can arise in our minds, too, though not in terms of doubting the Lord is coming for us someday, but because God's answer to our prayer is long in coming and our minds end up wondering or wandering. We wonder if He has heard us or maybe forgotten us, neither of which is possible. As Jeremiah 33:3 says, "Call to Me, and I will answer you, and show you great and mighty things, which you do not know."

God told us to call out to Him, and God said He will answer. Yes, Jeremiah wrote these words to the Jews, but the God of Israel is the unchanging God of the church. Maybe the answer to your prayer is no, maybe it is wait. But the promise we have from Him is that great and mighty things will be revealed to us in His time. So whenever God's response includes making us wait, remember and hang on to this important truth: He will answer in His time.

DAY 65

CHRISTIAN LIVING

We have all heard, and likely said, that Christianity is not a religion but a relationship, which is true. Yet in this relationship there is also responsibility. Matthew 28:16-20 says,

> The eleven disciples went away into Galilee, to the mountain which Jesus had appointed for them. When they saw Him, they worshiped Him; but some doubted. And Jesus came and spoke to them, saying, "All authority has been given to Me in heaven and on earth. Go therefore and make disciples of all the nations, baptizing them in the name of the Father and of the Son and of the Holy Spirit, teaching them to observe all things that I have commanded you; and lo, I am with you always, even to the end of the age." Amen.

There are two points for us to note: first, the duration of the directive, which is to the end of the age. That means you and I are included in this. The second is the content of the directive. We are to make disciples, baptize them, and teach them to observe our Lord's commands.

In the early days of the church, Christianity was referred to as The Way, and often, the practices and beliefs of Christians would cause commotion to arise in the places where the church was growing. Yet this did not change the content of the Great Commission, which is to make disciples, baptize them as a public statement of faith, and teach what Jesus has taught us to obey—all of that is how we grow. As 1 Timothy 4:1 says, "Now the Spirit expressly says that in latter times some will depart from the faith, giving heed to deceiving spirits and doctrines of demons."

This is the end result of diminishing the authority of Scripture and inserting human opinion or cultural sensitivities in its place. When we fail to stress the importance of the apostles' doctrines as we fellowship, break bread, and pray together with new disciples, we will leave people vulnerable to the enemy's efforts to insert his doctrines into their thinking.

DAY 66

DON'T MISS THE MESSIAH

We have all read a story about or seen in a movie the scenario of an unknown or long-lost rich person who left a fortune to their last surviving relative, and that person's life was changed dramatically. Many of us also know of the feeling of receiving a notice from a financial institution that reads "Paid in Full." And the greater the debt, the greater the sense of relief.

Imagine having a debt that is so large you could never pay it in full, no matter how many hours you worked or years you made payments on the debt. That is what Jesus came to do for us.

> He came to His own, and His own did not receive Him. But as many as received Him, to them He gave the right to become children of God, to those who believe in His name: who were born, not of blood, nor of the will of the flesh, nor of the will of man, but of God (John 1:11-13).

Jesus came and paid the unpayable sin debt of all mankind. Yet His fellow Jews, by and large, said, "We'll keep doing the works of the law and wait for someone else to come along." Many people today are doing much the same—they think they can work off their sin debt through works and good moral behavior. They've missed the Messiah, just like many Jews and others have.

In line with our simple analogy, the bill for our sin was sent to Jesus, and He marked it in His own blood: "Paid in Full." If your debt is paid in full, you don't keep sending payments, but rather, you live a debt-free life. You don't strain to make ends meet after they have already been met. You don't wish for someone else to come along to do what has already been done.

This is why Jesus could say, "If the Son makes you free, you shall be free indeed" (John 8:36).

DAY 67

THE SEVERITY OF THE TRIBULATION

Years ago, there was a bumper sticker that read, "Heaven doesn't want me and hell is afraid I'll take over." This type of thinking reveals how deeply people misperceive the gravity of eternity apart from God. Many think the same way about the coming great tribulation, including some Christians.

Mark 13:19-20 warns, "In those days there will be tribulation, such as has not been since the beginning of the creation which God created until this time, nor ever shall be. And unless the Lord had shortened those days, no flesh would be saved; but for the elect's sake, whom He chose, He shortened the days."

The current world population is more than 8.2 billion. If the rapture removes a billion, which is likely a generous estimation, that means the tribulation will be so severe that 7.2 billion people would be killed in less than seven years if Jesus didn't bring it to an end. We also know that the Antichrist brings a time of pseudo peace on the earth for a season, which will decrease the time frame of the cataclysmic events that would kill all if it weren't stopped by the Lord.

How bad will things get? Revelation 6:15-17 tells us:

> The kings of the earth, the great men, the rich men, the commanders, the mighty men, every slave and every free man, hid themselves in the caves and in the rocks of the mountains, and said to the mountains and rocks, "Fall on us and hide us from the face of Him who sits on the throne and from the wrath of the Lamb! For the great day of His wrath has come, and who is able to stand?"

To make light or little of the great tribulation is beyond foolish. It is the great day of God's wrath, and even those who experience it will ask, "Who is able to stand?" The answer is no one.

Time is running out. The night is far spent, and the day is at hand. Tell someone about Jesus today!

DAY 68

HOLD FAST TO SOUND WORDS

The Bible admonishes us to "hold fast the pattern of sound words" (2 Timothy 1:13), meaning to retain or remain joined to the Word of God, which the world clearly rejects. Later in the same letter, Paul warned Timothy that a time would come when people "will not endure sound doctrine, but according to their own desires, because they have itching ears, they will heap up for themselves teachers; and they will turn their ears away from the truth, and be turned aside to fables" (2 Timothy 4:3-4).

The Greek word translated "sound" means "free from mixture with error." We have to recognize that the Bible is a source of sound words greater than our own, and we need it to help keep our beliefs and actions free from error.

Psalm 19:7-11 has this to say about God's Word:

> The law of the Lord is perfect, converting the soul; the testimony of the Lord is sure, making wise the simple; the statutes of the Lord are right, rejoicing the heart; the commandment of the Lord is pure, enlightening the eyes; the fear of the Lord is clean, enduring forever; the judgments of the Lord are true and righteous altogether. More to be desired are they than gold, yea, than much fine gold; sweeter also than honey and the honeycomb. Moreover by them Your servant is warned, and in keeping them there is great reward.

The law, the testimony, the statutes, the commandments, the enlightenment, and the judgments of God are all contained in His Word, which is unmixed with error and thus perfect.

Paul told Timothy to hold fast to sound words because a time was coming when many wouldn't. We should heed his counsel today, as it will define faith and love as God sees it, and it will keep our lives from looking more like the world than the Word.

DAY 69

A WARNING FROM JESUS

When we consider Bible prophecies, the first thing we need to do is make sure we don't approach them like weather predictions and think that there is a percentage of a chance they will happen. Everything the Bible says about the last days will happen exactly as written, both the clearly stated and the implied.

In Matthew 24:4-8, Jesus told the disciples,

> Take heed that no one deceives you. For many will come in My name, saying, "I am the Christ," and will deceive many. And you will hear of wars and rumors of wars. See that you are not troubled; for all these things must come to pass, but the end is not yet. For nation will rise against nation, and kingdom against kingdom. And there will be famines, pestilences, and earthquakes in various places. All these are the beginning of sorrows.

When the disciples asked Jesus about the end of the age and the signs of His coming, He clearly stated there will be false Christs, wars and rumors of wars, international and ethnic tensions, famines, pestilences, and earthquakes. And all of this is preceded by an admonition to not be deceived, which implies there will be efforts to deceive people about the signs of His coming and the end of the age. Second Peter 3:3 says that some will scoff at the idea that Jesus is coming again at all.

We are living in such a time. The deceptions concerning the Bible and the last days' evidence is in full swing, and scoffers and deniers are all around us. The tragedy of this is that during the very time people ought to be more confident than ever that the Bible is 100 percent true, including the prophecies concerning the last days, instead, they have chosen to scoff at the idea of Christ's return.

DAY 70

GOD IS PRO-LIFE

The leading cause of death worldwide in 2024 was not cancer or heart disease, crime or war. The leading cause of death in the world was abortion. This reality pales in comparison to what has taken place since 1970. Globally, 1.5 billion babies have been murdered in their mothers' wombs.

In Ezekiel 16:20-23, God told the people of ancient Israel,

> You took your sons and your daughters, whom you bore to Me, and these you sacrificed to them to be devoured. Were your acts of harlotry a small matter, that you have slain My children and offered them up to them by causing them to pass through the fire? And in all your abominations and acts of harlotry you did not remember the days of your youth, when you were naked and bare, struggling in your blood. Then it was so, after all your wickedness—"Woe, woe to you!" says the Lord GOD.

This alone tells us how God feels about abortion and what our world has been doing to unborn children during these past 50 years and beyond.

Jesus said in Matthew 24:12 that because of abounding lawlessness in the last days, the love of many will grow cold. The word translated "cold" is a word used to describe a dead body. In other words, natural love and affection, like that of a mother for her unborn child, will die in the last days. The clear evidence of that is today's mantra "My body, my choice," with no concern for the life of the child in the womb.

Thankfully, those who have had an abortion in the past and have since come to Christ have all of their sins completely forgiven, including this one (Psalm 103:12), and the woes of the tribulation do not await them. This is further proof of the depth of the love of God for the world and that the blood of Jesus cleanses us from all sin and delivers us from the wrath to come!

DAY 71

GOD'S UNSTOPPABLE PLAN FOR ISRAEL

The fact that Nehemiah wrote about the mercies and deliverance of God for Israel more than 600 years after the time of the Judges, and after the Babylonian captivity, tells us this great man of God understood that God's plans for national Israel were not conditional on their behavior.

It is clear King David also had that same understanding when he wrote many of the psalms, including these words in Psalm 103:7-11:

> He made known His ways to Moses, His acts to the children of Israel. The LORD is merciful and gracious, slow to anger, and abounding in mercy. He will not always strive with us, nor will He keep His anger forever. He has not dealt with us according to our sins, nor punished us according to our iniquities. For as the heavens are high above the earth, so great is His mercy toward those who fear Him.

While many claim that ancient Israel's behaviors caused God to cast His people aside and replace them with the church, they seem to forget that God, according to Malachi 3:6, doesn't change. If we're going to learn anything from Israel's example, it should be that when we mess up and experience the consequences of doing so, God keeps His word and His promises to His people. As Lamentations 3:22-24 says, "Through the LORD's mercies we are not consumed, because His compassions fail not. They are new every morning; great is Your faithfulness. 'The LORD is my portion,' says my soul, 'Therefore I hope in Him!'"

Things were not good between the Lord and His chosen people at the time Jeremiah wrote Lamentations, and yet what did Jeremiah say? God's mercies are new every morning, as are His compassion and faithfulness. This is true for us as well and should be the lesson we learn from God's interactions with Israel.

Great is His faithfulness!

DAY 72

THE TIME IS ALWAYS RIGHT

It has been said that while on their deathbed, no one—no matter how wealthy or poor—ever wished they had more money, houses, or cars. The only thing they have wished for is more time.

We are all given a limited allotment of time, which is why Ephesians 5:15-16 says, "See then that you walk circumspectly, not as fools but as wise, redeeming the time, because the days are evil."

"Circumspectly" means "exactly or accurately," which, for Christians, obviously connects to the will of God. "Redeeming" means "to rescue from loss," or we might say, "to make it count." Time is our most precious commodity because of all that is related to it. Serving God and loving family are primary, and there are a host of other things that vie for our time—jobs, school, sports, and entertainment.

Paul exhorted the Christians at Ephesus to make their time count and to walk accurately because "the days are evil," which is a fitting description of our day. Walking accurately and making our time count is what we should be doing as well.

The reason time is such a precious commodity is because it is limited. We have only so much of it, and it seems quite possible that the church is running out of it! As Paul said in Romans 13:12, "The night is far spent the day is at hand." He then said, "Let us walk properly as in the day, not in revelry and drunkenness, not in lewdness and lust, not in strife and envy" (verse 13).

This hour in church history is late. Time is running out, and if there are things in your life that do not accurately reflect what you believe, now is the time to bring them in line with the will of God and start walking properly.

After all, as the saying goes, Christians are the only Bible some people will ever read.

DAY 73

WILL THE CHURCH GO THROUGH THE TRIBULATION?

The seventieth week of Daniel is a time of God's global wrath. The word *wrath* means "punishment, indignation, or vengeance." If Jesus satisfied the punishment we deserved by shedding His blood for our sins, then what is the purpose of the church going through the tribulation?

Consider also what the following passages say:

> Put to death your members which are on the earth: fornication, uncleanness, passion, evil desire, and covetousness, which is idolatry. Because of these things the wrath of God is coming upon the sons of disobedience (Colossians 3:5-6).

> They themselves declare concerning us what manner of entry we had to you, and how you turned to God from idols to serve the living and true God, and to wait for His Son from heaven, whom He raised from the dead, even Jesus who delivers us from the wrath to come (1 Thessalonians 1:9-10).

If the church goes through any of the tribulation, then Colossians 3:5-6, 1 Thessalonians 1:9-10, and 1 Thessalonians 5:9-10 are all wrong. And even more devastating than that, if we have to suffer God's wrath, the blood of Jesus was not sufficient propitiation for our sins.

The purpose of Daniel's seventieth week is for God to finally cause the tribulation-surviving Jews to look upon the One whom they pierced and mourn for Him as one mourns for an only Son (Zechariah 12:10). Those in the church already recognize that Jesus is the Holy One of Israel and don't need the tribulation to bring them to that conclusion. The Jews do. The church will be in heaven with the Lord while the seventieth week of Daniel is happening on the earth.

It has to be that way—the previous 69 weeks of Daniel prove it to be so.

DAY 74

THE DEITY OF JESUS

Though not completely unheard of, it is rare that someone would deny that a person named Jesus existed and lived during the timeframe that is consistent with the biblical record. Few would deny that Christianity is based on the teachings of Jesus and His original disciples. Most have their own opinion about who and what He was.

In Matthew 16:13-17, Jesus asked His disciples what they thought:

> When Jesus came into the region of Caesarea Philippi, He asked His disciples, saying, "Who do men say that I, the Son of Man, am?" So they said, "Some say John the Baptist, some Elijah, and others Jeremiah or one of the prophets." He said to them, "But who do you say that I am?" Simon Peter answered and said, "You are the Christ, the Son of the living God." Jesus answered and said to him, "Blessed are you, Simon Bar-Jonah, for flesh and blood has not revealed this to you, but My Father who is in heaven."

In Jewish culture, a firstborn son was the heir to all of his father's possessions and was thus equal to the father. It is for this reason that Jesus spoke a blessing over Peter, for Peter had stated that as the Christ, Jesus was the Son of God and thus equal to the Father.

Some argue Jesus never claimed to be God, and yet Jesus told Peter that his assessment of who He is, the Son of God, was a revelation from the Father. It may be true that Jesus never mouthed the words "I am God," but He proved He was equal to the Father in His actions and nature-defying miracles, and by actually fulfilling or keeping the law.

Consider this: if Jesus were merely a man, as many propose, His death would have been that of just a man and would be meaningless in terms of reconciling man to God. But He was not just a man—He is the God-man, the Christ, the Son of the living God.

DAY 75

THE HOUSE OF THE LORD

We have all heard it said that the church is people, not a place. While this is true, we also need to remember that since the days of the tabernacle, God has met His people in places set aside for that purpose. When it came to building a house for the Lord, Solomon had it right when he said, "Who is able to build Him a temple, since heaven and the heaven of heavens cannot contain Him? Who am I then, that I should build Him a temple, except to burn sacrifice before Him?" (2 Chronicles 2:6).

And yet at the dedication of Solomon's temple, God replied to his prayer concerning the house he had built for the Lord, saying, "Now My eyes will be open and My ears attentive to prayer made in this place. For now I have chosen and sanctified this house, that My name may be there forever; and My eyes and My heart will be there perpetually" (2 Chronicles 7:15-16).

Concerning His house, the Lord also said through Isaiah,

> Even them I will bring to My holy mountain, and make them joyful in My house of prayer. Their burnt offerings and their sacrifices will be accepted on My altar; for My house shall be called a house of prayer for all nations (Isaiah 56:7).

When the purpose of a place is worship and prayer to the King of kings and Lord of lords, that place—though made of brick and mortar, wood, and steel—becomes a sacred place of meeting for all the nations, and the eyes and heart of the Lord will be there.

It might be popular today to say you don't need to go to church to be a Christian. But the Bible indicates Christians should go to church and be equipped for the work of ministry and benefit from the fellowship of the brethren gathered in unity.

DAY 76

GOD'S FAITHFULNESS TO ISRAEL

Romans 11:16-18 says,

> If the firstfruit is holy, the lump is also holy; and if the root is holy, so are the branches. And if some of the branches were broken off, and you, being a wild olive tree, were grafted in among them, and with them became a partaker of the root and fatness of the olive tree, do not boast against the branches. But if you do boast, remember that you do not support the root, but the root supports you.

This arboricultural metaphor is a beautiful reminder of the relationship between Jews and Christians, and at the same time, is catastrophic to the extremely serious error of replacement theology, which says that the root we are grafted into has been severed and is no longer representative of God's chosen people, the Jews, and no branch can survive with severed roots. As Romans 11:29 says, in the same context as the above verses, "The gifts and the calling of God are irrevocable."

While there are a multitude of takeaways we can glean from God's ongoing relationship with the Promised Land and His chosen people, one of the most significant is that God is merciful. Another important reality is this: If God is omniscient (that is, He knows everything), then what would be the purpose of choosing the Jews if He knew He would later cast them off forever?

If that were true, the only lesson we could learn is that God will choose you because He loves you, and then later stop loving you and reject you. It is also curious that many who believe the church has replaced Israel also believe in eternal security—that those chosen by God cannot be lost. And yet they depart from that position when it comes to God's choosing of Israel.

The Jews are back in the land today because God is faithful to keep His promises to Israel and to His church.

DAY 77

THE INSPIRED AND INFALLIBLE WORD

Few things matter more in life relationships than a person's word. For someone to keep their word establishes their trustworthiness and reliability. It confirms that others can be confident they will follow through on the things they say and do.

This brings to mind the declaration in Psalm 119:162: "I rejoice at Your word as one who finds great treasure." Would the psalmist have been able to say that if inconsistencies or errors were found in God's Word? How could anyone know what is true and what isn't? And if God's Word isn't trustworthy, wouldn't that call into question the reliability of God Himself?

The psalmist reminds us that God's Word should draw our thoughts to the Lord's nature and character, His goodness and kindness. Our thoughts should frequently turn to the Word of God, who became flesh and dwelt among us (John 1:14). Acts 4:12 says, "Nor is there salvation in any other, for there is no other name under heaven given among men by which we must be saved."

To state or imply that salvation can be had by doing good is to esteem one's name (character) above God's Word. If His Word says, "Believe on the Lord Jesus Christ, and you will be saved" (Acts 16:31), then we are to add nothing to that. If the Word says to repent and be converted, then that's what we should say to others.

When it comes to salvation, anything that is added to the blood of Jesus or that is done to amend the gospel message or that broadens it into universalist thinking is equal to saying, "The Bible is wrong," which is to say God is wrong.

There is no way to be saved other than through the shed blood of Jesus Christ. It may make people feel good to say you don't have to believe in Jesus, and it's enough to simply be a good person. But that's not true, and the consequences for such thinking are catastrophic.

DAY 78

WORDS OF COMFORT

There is no question that we live in a time during which the signs of the Lord's return for His church are plentiful. Some are in the news every day, others we can see clearly in society, and still others are more subtle yet no less significant.

In Matthew 24:37-39, Jesus said,

> As the days of Noah were, so also will the coming of the Son of Man be. For as in the days before the flood, they were eating and drinking, marrying and giving in marriage, until the day that Noah entered the ark, and did not know until the flood came and took them all away, so also will the coming of the Son of Man be.

Noah was building a massive ship on dry land on a planet that had never seen rain, and while doing so, he was preaching righteousness (2 Peter 2:5), which would most certainly include warnings of impending judgment. Yet the response to his preaching and the visible evidence that something cataclysmic was coming was indifference—eating and drinking, buying and selling, marrying and giving in marriage, a business-as-usual kind of attitude toward impending judgment.

This description of the mentality of man on the earth before the time of God's global wrath via the flood is given as a parallel to what conditions will be like before God pours out His global wrath during the seventieth week of Daniel, or the great tribulation. This brings us to a magnificent and comforting truth: "God did not appoint us to wrath, but to obtain salvation through our Lord Jesus Christ" (1 Thessalonians 5:9).

Someday, perhaps even today, the Lord Himself will descend from heaven, announced by the shout of an archangel and the blast of the trumpet of God. Believers alive at the time will be instantly and permanently transformed into their new and glorious bodies (Philippians 3:21) and meet the resurrected believing dead in the air, who will also have received their new bodies.

IT'S DIABOLICAL

There is a growing number of people today who say that as long as you believe in Jesus and that He was raised from the dead, the rest of what you believe is of no consequence. You can believe some of the Bible or none of the Bible, or even things outside of the Bible, and still expect to arrive in heaven.

The problems with this thinking are many, not the least of which is this: "The entirety of Your word is truth, and every one of Your righteous judgments endures forever" (Psalm 119:160).

The Word of God—penned by 40 different authors in three different languages on three different continents over a period of 1,500 years—is entirely true, and the judgments within its pages endure forever.

Remember, among His characteristics, Jesus said He is the truth, along with the way and the life (John 14:6). In John 1:1, He is revealed as "the Word," who is God.

The point is that if you say you have a relationship with the Lord, you cannot distance yourself from His Word. He is the Word, and the entirety of the Word is truth.

Antisemitism is sin. It doesn't matter what one's opinion may be about Hamas and the Palestinians. It does not matter what anyone thinks about who was in the land first, simply because God said, "I will plant them in their land, and no longer shall they be pulled up from the land I have given them" (Amos 9:15).

It is the devil who is driving the global antisemitism of the day, and no Christian, under any circumstances, should ever side with the father of lies (John 8:44). What we believe matters, and the salad-bar approach to accepting some parts of the Bible but not others is nothing less than diabolical.

God is always right, and falling for the devil's twisting of Scripture never leads to anything good. Just ask Adam and Eve.

DAY 80

NONE OF THESE THINGS MOVE ME

In Acts 20:22-24, Paul wrote,

> Now I go bound in the spirit to Jerusalem, not knowing the things that will happen to me there, except that the Holy Spirit testifies in every city, saying that chains and tribulations await me. But none of these things move me; nor do I count my life dear to myself, so that I may finish my race with joy, and the ministry which I received from the Lord Jesus, to testify to the gospel of the grace of God.

The word "none" in this passage can also be translated as "no one," and the Greek word translated "move" has many meanings and could be read "make me transgress" or "change my purpose." Paul said he knew chains and tribulations were ahead wherever he went, but no one was going to persuade him to change his purpose.

If we knew great difficulties were coming, could we say the same? Would someone be able to persuade us to change our purpose or make us transgress? This is probably why the Lord gives us directions one step at a time. If we knew of hardships in advance and how to avoid them, we could easily fall into a trap.

It is equally important that Paul said no one could make him transgress, or violate a command. Jesus made it clear that in this life we will have tribulation (John 16:33), but in Him we will have peace, even in tribulation. This is what Paul had and described as the peace "which surpasses all understanding," which will "guard your hearts and minds" (Philippians 4:7).

Paul also prepared Timothy for what he could expect. In 2 Timothy 4:5, he wrote, "Be watchful in all things, endure afflictions, do the work of an evangelist, fulfill your ministry."

Evangelizing and doing the work of the ministry will bring afflictions, but we cannot let anyone move us from our purpose. We must fulfill our calling to tell others about Jesus.

DAY 81

THE IMPORTANCE OF PRAYER

In Matthew 6:7, Jesus said, "When you pray, do not use vain repetitions as the heathen do. For they think that they will be heard for their many words."

There is a movement in the church today that resorts to repeating biblical phrases or passages in the hopes of obtaining the meaning of them "for you." This is the practice of the heathen, and repeating words or phrases found in the Bible hundreds or thousands of times is not earnest prayer. Daniel provides an example of true prayer:

> At the beginning of your supplications the command went out, and I have come to tell you, for you are greatly beloved; therefore consider the matter, and understand the vision: "Seventy weeks are determined for your people and for your holy city, to finish the transgression, to make an end of sins, to make reconciliation for iniquity, to bring in everlasting righteousness, to seal up vision and prophecy, and to anoint the Most Holy" (Daniel 9:23-24).

Wouldn't it be wonderful if our prayer life looked like Daniel's! We pray, and before we say amen, God dispatches an angel to tell us His answer, then has the angel explain the answer and even provide a timeline of future events that reveals how and when the answer will be fulfilled. Yet we all recognize that is not how our prayers are normally answered.

The disciples had noticed that Jesus' prayer life was different than theirs. That's why they asked Him to teach them how to pray. In His answer, He said to honor God, pray that God's will be done on Earth, petition God for provision, ask for forgiveness and a forgiving spirit, request deliverance from the temptations of the evil one, and all of that is followed by another proclamation of God's greatness, acknowledging that His is the kingdom, the power, and the glory forever.

Notice that less than 10 percent of the model prayer included petitions for needs. It is important that we know how to pray if we hope to have a powerful prayer life.

DAY 82

CRISIS OF TRUST

Nothing is more important to any type of relationship than trust. When trust is broken, there are always companion issues that follow. In a marriage, heartbreak is often the outcome. In friendships, a diminished relationship is usually the consequence. In politics, suspicion is the end result.

While trust is often broken in this life, there is still one place where we can be assured that will never happen. We can always trust the Word of God and the God of the Word—and yes, they are inseparable. God is never wrong, and His Word is always trustworthy and true.

In Proverbs 3:5-6, we are told to "trust in the LORD with all your heart, and lean not on your own understanding; in all your ways acknowledge Him, and He shall direct your paths."

Significant trust is necessary on our part in our relationship with God. We must acknowledge He has a better understanding of all things to the point we allow Him to direct our paths. When we extend that level of trust, the end result is the assurance God knows what is best for us.

As we watch the world spiral out of control, we can trust what God's Word says about the end of the story. Israel will not be destroyed, and the devil and his two servants during the tribulation will be defeated when our Lord returns. There will be peace on Earth when the Prince of Peace rules for 1,000 years, and the best part about all this is that we can live with those assurances even before they happen.

Psalm 119:160 says of God, "The entirety of Your word is truth, and every one of Your righteous judgments endures forever."

God's Word says Christ is coming back for us, and then later, He will return to Earth with us. Trusting in these facts alone should change how we view everything we encounter and endure until He comes. Job went as far as to say, "Though He slay me, yet will I trust Him" (Job 13:15). We can trust God to the same extent today.

DAY 83

NO WEAPON WILL PROSPER

We need to be careful about applying Old Testament passages relating to Israel to ourselves. Yet there are some promises that, because they have to do with the unchanging nature and character of God, we who are in the church can appropriate them for ourselves. Here is a prime example:

> "No weapon formed against you shall prosper, and every tongue which rises against you in judgment you shall condemn. This is the heritage of the servants of the LORD, and their righteousness is from Me," says the LORD (Isaiah 54:17).

The scope of this promise includes those who serve the Lord and those who have received imputed righteousness from Him. That tells us these words written to Israel are not limited only to Israel. We, as Christians, are servants of the Lord, and we as Christians have been made righteous through Christ. That means the weapons formed against us will not prosper as we, too, are God's chosen people, not by birth but by faith.

The Hebrew word translated "prosper" means "to push forward or advance," and can be translated as "to succeed." We can read this as saying the weapons of the enemy will not achieve their intended result against those who are the Lord's servants and made righteous through belief in Him.

In Ephesians 6:16, we read that by "taking the shield of faith...you will be able to quench all the fiery darts of the wicked one." Paul tells the church at Ephesus that the fiery darts aimed at them can be quenched with the shield that comes through saving faith.

It is important to note that Isaiah and Peter aren't saying that weapons won't be formed and fiery darts will never be fired. Rather, they both say we don't have to be victims of them when they are. You may be thinking, *But what about the millions of martyrs who lost their lives over the centuries?* All who are absent from the body are now present with the Lord, so in their case, the devil lost again!

DAY 84

THE MIND OF CHRIST

At a time when there is so much delusion in people's thinking and they have exchanged the definitions of good and evil, we need to remember that among the many benefits of knowing the Lord and being saved by His grace is this: "God has not given us a spirit of fear, but of power and of love and of a sound mind" (2 Timothy 1:7).

Having a sound mind while the world has lost its mind is a huge blessing! Part of that soundness of mind is the result of having not been given a spirit of fear, but instead, of power and love.

First Corinthians 2:16 says, "For 'who has known the mind of the Lord that he may instruct Him?' But we have the mind of Christ." The fearless power we have been given will manifest itself in loving our enemies, doing good to those who hate us, and praying for those who spitefully use us, just as the Lord did. This mind of Christ will also give us discernment during this age of lies and misinformation and keep us from getting blown about by every wind of doctrine (Ephesians 4:14).

Christ's mind is revealed to us through His Word, which lights our path. Be careful of the thinking many have today, that says, "Because I am saved by grace, anything I do and believe is okay, even when it contradicts the Word of God." The mind of God is revealed in the Word of God, and the mind of the Christian needs to know the Word in order to be guided by it.

What a blessing it is to know that our faith in Christ has come with a peace that surpasses all understanding and guards the heart and mind through Christ Jesus (Philippians 4:7)!

In Psalm 119:11, we read, "Your word I have hidden in my heart, that I might not sin against You." Make sure you are hiding God's Word in your heart each day, and your steps will be ordered by the Lord.

DAY 85

THE FIRST RESURRECTION

Some Christians find the idea of the first resurrection to be somewhat confusing, and it is more easily understood when we consider two facts. One, the first resurrection refers to a category of people, not only an event. It is not dissimilar to being "in Christ." Revelation 20:6 says, "Blessed and holy is he who has part in the first resurrection. Over such the second death has no power, but they shall be priests of God and of Christ, and shall reign with Him a thousand years."

While there are many who would be considered "blessed" in this world, there is only one way to become holy, and that is to be in Christ. It is only those who are in Christ who are "a new creation; old things have passed away; behold, all things have become new" (2 Corinthians 5:17).

Two, we need to remember that a new and glorified body awaits those of us who are part of the first resurrection. As 1 Corinthians 15:20 says, "Now Christ is risen from the dead, and has become the firstfruits of those who have fallen asleep."

The resurrection of Christ from the dead and His bodily ascension from this life into the eternal realm have paved the way for those who take part in the first resurrection—they will follow Him into heaven in the same way. First Corinthians 15:50 describes this as our final victory, saying that "flesh and blood cannot inherit the kingdom of God; nor does corruption inherit incorruption."

Our corruptible bodies, which have been ravaged by the consequences of sin, are incapable of eternal existence. Yet because we are in Christ and will be part of the first resurrection, the sting of sin's consequences is overcome by Christ's victory over death.

This means a new, immortal, and incorruptible body awaits us at the first resurrection!

DAY 86

FULFILL YOUR CALLING

We live in a world that has largely turned its back on God, and at a time during which people in many churches have rejected sound doctrine and preferred to attend places that teach fables. In 2 Timothy 4:5, Paul told Timothy, "Be watchful in all things, endure afflictions, do the work of an evangelist, fulfill your ministry."

The word "watchful" is elsewhere translated as "be sober." In other words, because the last days will be a season of afflictions, our full and undiminished attention is going to be required of us.

The word "fulfill" means "to entirely accomplish." Paul also told the church at Ephesus that the purpose of the church gathering is to equip the saints "for the work of ministry, for the edifying of the body of Christ" (Ephesians 4:12). In Luke 19, Jesus said in the parable of the minas to "do business till I come" (verse 13).

While we all recognize that each day that passes brings us closer to the unknown day and hour of the rapture, each day also draws us closer to a time of tribulation like the world has never seen. Thus, the admonitions to do business and fulfill the ministry of evangelism until He comes are more vital with the passing of each day.

We are living around people who will go into the great tribulation, and as students of Bible prophecy, we know how terrible things will be on Earth. Let that be a motivation to do what the Word and Holy Spirit have equipped us to do and fulfill our ministries of evangelizing the lost.

Time is short and, as stated in the parable of the minas, the Master is about to return. We don't want to report to Him, like the wicked servant, that we did nothing with what He gave us.

DAY 87

THE LORD IS WITH US

Sometimes the responsibilities the Lord asks and expects of us can be intimidating. Can you imagine how Joshua felt when the Lord tapped him to replace Moses? Yet the Lord gave Joshua a reminder that we would do well to remember:

> No man shall be able to stand before you all the days of your life; as I was with Moses, so I will be with you. I will not leave you nor forsake you. Be strong and of good courage, for to this people you shall divide as an inheritance the land which I swore to their fathers to give them (Joshua 1:5-6).

The Lord did not say, "You're not Moses, so there's not much I can do through you." Rather, God assured him that just as He had been with Moses, He would be with Joshua. God has made a similar promise to us: "He Himself has said, 'I will never leave you nor forsake you.' So we may boldly say: 'The LORD is my helper; I will not fear. What can man do to me?'" (Hebrews 13:5-6).

Is this not the same promise God made to Joshua? That the Lord would be with him and he would not be left to lead Israel in his own strength? We need to remember that the things God accomplished through Moses were manifestations of His power. He told Joshua, and Hebrews tells us, that we don't have to worry or wonder whether we can do what God has asked of us because these responsibilities are not about us and our power, but about God and His power.

So if the Lord asks you to do something that you find to be intimidating, remember: If He called you to it, He will enable you to do it, so do not fear—the Lord is your helper.

DAY 88

HAVING JOY IN THE LAST DAYS

In Psalm 103:1-5, we read these words of joyous praise:

> Bless the Lord, O my soul; and all that is within me, bless His holy name! Bless the Lord, O my soul, and forget not all His benefits: who forgives all your iniquities, who heals all your diseases, who redeems your life from destruction, who crowns you with lovingkindness and tender mercies, who satisfies your mouth with good things, so that your youth is renewed like the eagle's.

King David hit the nail on the head in his reminder of the benefits and blessings of knowing the Lord. God, through Christ, has forgiven all of our sins, and someday, we will all live with perfect and eternal health. He has redeemed us from destructive life patterns and actions and crowned us with His lovingkindness and tender mercies. He also satisfies our mouth with good things, and someday will renew our youthful strength and stamina.

Yet we live in a world filled with people who say their way is the right way. Their way is the way of tolerance, and yet they tolerate only those who think like them. There are people in power today who say our world would be better if there were fewer of us. They have polarized the planet and set people at odds with one another, setting the stage for the hatred that will dominate during the tribulation. So how do we maintain our joy in times such as these?

Colossians 3:2 gives us the answer: "Set your mind on things above, not on things on the earth." When the world tries to take control of our everyday lives and thoughts, set your mind on things above. When the world tries to pit us against each other, set your mind on things above. When the world confuses fame with wisdom and authority, set your mind on things above. When the world tries to undermine your health and well being, set your mind on things above, where Christ is, and not on the earth below.

DAY 89

COMING IN THE CLOUDS

In an age when the subject of Bible prophecy is ignored and even disparaged, it is noteworthy that even though Paul was in Thessaloniki for only "three Sabbaths" (Acts 17:2), he communicated truths concerning the rapture of the church and the coming day of the Lord during his brief visit. Afterward, when the Thessaloniki believers asked a question about the rapture, Paul wrote,

> I do not want you to be ignorant, brethren, concerning those who have fallen asleep, lest you sorrow as others who have no hope. For if we believe that Jesus died and rose again, even so God will bring with Him those who sleep in Jesus. For this we say to you by the word of the Lord, that we who are alive and remain until the coming of the Lord will by no means precede those who are asleep. For the Lord Himself will descend from heaven with a shout, with the voice of an archangel, and with the trumpet of God. And the dead in Christ will rise first. Then we who are alive and remain shall be caught up together with them in the clouds to meet the Lord in the air. And thus we shall always be with the Lord. Therefore comfort one another with these words (1 Thessalonians 4:13-18).

The early church believed in the bodily resurrection of the "dead in Christ" and often referred to death as sleep, meaning it was a temporary state.

In a time when much of the world is gathered in opposition against Israel and the church is viewed largely as the enemy of a more enlightened culture, it is good to know and remember that this world is not our home; this life is not all there is. A pain- and problem-free future awaits us in which we will never grow old and never experience sickness or disease or feel sorrow or pain, including the emotional pains of life that often stain our faces with tears.

This transition will happen in the twinkling of an eye, perhaps even today!

DAY 90

LIFE BEGINS AT CONCEPTION

It is quite amazing that people today can repeat the mantra "trust the science" yet don't do that themselves and don't even know what a woman is. There is no new evidence that inside a pregnant mother's womb is anything other than a human baby. There is no new scientific proof that says the baby, at such-and-such a time during the pregnancy, becomes human.

The pro-choice crowd has decided that they can make things up that are anti-science and untrue—such as "It's not a baby until it breathes air," or "It's not human until it has sentience" (the ability to perceive or feel things). How foolish to think that a baby who reacts to touch can't feel its precious little body being torn apart during an abortion. The force behind the "my body, my choice" movement is not science, but Satan.

Matthew 24:12 describes well the prevailing condition of our culture: "Because lawlessness will abound, the love of many will grow cold." Since 1970, the number of children estimated to have been killed in their mother's womb ranges from 1.72 to 2.15 billion.

Remember when King David had an adulterous encounter with Bathsheba? She became pregnant, and later, after David arranged for the death of her husband, he married Bathsheba. As a consequence of his sin, shortly after the child was born, it became gravely ill and died. David surprised his attendants when, upon hearing about the child's death, he said to them,

> While the child was alive, I fasted and wept; for I said, "Who can tell whether the LORD will be gracious to me, that the child may live? But now he is dead; why should I fast? Can I bring him back again? I shall go to him, but he shall not return to me" (2 Samuel 12:22-23).

David believed that when his infant child died, he would go to where David would later go—in the presence of God. This informs us that someday in the New Jerusalem, we can expect to meet a massive number of humans who were slain while in the womb because they were actually children, not blobs of tissue.

DAY 91

THE GOD OF RESTORATION

The nation of Israel teaches us many lessons about human nature and the nature of God. After the people of Israel had forsaken the sabbatical year for 490 years, the Lord told them what He would do in response to their disobedience: "This whole land shall be a desolation and an astonishment, and these nations shall serve the king of Babylon seventy years" (Jeremiah 25:11).

Yet in the midst of warning about the consequences for their sin, the Lord called for His people to remember His great love for them:

> After seventy years are completed at Babylon, I will visit you and perform My good word toward you, and cause you to return to this place. For I know the thoughts that I think toward you, says the Lord, thoughts of peace and not of evil, to give you a future and a hope. Then you will call upon Me and go and pray to Me, and I will listen to you (Jeremiah 29:10-12).

This is true for us as well. The Lord does not change, and when we disobey and experience the consequences of our sin, the Lord wants us to remember His nature and character, that His thoughts toward us are of peace, and His discipline does not negate our future hope. In Joel 2:25-26, God told Israel,

> I will restore to you the years that the swarming locust has eaten, the crawling locust, the consuming locust, and the chewing locust, My great army which I sent among you. You shall eat in plenty and be satisfied, and praise the name of the Lord your God, who has dealt wondrously with you; and My people shall never be put to shame.

Our God is a God of restoration, even when what needs to be restored is the result of our own failures. We know from God's dealings with Israel that He is abundant in mercy and ready to pardon, and His thoughts toward us are not of evil.

DAY 92

FULLNESS OF JOY

In a world filled with negative thoughts and events, it is nice to have something to look forward to. The Bible continually reminds us that this world is not our home, and John the Beloved even warns us of the danger of loving it or the things of it (1 John 2:15).

In John 16:33, Jesus said, "These things I have spoken to you, that in Me you may have peace. In the world you will have tribulation; but be of good cheer, I have overcome the world."

While this passage is familiar to most Christians, it does not seem to make the list of "favorite life verses" for many. But Jesus' words help to highlight the contrast between this life and the next, and underscore why we need to keep looking forward to our eternal home and existence. The Greek word translated "tribulation" in no way refers to events such as those during the great tribulation. Rather, the word means "pressures, afflictions, anguish, burdens, persecution, troubles." This is clearly a fitting description of life, as we know it, in this fallen world.

One of the many reasons why we have to keep looking ahead and remembering what we are looking forward to is stated in Psalm 16:11: "You will show me the path of life; in Your presence is fullness of joy; at Your right hand are pleasures forevermore."

For born-again believers, this life will end in a place and existence filled with joy and pleasure that will last forever. A key truth we want to keep in mind about this wonderful reality is that the Lord's presence is already in us, which is why we can be filled with joy and enjoy this life even though we are surrounded by temptations and tribulations.

Life in this world can be hard, but life in the next one isn't and never will be. Keep your eyes on the prize and remember what is in your future!

DAY 93

GOD'S PLANS

In the book of Romans, the apostle Paul gave us a wonderful reminder that many of us need to heed today: "Whatever things were written before were written for our learning, that we through the patience and comfort of the Scriptures might have hope" (15:4).

If we were to paraphrase Paul's statement, we could say the Old Testament (the things "written before") was given to us for our learning, patience, comfort, and hope. Yet sadly, many in the church today marginalize the Old Testament to secondary status even though its contents are just as inspired as those found in the New Testament.

Some say, "Read only the red letters," pointing to the words of Jesus printed in red in many Bibles. There are two major problems with such thinking: First, there were no red letters in the original Greek manuscripts. And second, such statements diminish the inspiration of the rest of the Bible and are an insult to the third member of the triune Godhead, the Holy Spirit, who inspired all that is written in the Scriptures, including the Old Testament.

In Genesis 18:17-18, God said, "Shall I hide from Abraham what I am doing, since Abraham shall surely become a great and mighty nation, and all the nations of the earth shall be blessed in him?"

It is the Lord's desire to make known His plans to His people, and down through the ages, He has continually revealed what His will is for the present and what awaits us in the future. For some, He revealed the near future, as with Abram and Sarai having a child. And for others, He has revealed the distant future, as with Daniel, who was told of things that would happen "many days in the future" (Daniel 8:26).

If you're searching for God's plan for your life, read your Bible. You may not find your name there, but you will find His will.

DAY 94

DARE TO SHARE

If there is one thing in our world that is a rare commodity, it is good news. The media bombards us daily with bad news or negative information. Political leaders have adopted the practice of tearing down their opponents instead of promoting their own merits and qualifications. Some parts of the world are quaking and shaking, some areas are flooded from torrential rains, while still others are experiencing severe drought. International tensions abound, racial strife is increasing, and in this information age, all of this inundates us with bad news.

Yet in the midst of all that is happening in the world, there is good news—news that is so good it makes all the bad news more bearable. And while this good news is available to all, billions have not yet heard it. That is why, in Mark 16:15, Jesus said, "Go into all the world and preach the gospel to every creature."

Think about the number of spiritually lost and hopeless people we encounter on any given day and the unknown stories of their lives. Many cloak their faces with a smile that hides sorrow, hopelessness, and despair. In light of recent statistics, it is almost certain that you will walk by people today who are considering ending it all—for them, the bad news is too much, the pain is too deep, the trauma is too much to bear. And yet, we are in possession of good news that can restore hope, heal broken hearts, and set captives free—and therefore, we must not be fearful or keep silent.

Good news is such a rare commodity today, and news that can help people to endure all that is happening in the world without losing hope or peace can only be found in Christ. We are His ambassadors, representatives in a foreign land of the heavenly kingdom. And we have been entrusted with life-changing news about eternity that billions are in need of.

Tell someone about Jesus today!

DAY 95

WHAT THE LAST TRUMPET COMMUNICATES

If you have seen a Western movie, chances are you have heard the trumpet signal used to tell cavalry troops to charge. A military trumpeter is also tasked with sounding the notes for retreat when it is time to pull back. On military bases, "Taps" is played at the end of the day to signal lights out, and military funerals are often accompanied by the playing of "Taps" to indicate the end of a veteran's time here on Earth.

Different uses of a trumpet have different meanings. In 1 Corinthians 14:7-8, we read, "Even things without life, whether flute or harp, when they make a sound, unless they make a distinction in the sounds, how will it be known what is piped or played? For if the trumpet makes an uncertain sound, who will prepare for battle?"

The context of Paul's statement to the Corinthians is that of the importance of the interpretation of tongues, which is necessary so that the church can be edified. But his choice of illustration here makes the point that trumpets, when used to make certain sounds, communicate specific messages.

During the trumpet judgments in Revelation, seven trumpets will be sounded, with six to announce specific types of judgment coming upon the earth. The seventh will make a great announcement over all creation: "Then the seventh angel sounded: And there were loud voices in heaven, saying, 'The kingdoms of this world have become the kingdoms of our Lord and of His Christ, and He shall reign forever and ever!'" (Revelation 11:15).

In an age where up is down and down is up, and evils are now considered good, it is reassuring to know that someday, the Lord will return to Earth and reign and we will be with Him!

Paul told us the last days would be perilous, and indeed they are. And yet we know that someday, things are going to turn around. Wars will cease, evil will be held in check, Satan will be bound, and there will be peace on Earth. Keep that in mind as you make your way through these last days!

DAY 96

THE CONFESSION OF OUR HOPE

One of the greatest testimonies of the grace and mercy of God, outside that of the nation of Israel, is the restoration of the apostle Peter—a man who walked with Jesus and walked on water. A man who saw Jesus heal and, by God's power, healed others himself (Matthew 10:8). A man who also said this:

> "Even if all are made to stumble because of You, I will never be made to stumble." Jesus said to him, "Assuredly, I say to you that this night, before the rooster crows, you will deny Me three times." Peter said to Him, "Even if I have to die with You, I will not deny You!" And so said all the disciples (Matthew 26:33-35).

Peter not only denied the Lord, he did so three times. The second time, Peter denied Him with an oath, and the third time, with cursing and swearing, saying, "I do not know the Man!" (Matthew 26:74). Yet in Acts chapter 2, we find Peter, the thrice denier, preaching the first gospel message that opened the church age, and doing so with thunderous power and authority. The Lord's grace toward Peter brings to mind Lamentations 3:21-23: "This I recall to my mind, therefore I have hope. Through the LORD's mercies we are not consumed, because His compassions fail not. They are new every morning; great is Your faithfulness."

If you have had a great failure or denial of the Lord in your life, either in thought or deed, take heart: God's mercies are new every morning, and His faithfulness toward you is great! As 2 Timothy 2:13 says, "If we are faithless, He remains faithful; He cannot deny Himself."

Dear friend, God is faithful! This isn't something He does; it is what He is. He cannot deny His very nature. If you have fallen or failed, get up and keep going, for His mercies endure forever, and His faithfulness is great!

DAY 97

THE CHURCH AND ISRAEL

We are in a unique season of history as we watch world events unfold that indicate a change is near, even at the doors! That change is the transition from the church age to the seventieth week of Daniel, which requires the removal of the church from the earth.

After all, the church was not present during any of the first 69 now-fulfilled weeks of the 70 determined for Daniel's people and the holy city (Daniel 9:24). This precedent implies the removal of the church before the seventieth week can begin.

The last time the Jews had possession of Jerusalem at the same time the church existed, though in its infancy, was right after Jesus' ascension. Now, for the first time in history, not only are the Jews in possession of Jerusalem again, but the nation of Israel and the church exist simultaneously! Could it be that this unprecedented situation has happened right before Jesus comes for His church, and then with His church at the second coming?

Paul wrote this about the rapture in 1 Thessalonians 4:15-18:

> This we say to you by the word of the Lord, that we who are alive and remain until the coming of the Lord will by no means precede those who are asleep. For the Lord Himself will descend from heaven with a shout, with the voice of an archangel, and with the trumpet of God. And the dead in Christ will rise first. Then we who are alive and remain shall be caught up together with them in the clouds to meet the Lord in the air. And thus we shall always be with the Lord. Therefore comfort one another with these words.

With the world a delusional mess, the Middle East powder keg exploding, and many within the church not enduring sound doctrine, we should expect to hear, at any time, the trumpet of God calling us to meet the dead raised up in Christ and the Lord Himself in the air. What a wonderfully comforting thought!

DAY 98

THE MASTER OF DECEPTION

Deception has always been the primary weapon of Satan's arsenal. It was the weapon he deployed in the beginning with Eve: "Now the serpent was more cunning than any beast of the field which the Lord God had made. And he said to the woman, 'Has God indeed said, "You shall not eat of every tree of the garden"?'" (Genesis 3:1).

Eve replied that if they did eat of the tree, they would die. Satan then told Eve the opposite of what was true—in essence, saying, "You will not die; God knows that if you do eat from it you'll be like Him, and He doesn't want you to be like Him." God had said if they disobeyed, they would cease being like Him, and Satan twisted God's words to mean the opposite. This brings to mind 2 Timothy 4:3-4:

> The time will come when they will not endure sound doctrine, but according to their own desires, because they have itching ears, they will heap up for themselves teachers; and they will turn their ears away from the truth, and be turned aside to fables.

A fable is distinct from a myth, which is comprised of strictly fictional beings and events. Fables, however, make use of literal things in conjunction with fabrications—like the fable of the old woman who lived in a shoe and had so many children she didn't know what to do. Old women, shoes, and children are all nonfictional elements, but the idea of an old woman living in a shoe with countless children makes it a fable.

Some preachers use words found in the Bible to create fables that people would rather hear in place of the truth. When you go to a church, don't simply listen to a preacher's vocabulary, find out about their dictionary—what they mean when they use terms found in the Bible, like *prosperity* or *success*. Our best defense against fables is the truth!

DAY 99

JESUS IS KING

It has been said that in the beginning, God created man in His own image, and in the end, man returned the favor—meaning man created God as they imagine Him. Sadly, there are multitudes of people who simply aren't happy with God no matter what He does or what His purposes are.

God the Son came into the world as a Savior, and most of His own people said, "We're not in need of a Savior; we need a political leader to get us out from under Roman oppression and rule." The Bible promises that Jesus will return someday to sit on the throne of David and rule as an earthly King, and yet there are people today who say, "We aren't interested in a ruler; we need a Savior who forgives us and asks and expects nothing of anyone."

Dr. J. Vernon McGee once said, "This is God's universe, and God does things His way. You may have a better way, but you don't have a universe."[4]

Hebrews 9:27-28 helps us to have a right perspective: "It is appointed for men to die once, but after this the judgment, so Christ was offered once to bear the sins of many. To those who eagerly wait for Him He will appear a second time, apart from sin, for salvation."

Hebrews is telling us that the Lord Jesus is coming again for a purpose that is distinct from shedding His blood for the sins of the whole world (1 John 2:2). The word translated "salvation" means "to bring to safety, to deliver."

Jesus is coming again to deliver us and bring us to safety. He is coming on a warhorse to tread the winepress of the fierceness and wrath of Almighty God. Some may not like that idea or believe this about God's plan, but no one can change or stop it. Some might think it would be better for Him to just forgive everyone universally. But this is His universe, and He does what He pleases.

DAY 100

THE ERRORS OF UNIVERSALISM

While the Bible is filled with figures of speech and illustrations, there is nothing more dangerous to our understanding of the Bible—and especially Bible prophecy—than allegorizing or spiritualizing that which is to be taken literally. We are to accept God's Word for what it says.

In Psalm 42:1, we read, "As the deer pants for the water brooks, so pants my soul for You, O God." The word "as" indicates this is an illustration of the literal truth of longing for God. The soul does not literally pant, but it should possess a thirst for the things of God.

Consider what is said in Revelation 4:7: "The first living creature was like a lion, the second living creature like a calf, the third living creature had a face like a man, and the fourth living creature was like a flying eagle." In this verse, the word "like" is used in its prepositional form to indicate a similarity rather than an absolute or a literal likeness. The Bible is always careful to identify word pictures, metaphors, and figures of speech so we can determine the literal from the allegorical.

Because 1 John 2:2 says Jesus died for the sins of the whole world, there are those who, under the banner of universalism (which teaches that everyone on Earth will be saved), teach what is called *theosis*, also known as divinization, or the process of becoming like God. Universalists teach that all souls will ultimately be reconciled and conformed to the image of the glorified resurrected Christ, whether they are born again or not.

To say this is to take the text beyond its context and a failure to let scripture interpret scripture. If everyone is saved because Jesus died for the sins of the whole world, then what is the purpose of the Great Commission? Why would there ever be a great tribulation? Why would Romans 6:23 say, "The wages of sin is death"?

Universalism is not true; you must be born again!

DAY 101

THANK YOU FOR THE CROSS

It has been said, "The ground is level at the foot of the cross," which reminds us that no matter our past, no matter our present station in life, no matter our ethnic or cultural background, whosoever will may come and find forgiveness and reconciliation with God through the cross of Jesus Christ! This is one of the many reasons the gospel is good news.

First Corinthians 1:18 proclaims this incredible truth: "The message of the cross is foolishness to those who are perishing, but to us who are being saved it is the power of God."

Most people readily and easily understand and accept the concept of debt and repayment, and yet when it comes to the "wages of sin" (Romans 6:23) or the debt accrued by our sin and the repayment of that debt, the same concept is deemed as foolishness.

The world needs a strong gospel today, the very power of God manifested through His Word and the message of Christ and Him crucified. Many today are seeking signs that there is a God, and others are saying that believing the Bible is foolish. If Paul were writing to our world today, he would have written the same truths he did to the believers at Corinth. The wisdom of man can do nothing to pay man's sin debt; the disputer or debater of this age is foolish compared to the wisdom of God.

Again, most understand the concept of debt and repayment, but for God to allow sin to go unpunished would leave our sin debt unpaid and would deny His just nature. Therefore, just as one man, Adam, introduced death and separation from God into the realm of human existence, so, too, God became a man in the person of Jesus Christ to pay the sin debt of others by dying a death He did not deserve, thus satisfying God's justness while paying the sin debt of the whole world.

He paid a debt He did not owe because we owed a debt we could not pay.

DAY 102

ARE YOU READY?

The concept of "casting off" and "putting on" is one that runs consistently through the Scriptures in various forms and phrases. The "works of darkness" Paul spoke of to the church at Rome (Romans 13:12) were called "evil" deeds by Jesus in John 3:20. Peter called them "the will of the Gentiles" in 1 Peter 4:3, and in every use of such terms, there is either the implied or direct call to "cast them off" prior to the directive to "put on the new." That's what we see in Colossians 3:8-10:

> Now you yourselves are to put off all these: anger, wrath, malice, blasphemy, filthy language out of your mouth. Do not lie to one another, since you have put off the old man with his deeds, and have put on the new man who is renewed in knowledge according to the image of Him who created him.

Imagine never taking off the clothes you wore all day and trying to put on a new set of clothes over them. You might be able to pull this off for a day or two, but to continue doing this would soon become impossible. The same is true about being a new creation in Christ. The new you doesn't fit over the old you; the old you must be cast off and the new you must be put on.

This is one of the most significant ways we can be confident we are ready for when the Lord appears in the air and the dead in Christ are raised and we who are alive and remain are taken up to meet them to forever be with the Lord (1 Thessalonians 5:16-17).

Jesus is coming again, and until then, we are to cast off the works of darkness and walk in His marvelous light. No matter how crazy the world may get, God is still on the throne, His will cannot be averted, and His Word is going to be fulfilled, even though Satan opposes it and people question and doubt it. His will is going to be done on Earth as it is in heaven.

DAY 103

JERUSALEM, JERUSALEM

In a world that is spiraling out of control on every level, it is good to know that someday, God's will is going to be done on Earth as it is in heaven. Jesus promised,

> Let not your heart be troubled; you believe in God, believe also in Me. In My Father's house are many mansions; if it were not so, I would have told you. I go to prepare a place for you. And if I go and prepare a place for you, I will come again and receive you to Myself; that where I am, there you may be also (John 14:1-3).

One reason there is no need for our hearts to be troubled is because we know the end of the story and many of the events that lead to it, including the fact Jerusalem will take center stage on the world scene:

> Thus says the LORD, who stretches out the heavens, lays the foundation of the earth, and forms the spirit of man within him: "Behold, I will make Jerusalem a cup of drunkenness to all the surrounding peoples, when they lay siege against Judah and Jerusalem. And it shall happen in that day that I will make Jerusalem a very heavy stone for all peoples; all who would heave it away will surely be cut in pieces, though all nations of the earth are gathered against it" (Zechariah 12:1-3).

The nations of the world are gathering against Jerusalem today. The United Nations is constantly condemning Israel through its antisemitic resolutions while it remains silent about the atrocities committed against Christians and Jews around the world, as well as the human rights violations committed by tyrannical and oppressive governments.

This is a clear sign that the seventieth week of Daniel is on the near horizon and that the church is soon headed to the Father's house so that we may be where the Lord is.

Perhaps even today!

DAY 104

A GOOD WITNESS

It has been said that if you believe we are living in the last days, then you should act like it! Jesus Himself made it clear that there will be an entire generation of people who will bypass death and go to the place He has prepared for them to be with Him forever (John 14:3).

If we believe that this time is near and this day is approaching, then it should stir our hearts to do two things: First, tell unbelievers how to avoid the tribulation through faith in Christ. And second, prepare unsaved people for what this time is going to bring.

We need to tell others that the days to come are prophesied in the Bible and give them specifics about the events that will take place. If they end up remaining on Earth during the tribulation and see Bible prophecy unfold right before their eyes, hopefully they will remember the gospel message we shared with them.

The invitation of the gospel is for everyone. Romans 10:12-13 says, "There is no distinction between Jew and Greek, for the same Lord over all is rich to all who call upon Him. For 'whoever calls on the name of the Lord shall be saved.'"

Time is short, and we are quickly closing in on the seventieth week of Daniel, which is preceded by the rapture of the church. If we believe that, then we should act like it! We should tell Jew and Gentile alike what is coming and how they can avoid the time of tribulation such as the world has never seen.

Acts 1:8 makes our calling clear: "You shall receive power when the Holy Spirit has come upon you; and you shall be witnesses to Me in Jerusalem, and in all Judea and Samaria, and to the end of the earth."

It is time for the church to be bold, strong, and of good courage. We are to live in a manner that is distinct from a lost and perishing world, as witnesses who act and live like the end is at hand.

DAY 105

JESUS, THE GREAT "I AM"

In this age during which information is collected by various groups in an effort to track our spending patterns, identify our likes and dislikes, and even monitor trends in an effort to do better target marketing of any given product, there are Christian groups who also conduct surveys and monitor trends within the church.

One recent survey sought to examine the beliefs of evangelical Christians regarding certain key theological precepts. The most disturbing of the findings was that 73 percent of people who consider themselves evangelical Christians believe that Jesus is the first and greatest created being of God,[5] which is a clear denial of His deity.

Colossians 1:15-17 is clear on this truth:

> He [Jesus] is the image of the invisible God, the firstborn over all creation. For by Him all things were created that are in heaven and that are on earth, visible and invisible, whether thrones or dominions or principalities or powers. All things were created through Him and for Him. And He is before all things, and in Him all things consist.

Add to this Jesus' seven "I am" statements recorded in John's Gospel, linking Him back to the conversation Moses had with God at the burning bush in Exodus 3, and there is no question the Bible declares that Jesus is not a created being but is God the Son, eternally existent and uncreated.

The scribes and Pharisees were unwilling to see the evidence and confess Yeshua as the Savior and Redeemer of Israel. For those polled today, however, we could say they are unable to see the deity of Jesus largely because there are so many churches that do very little, if any, Bible teaching. That leaves those who may want to know who Jesus is left with the options of either asking unsaved friends or, as the saying goes, "googling it."

Jesus told the religious elite that their search of the Scriptures should have led them to Him (John 5:39). The same should be true for any who search the Scriptures today.

DAY 106

PEACE IN THE BIRTH PANGS

Something we don't think about often is that when Adam fell, creation fell too. It was never God's desire that we live in a climate of fear of natural disasters, shifting tectonic plates, tornadoes and hurricanes, and other such calamities.

Life in a fallen world is far different than life in the initial created world. Adam and Eve went from walking in the garden with the Lord during the cool of the day to being barred from the garden by an angel with a flaming sword. The angel guarded the way to the tree of life, which, if Adam and Eve had eaten from it in their sinful state, their fallen condition would have become eternal.

Romans 8:22 says, "We know that the whole creation groans and labors with birth pangs together until now." We live in a time during which the travails of the earth are increasing in frequency and intensity in a labor-pain-like fashion. Earthquakes are increasing, weather phenomena are getting more intense, and plagues are sweeping the globe. It seems that as soon as one disaster subsides, another comes.

How do we keep from being overwhelmed at such a time as this? Remember that Jesus has overcome the world and will someday create a new heaven and new earth in which righteousness dwells. No earthquakes or hurricanes, no famines or plagues. What man caused in the garden, Jesus conquered on the cross!

In this life, we will experience the consequences of being in a fallen world. So as the world groans and awaits its deliverance from the curse, let's remember there is coming a day when the curse will be lifted, and Psalm 16:11 will become true for us: "You will show me the path of life; in Your presence is fullness of joy; at Your right hand are pleasures forevermore."

DAY 107

JESUS AND THE PASSOVER

Of the many aspects of God's character and nature we should be grateful for, a key one is His willingness and desire to communicate with man. God has made known His love and plans for the people of Israel in every way imaginable and revealed Himself through miracles and wonders so that they, and the world, might know He is a good and loving God who is righteous and holy. It is also true that for about 1,500 years, between the time the first Passover lamb was offered and Jesus' death on the cross, God made it clear to Israel that blood had to be shed to cover man's sin.

God also explained to Israel—through the Passover lamb—that not just any shed blood was sufficient, but that the blood had to be innocent blood. That's why John the Baptist's words in John 1:29 are so significant: "Behold! The Lamb of God who takes away the sin of the world!" And the writer of Hebrews wrote, "We do not have a High Priest who cannot sympathize with our weaknesses, but was in all points tempted as we are, yet without sin" (4:15).

The blood of bulls and goats was not sufficient to bring about our forgiveness and salvation. Better blood was required even than that of the innocent Passover lambs offered through the centuries. The better blood was that of our sinless Savior, who came to take away the sins of the world.

For 33 years, Jesus lived on the earth, and three of those years were spent in public ministry, during which He proved Himself to be the One whom the Passover and Feast of Unleavened Bread were pointing to. He is the Lamb of God, and as such, is innocent of all sin.

No ordinary man could shed their blood for the sins of the whole world. Not even the shed blood of an extraordinary man could accomplish that. Only the God-man, Jesus Christ, could pay the sin debt of the whole world with His shed blood!

DAY 108

ABRAHAM, ISAAC, AND JACOB

May 14, 1948, was a day of great prophetic significance. It began the final march toward the end of the church age and the beginning of the seventieth week of Daniel. The fig tree Jesus spoke of in Matthew 24:32 has "become tender and [put] forth leaves." The Greek word translated "tender" means "to be full of sap." The sap carries nutrients through the branches and leaves, making the tree ready to bear fruit.

Satan is well aware of the sequence of events that will take place during the last days, and his desire is to destroy the fig tree before it bears the fruit of Zechariah 12:10:

> I will pour on the house of David and on the inhabitants of Jerusalem the Spirit of grace and supplication; then they will look on Me whom they pierced. Yes, they will mourn for Him as one mourns for his only son, and grieve for Him as one grieves for a firstborn.

Satan has attempted this through the Holocaust and the current rise in antisemitism. He has also done this through spiritual deception, convincing some that the church is the new Israel. To others he has given false messages about the Bible being corrupted. They claim that a "new and improved" word from God has now come. This is what Mormons and Muslims have done. They use familiar-sounding terminology but they have an altogether different dictionary. Both have in their writings a place for someone called Jesus, but it is not the Jesus of the Bible.

In contrast, God said in Matthew 22:32, "I am the God of Abraham, the God of Isaac, and the God of Jacob...God is not the God of the dead, but of the living."

The Jesus of the Bible, the real Jesus, is God in human flesh. He is the God of Abraham, Isaac, and Jacob, and besides Him, there is no other! Make sure you check a person's dictionary when you hear spiritual-sounding vocabulary that could be deceiving!

DAY 109

CHRIST IN YOU

One of the most encouraging aspects of Scripture is that many of those who wrote it or were written about had failures in their lives, and yet God used them in great and mighty ways. The apostle Paul would certainly qualify as a great example. He was a former Pharisee who persecuted the church and consented to the death of the church's first martyr, Stephen. Yet later, he wrote this:

> I have been crucified with Christ; it is no longer I who live, but Christ lives in me; and the life which I now live in the flesh I live by faith in the Son of God, who loved me and gave Himself for me (Galatians 2:20).

This personalized perspective of the work of Christ on the cross was likely a major contributing factor to Paul's usability. He didn't simply write that in Christ we are new creations from which old things have passed away (2 Corinthians 5:17). He lived this truth, and God used him mightily because of it.

The same is true for all who believe the gospel truth: They are new creations, the past is dead, the future is bright, and God wants to use them mightily. But if we spend our lives in the past or drag it into the present, then the past will become our primary focus and we'll spend our lives as the walking wounded rather than as warriors in Christ.

While it is true that life brings hurtful things our way and that past sins can have lifelong consequences, those things do not comprise our identity. Do not allow the devil to exploit memories of sins that were nailed to the cross. Remember, Jesus died for you and gave Himself for you so that you might then live—in spite of the past—for Him as He brings glory to the Father through the good works He does in you. You are no longer what you used to be, but you have become free indeed!

DAY 110

THE GOD OF MIRACLES

How fortunate we are to serve a loving and all-powerful God! Our God rides the clouds and measures the universe with the span of His hand. He sets the boundaries for the seas, He names and numbers the stars, He commands light to shine out of the darkness, He is not bound by the laws of nature, nor is He limited by difficult circumstances. When He tells the lame to walk, they can. When He commands the blind to see, they do. When He says to the leper "Be clean," they are. And someday, He will say to the dead in Christ and those who are still alive in Christ, "Meet Me in the clouds," and they will!

Scripture repeatedly confirms the greatness of God's power in passages like these:

> Ah, Lord God! Behold, You have made the heavens and the earth by Your great power and outstretched arm. There is nothing too hard for You (Jeremiah 32:17).

> By faith Enoch was taken away so that he did not see death, "and was not found, because God had taken him"; for before he was taken he had this testimony, that he pleased God (Hebrews 11:5).

Because God is all-powerful, it is no harder for Him to make millions bypass death than it is for Him to do the same with one person. If God can part the Red Sea for His people to cross over safely, if He can cause the waters of a river during flood season to stand up in a heap so His people can enter the Promised Land, if Jesus can tell a man blind from birth to open his eyes and see and a lame man to rise up and walk, and if He can calm a stormy sea and walk on water, then causing millions who have faith in Him to bypass death and meet Him in the air with the resurrected dead in Christ is not only possible, it's proven.

DAY 111

LAST-DAYS SCOFFERS

The apostle Peter said, in his second epistle, that he wanted to stir up the minds of his readers to the words of the holy prophets and apostles of the Lord. He opened this section of the letter with this statement about the last days:

> Knowing this first: that scoffers will come in the last days, walking according to their own lusts, and saying, "Where is the promise of His coming? For since the fathers fell asleep, all things continue as they were from the beginning of creation" (2 Peter 3:3-4).

Peter went on to say that they "willfully forget" (verse 5), which means they choose to ignore that in the past, God has judged the world, and things have not continued in the same way since the beginning. His point is that this will happen again, not with a flood of water, but with fire (verses 6-7). Peter then says:

> Beloved, do not forget this one thing, that with the Lord one day is as a thousand years, and a thousand years as one day. The Lord is not slack concerning His promise, as some count slackness, but is longsuffering toward us, not willing that any should perish but that all should come to repentance (verses 8-9).

Peter also points out that God dwells outside of time and that 1,000 years and one day are equal to Him, so we cannot look at the length of time that God waits to judge the world and assume He has had a change of heart regarding global judgment. God is waiting because of His desire that all would come to know Him and repent. Think about the number of people who have been saved in the past ten years, or ten months, or even ten weeks or minutes, who will now escape the wrath that will come upon the whole world, and most importantly, the fires of hell.

Judgment is coming, and we are to seek to rescue from death as many as we can before it does.

DAY 112

THE LORD WILL GATHER HIS PEOPLE

The Bible is filled with wonderful reminders of the unchanging nature and character of God, including His faithfulness, and no reminder is clearer than in His relationship with the nation of Israel. The special nature of this relationship is evident in Genesis 32:28, where God told Jacob, "Your name shall no longer be called Jacob, but Israel; for you have struggled with God and with men, and have prevailed."

Through Israel, we see the transforming power of having a relationship with God. Jacob, whose name means "heel catcher," or figuratively, "supplanter" (which means "a schemer"), is renamed by God as Israel. This name signifies that Jacob's encounter with God changed him from someone who, by name and reputation, was a schemer to a man who bore the illustrious moniker "prince of God." This reminds us that God has long been in the business of taking imperfect and sinful people and doing a work in them that reflects His majesty, power, glory, and faithfulness to a lost and dying world. We see an example of this in Joel 3:1-2:

> Behold, in those days and at that time, when I bring back the captives of Judah and Jerusalem, I will also gather all nations, and bring them down to the Valley of Jehoshaphat; and I will enter into judgment with them there on account of My people, My heritage Israel, whom they have scattered among the nations; they have also divided up My land.

"In those days and at that time" is defined for us in Joel 2 when the Lord says it is a time of restoring what the swarming, crawling, consuming, and chewing locusts have eaten. This speaks of the years of the Diaspora, during which the Jewish people were scattered among the nations.

We cannot ignore the proximity of the regathering of God's people into their national homeland and the gathering of the nations who have opposed Israel into the Valley of Jehoshaphat for judgment. This should remind us the hour is late, and Jesus is coming for us soon!

NO OTHER NAME

One of the most important passages in all the Bible is found tucked away in Psalm 138:2: "I will worship toward Your holy temple, and praise Your name for Your lovingkindness and Your truth; for You have magnified Your word above all Your name."

Think about the profoundness of those last few words—the Lord has magnified His word above all His name. If someone were to say the word *liar* to us, we would remember a person who lied to us or a time when a lie hurt us. In a similar way, the psalmist is saying that God's Word should draw our thoughts to the Lord's nature and character, His goodness and kindness.

An example of how God's Word magnifies Him and His goodness is found in John 1:12: "As many as received Him, to them He gave the right to become children of God, to those who believe in His name." As it pertains to salvation, anything that is added to the blood of Jesus or that amends the gospel message or broadens it into a universalist message is equal to saying the Bible is wrong, which is to say God is wrong. Scripture warns against rejecting God's truth and embracing lies:

> The coming of the lawless one is according to the working of Satan, with all power, signs, and lying wonders, and with all unrighteous deception among those who perish, because they did not receive the love of the truth, that they might be saved. And for this reason God will send them strong delusion, that they should believe the lie, that they all may be condemned who did not believe the truth but had pleasure in unrighteousness (2 Thessalonians 2:9-12).

There is no other way to be saved than through the shed blood of Jesus Christ. Some people might feel good when they say we don't have to believe in Jesus to be a good person, but it's not true, and the consequences for such thinking are catastrophic.

DAY 114

THE JEWS, JESUS, AND JERUSALEM

The gospel is often described as the good news, and so it is. This term, however, is too often limited to one aspect of the good news, and that is the salvation that comes exclusively through Jesus Christ, which is good news indeed! The Greek word translated as "gospel" literally means "good message," and also means "the reward of good tidings."

While the gospel is the good news that a Savior has entered into the world, who is Christ the Lord, the good news is also that He has gone to prepare a place for us in His Father's house, and that He is coming again to receive us unto Himself so that where He is we might be also. The good news is also that He is going to return and bring peace on Earth, and the good news is that when He does, we will be coming with Him. And the good news is that He is going to rule and reign in righteousness, and of His kingdom there will be no end!

Where is Jesus coming back to? The Mount of Olives, which is in Jerusalem, the capital city of the Jews. In Zechariah 12:10, God tells us what will happen at the time:

> I will pour on the house of David and on the inhabitants of Jerusalem the Spirit of grace and supplication; then they will look on Me whom they pierced. Yes, they will mourn for Him as one mourns for his only son, and grieve for Him as one grieves for a firstborn.

In order for the Jews to look upon Him whom they pierced when Jesus returns to the Mount of Olives, the Jews need to be back in the land and in full possession of Jerusalem. The good news is that they are! Which means that the season of the Jews being scattered among the nations without a homeland has come to an end, and the prophetic clock is moving forward to the day when Jesus returns to Earth with the church.

DAY 115

NEHEMIAH'S JOURNEY

The book of Nehemiah is a story of courage, boldness, steadfastness, and faithfulness in spite of incredible opposition to the work of God. Nehemiah's story begins in the palace of the king of the Persian Empire, Artaxerxes. When Nehemiah heard about the desolate condition of Jerusalem, he could not hide his despair from the king. He appeared before the king with a sad countenance, which was a violation punishable by death or banishment.

Yet because of Nehemiah's proven faithfulness to the king even as a captive, he was able to ask the king to show him favor. And not only did the king allow Nehemiah to rebuild the wall and much of the city of Jerusalem, he also helped to finance the project.

As the work on the wall progressed, Nehemiah faced opposition:

> Now it happened when Sanballat, Tobiah, Geshem the Arab, and the rest of our enemies heard that I had rebuilt the wall, and that there were no breaks left in it (though at that time I had not hung the doors in the gates), that Sanballat and Geshem sent to me, saying, "Come, let us meet together among the villages in the plain of Ono." But they thought to do me harm. So I sent messengers to them, saying, "I am doing a great work, so that I cannot come down. Why should the work cease while I leave it and go down to you?" But they sent me this message four times, and I answered them in the same manner (Nehemiah 6:1-4).

This reminds us that opposition to the Jews returning to their national homeland is nothing new. Also, Nehemiah teaches us some vital lessons about what to do when hostility comes our way. When our adversaries invite us to "meet together...in the plan of Ono" with the intent to harm us, our response should always be, "Oh no, I am doing a great work and will not stoop down to your level."

Remember, the One who is in you is greater than anyone who is after you!

DAY 116

FORETOLD AND FULFILLED

Anyone who has visited Israel has experienced the awe and wonder of the land that is home to God's chosen people, the Jews. The history, the culture, Mount Carmel, the Valley of Tears, Magdala, and a host of other places remind us of what a special place Israel is.

One of the most awe-inspiring sights, however, is not built with ancient stones, nor is it a site with historical significance, like the Valley of Elah, where David and Goliath met. This site is the Jezreel Valley, a rich and fertile farmland that stands as evidence that God is faithful to His promises. This lush valley was barren and dormant for nearly 2,000 years, and yet today, it is teeming with crops and flowers. This is a fulfillment of a prophecy in Ezekiel 36:34–36:

> The desolate land shall be tilled instead of lying desolate in the sight of all who pass by. So they will say, "This land that was desolate has become like the garden of Eden; and the wasted, desolate, and ruined cities are now fortified and inhabited." Then the nations which are left all around you shall know that I, the LORD, have rebuilt the ruined places and planted what was desolate. I, the LORD, have spoken it, and I will do it.

With all that is going on in relation to Israel today, we can take heart in the fact that because God brought the Jews back into their national homeland, and because God has blessed the land and it has flourished as He promised it would, the enemies of Israel will not prevail! For no man, country, demon, or devil can cause God's promises to be thwarted or reversed.

We also find personal encouragement here, which is this: When we go through a long, dry season in life and we feel as though the things God has promised are never going to happen, we can be assured that God always keeps His word, and our enemies cannot do anything to change that.

DAY 117

THE RAPTURE: A MYSTERY AND BLESSED HOPE

The Bible refers to the rapture as a mystery. When Paul described the rapture in 1 Corinthians 15, he started by saying, "Behold, I tell you a mystery…" (verse 51). Then he wrote about the instant translation of mortal human beings into immortal and incorruptible beings. Paul also wrote in 1 Thessalonians 4 that as the church is taken up in the rapture, the dead in Christ will rise first, and we who remain will be raised up as well, and all of us will meet the Lord in the air. Not only will we be changed into immortal bodies, but we will change location as well.

It is important to recognize that the rapture is described as a mystery, not a secret. The Bible uses both terms: Secrets are things we don't know that God reveals, and mysteries are things the Bible reveals that need investigation to be understood. A mystery is not something that is hidden like a secret, but rather, something that is transformed from shadow to substance. In the Bible, the greatest example of a mystery is the church. It was no secret that God was going to save the Gentiles, as multiple Old Testament passages stated so (for example, Isaiah 60:3; Jeremiah 16:19; Amos 9:12). The mystery here—something requiring further investigation—was that from the Jews and Gentiles God was creating "one new man" through His Son, bringing down the wall of separation between Jew and Gentile (Ephesians 2:14-15).

Paul also said in 1 Corinthians 15 that when Christians receive their immortal, incorruptible bodies, they will do so "in the twinkling of an eye" (verse 52). This transformation will happen so quickly that Christians all over the world will simply disappear. This will not be a gradual event; it will be instant. In a split second, the church will be taken up to be with the Lord forever. And the Bible describes the rapture as "the blessed hope" (Titus 2:13).

DAY 118

GOD RAISES NATIONS AND SETS THEM DOWN

We live in a time when many in our world believe that to love someone is to accept them "as they are," and regardless of what they do. To many, a God who would judge or not accept people as they are is not a God they are willing to accept. Yet it's interesting that these same people will express an accusatory tone toward God when something bad happens, and demand an explanation for why He would allow it to take place if He is indeed a God of love. They want God to accept everything that anyone thinks, says, or feels, and yet they get upset at God when something they don't like happens. This is the proverbial "have your cake and eat it too" mindset.

The truth is that justice and love are completely consistent characteristics, and there is no greater example of this than what we see in God's relationship with the nation of Israel: "You are a holy people to the Lord your God; the Lord your God has chosen you to be a people for Himself, a special treasure above all the peoples on the face of the earth" (Deuteronomy 7:6).

God set His love on the nation of Israel, and in that love we find His justice that deals with their disobedience. Because they forsook God's commanded Sabbath year for 490 years, He sent them into captivity in Babylon for 70 years to let the land rest. As Jeremiah 25:11 says, "This whole land shall be a desolation and an astonishment, and these nations shall serve the king of Babylon seventy years." God loved His people, and yet He did not turn a blind eye to their disobedience.

While the following declaration in Hebrews 12:6 is not our favorite truth, it is the truth nonetheless: "Whom the Lord loves He chastens." So when we get away with sin without consequence, there is reason for concern, because God's discipline is evidence of His great love for us!

DAY 119

DOING GOOD VERSUS FEELING GOOD

Can you imagine what our world would be like if everyone did just one thing that God has said to do or not do? Pick any of the Ten Commandments. For the whole world to obey just one of them would make for a different and far better world. For example, what if no one ever lied? Or imagine a world in which no one ever committed adultery, or no one ever stole anything. Or better yet, everyone believed in the one true and living God. Broaden this out beyond the Ten Commandments and the same result is true.

If everyone obeyed God, the world would be different, but they don't. However, you can make a difference by your obedience. Imagine the impact of living out Matthew 5:43-44:

> You have heard that it was said, "You shall love your neighbor and hate your enemy." But I say to you, love your enemies, bless those who curse you, do good to those who hate you, and pray for those who spitefully use you and persecute you.

Your light can shine in the darkness, your soul can be satisfied in drought, your bones can be strengthened, and your life can be like a well-watered garden simply by doing what the Lord has said to do, and by not doing what He has prohibited.

People often say they want to change the world. The best place to start is with our own lives. The people we encounter every day make up our world, and we can have an influence on them. This is vitally important for us to recognize because we are deep into the perilous times Paul spoke of in 2 Timothy 3:1-7, and there isn't much going on around us that is good.

As Christians, when we do good, we feel good. And obeying God, no matter what is happening around us, is the greatest weapon we have for keeping our minds and hearts guarded in Christ Jesus.

DAY 120

WE'RE ADOPTED

Today, there are people who defend their lifestyle choices and immoral actions by saying, "We are all God's children," which is not true. John 1:12 is clear about this: "As many as received Him, to them He gave the right to become children of God, to those who believe in His name."

God's children are those who have received Him as Savior and Lord. They alone have the right to "become" His children. If a person must, through belief in His name, "become" His child, that means prior to that decision, he or she was not His child. We are all born in sin and alienated from God (Colossians 1:21), but through Christ, we are adopted as sons and daughters of the Most High.

At the time of Jesus, the Roman practice of adoption was common, and it was customary for a father to leave his wealth to his son(s). If a suitable heir was not available, then a young man who could manage the father's wealth was sought out and adopted. All of that man's debts were forgiven, and he would be given all the rights and benefits of a natural-born son.

This is what happened with us through Christ. When our sin debt was forgiven, we became sons and daughters of God, and we now enjoy all the rights and benefits that belong to His children. Galatians 4:4-5 says that "when the fullness of the time had come, God sent forth His Son, born of a woman, born under the law, to redeem those who were under the law, that we might receive the adoption as sons."

It was also true in ancient Roman culture that a father could disown his son, but an adopted son's status could not be reversed. The same is true for those of us who have been adopted by God. We, as born-again believers, can say with assurance that we are children of God and nothing can change that. Nothing can separate us from His love (Romans 8:35-39), and no one can snatch us from His hand (John 10:28-29). That's the best news you'll hear all day!

DAY 121

HIS PEOPLE, HIS LAND

Today's global hatred of the Jewish nation of Israel reveals the extent of the spiritual war raging all around our world.

Make no mistake: Antisemitism is demonic in nature. The devil is the driving force behind the anti-Israel sentiment we see growing all around us. The most tragic aspect of this hatred is that it has blinded the eyes of millions to the fact that the rebirth of the nation of Israel is nothing short of a miracle and an undeniable fulfillment of Bible prophecy. Upon reading that, your mind might quickly gravitate to the prophecy in Ezekiel 37 about the valley filled with dry bones. Ezekiel wrote that 2,600 years ago, but prophecies relating to the regathering of the Jews to their land go much farther back in history:

> Now it shall come to pass, when all these things come upon you, the blessing and the curse which I have set before you, and you call them to mind among all the nations where the LORD your God drives you, and you return to the LORD your God and obey His voice, according to all that I command you today, you and your children, with all your heart and with all your soul, that the LORD your God will bring you back from captivity, and have compassion on you, and gather you again from all the nations where the LORD your God has scattered you (Deuteronomy 30:1-3).

Moses' words predate Ezekiel's prophecy by some 800 years, yet predicts the same event that we are now privileged to see right before our eyes. This should remind us that our God knows the beginning from the end and all that happens in the middle (Isaiah 46:10). God has brought His people back into their land and has prospered and multiplied modern Israel more than in times past, and both Moses and Ezekiel said this would happen.

This means the seventieth week of Daniel—and the rapture that precedes it—must be in the near future.

DAY 122

GREATER IS HE WHO IS IN YOU

While it is true that all of us have gone through dry seasons spiritually, it is also true that such times are just that—seasons. With that in mind, we should find great encouragement in these words:

> In Him you also trusted, after you heard the word of truth, the gospel of your salvation; in whom also, having believed, you were sealed with the Holy Spirit of promise, who is the guarantee of our inheritance until the redemption of the purchased possession, to the praise of His glory (Ephesians 1:13-14).

This great promise should remind us that because the Holy Spirit is within us, no matter how or what we feel, our inheritance of a future in heaven is guaranteed. We also need to keep in mind what the indwelling of the Holy Spirit assures us of: "You are of God, little children, and have overcome them, because He who is in you is greater than he who is in the world" (1 John 4:4).

In this passage, "them" refers to every antichrist spirit that is in the world. They have been overcome by the One who is in us. The word "overcome" means "to get the victory." In other words, because the Spirit of the living God is in us, we can "get the victory" over anything that the devil throws at us.

This is true even during the dry seasons of life, and it is certainly true during the times of trial we all experience. We need to note that "overcome" implies that the victory is assured by acting on the power we have been given. It doesn't mean we sit back and let the Spirit fight our battles. Rather, it means that through the Spirit, we get the victory during all forms of spiritual warfare simply because the one who is after us is not greater than He who is in us!

DAY 123

GOD LOVES TO DECLARE HIS PLANS

Imagine going through life without the Word of God. You wouldn't know what's going on or where things are going. You wouldn't know that the delusion that much of the world is under is actually a sign that something wonderful is going to happen to the church. You wouldn't know what to think about the rebirth of the nation of Israel. You wouldn't have the comfort that comes from knowing the truth. And the greatest tragedy of all is that you wouldn't know about the One who came into the world to save us.

All these things and more have been declared to us by God:

> Remember the former things of old, for I am God, and there is no other; I am God, and there is none like Me, declaring the end from the beginning, and from ancient times things that are not yet done, saying, "My counsel shall stand, and I will do all My pleasure" (Isaiah 46:9-10).

The true and living God of the Bible, who dwells outside of time and knows all, has told man how things began and how things will end and how we should live in the middle. He has told us about the nation and people He chose so that through them, He could send the Savior of the world. He has revealed to us how this Savior would be born, where He would be born, where He would live, how He would die, and the fact He would be resurrected. He put all this information in His book.

We need not live without knowledge of the past, or of what's coming in the future. The God who knows the end from the beginning has given us His Word, and both testaments are living and powerful. The law, the history, the poetry, and the prophecies are all what make the Bible the inspired Word of God. And, as God said in Isaiah 55:11, "So shall My word be that goes forth from My mouth; it shall not return to Me void, but it shall accomplish what I please, and it shall prosper in the thing for which I sent it."

Amen to that!

DAY 124

BE HEAVENLY MINDED

It has been said, "Some people are so heavenly minded they are no earthly good." The fact is, nothing could be further from the truth! We need to be heavenly minded every day. When we do so, we will be reminded that the future is far better than the present, and that this world is not our home.

Consider Paul's words in 1 Corinthians 3:9-15:

> We are God's fellow workers; you are God's field, you are God's building. According to the grace of God which was given to me, as a wise master builder I have laid the foundation, and another builds on it. But let each one take heed how he builds on it. For no other foundation can anyone lay than that which is laid, which is Jesus Christ. Now if anyone builds on this foundation with gold, silver, precious stones, wood, hay, straw, each one's work will become clear; for the Day will declare it, because it will be revealed by fire; and the fire will test each one's work, of what sort it is. If anyone's work which he has built on it endures, he will receive a reward. If anyone's work is burned, he will suffer loss; but he himself will be saved, yet so as through fire.

Thankfully, the judgment seat of Christ is not where eternal destinies are determined. We are saved by grace through faith and not of works (Ephesians 2:8-10). But, as those who are saved, our works will be judged and tested by fire to reveal their level of purity and the motivation behind them. The judgment seat of Christ is about rewards, not salvation. This is why the adage I quoted above is so far off base. The truth is that when we are more mindful of heaven, we will do more earthly good.

When we remember that someday we will stand before the judgment seat of Christ, we will, like Joshua, choose this day, and any other, to serve the Lord.

DAY 125

AN ORDAINED ORDER, PART 1

In 2022, the United Nations General Assembly passed more resolutions critical of Israel than against all other nations combined. The General Assembly approved 15 anti-Israel resolutions in 2023 versus 13 resolutions criticizing other countries, according to the monitoring group UN Watch.

Russia was the focus of six resolutions that condemned its invasion of Ukraine. North Korea, Afghanistan, Myanmar, Syria, Iran, and the US were hit with one resolution each. Saudi Arabia, China, Lebanon, Turkey, Venezuela, and Qatar, which have poor human-rights records or were involved in regional conflicts, were not dinged by any resolutions critical of them.

Why the imbalance? Why were there no resolutions against countries that execute dissidents? The question becomes even more perplexing when you consider that Israel is the only democracy in the Middle East and the only country that practices the free exercise of religion.

The answer is simple: Israel is pivotal to the end-times scenario and is the central focus of the coming great tribulation. Even so, Psalm 94:14 assures us that "the Lord will not cast off His people, nor will He forsake His inheritance."

The criticism leveled against the nation of Israel by the UN and the rest of the world has a spiritual origin and is driven by Satan's desire to eliminate the Jews and thus invalidate God's Word.

Of all the nations on the earth, God chose Israel as His own special people. Of all the nations on the earth, God brought His Son into the world through the nation of Israel. Of all the nations on the earth, salvation is offered to the world through the Jews, and the message of redemption came to the Jews first, then to the Greek (meaning the Gentiles).

After nearly 2,000 years of being scattered among the nations, the fact the Jews are back in their homeland should tell us that whatever God has said He will do will come to pass, even when it seems impossible to man!

DAY 126

AN ORDAINED ORDER, PART 2

In Acts 1:8, Jesus said, "You shall receive power when the Holy Spirit has come upon you; and you shall be witnesses to Me in Jerusalem, and in all Judea and Samaria, and to the end of the earth."

We need to remember that the power of the Holy Spirit that came on Pentecost came to the Jews first in order that they might be witnesses in Jerusalem and Judea, then to the ends of the earth.

God is a God of order, and we can take heart in the fact that all He promised to and about Israel is coming to pass just as He said it would. Jerusalem is where the church was born, as written in Acts 1:8, and Jerusalem is now a burdensome stone to all nations, as prophesied in Zechariah 12:3.

On Pentecost, the Jews who tarried in Jerusalem, as Jesus told them to, received the power to be witnesses. The church began to spread from Jerusalem, to Judea, then on to Samaria, and is continuing to spread to the ends of the earth. This will continue even during the tribulation, during which God will appoint 144,000 Jews as witnesses.

The world is a mess right now, but there is good on the horizon for those who love God. One day, we will meet the Lord in the air, and from that point onward, we will always be with Him. How do we know? Jesus said He would come again to receive us unto Himself so that where He is, we will be too (John 14:3). He has never failed to keep a promise, and Israel is the greatest proof of that we could ever want.

For this reason, Hebrews 10:23 says, "Let us hold fast the confession of our hope without wavering, for He who promised is faithful." Hold fast, saints. One day, He will come for us. And we should live every day like that might happen today!

DAY 127

GOD'S LOVE FOR PEOPLE

In Amos 9:14-15, God promised,

> "I will bring back the captives of My people Israel; they shall build the waste cities and inhabit them; they shall plant vineyards and drink wine from them; they shall also make gardens and eat fruit from them. I will plant them in their land, and no longer shall they be pulled up from the land I have given them," says the LORD your God.

Notice that the Lord placed upon Himself the responsibility of bringing the people back into the land. And He stated that once He planted them there, they would never again be uprooted from the land He had given them. The fact that God took responsibility for the return of the Jews implied that this return would occur through a supernatural means, and thus against all odds—and, as is usual with God's will, to the displeasure of the enemies of God's people.

Within hours of declaring statehood on May 14, 1948, Israel was attacked by five Arab countries, yet the Jewish people were not uprooted from the land God had given to them.

In Zechariah 12:3, God said there is coming a day when He "will make Jerusalem a very heavy stone for all peoples; all who would heave it away will surely be cut to pieces, though all nations of the earth are gathered against it."

Someday, all the nations will come against Israel. The word "gathered" means "to be united in purpose," and in this context, the purpose is Israel's destruction. For centuries, God supernaturally protected His chosen people, and for the most part, they did not assimilate into the countries and cultures into which they were scattered.

The rebirth of Israel put into motion a series of prophetic events that will lead to the salvation of the Jews when they recognize Jesus of Nazareth, the One whom they pierced, is the King of kings and Lord of lords, the Holy One of Israel, their Savior.

DAY 128

GENTILES AND THE LAW

It is quite popular today for some in the church to incorporate the rituals of the law into their practices. Yet for a born-again Christian, who has a personal relationship with the One who fulfilled the law, to seek to go back under the law is like taking a photograph of your spouse with you to dinner instead of your actual spouse.

Eating dinner with a photograph might stir up thoughts, memories, and feelings, but you would have no actual relationship or interaction with the photo. This is true of Christians who think they are somehow more complete by observing the law, as the New-Testament-era Judaizers said. Paul constantly battled against the Judaizers, who were trying to get Christians to observe Jewish traditions.

The feast days and Sabbath observances of the Jews were all "photos" pointing to the One who would come and fulfill them. Christians who want to observe them are certainly permitted to do so. But why fill your life with something that has been fulfilled and become obsolete when you already have a relationship with the One all the feast days and rituals were pointing to? Hebrews 10:1 says,

> For the law, having a shadow of the good things to come, and not the very image of the things, can never with these same sacrifices, which they offer continually year by year, make those who approach perfect.

Seder dinners, mezuzahs containing the Shema on the doorpost of your home, and other such things are beautiful images, but they are just that—images. They, like any photograph, are not a replacement for the person, nor can a relationship be had with them.

DAY 129

HE'S COMING SWIFTLY

It has been said, "What problem do you have that the rapture wouldn't solve?" The wonderful thing about the answer is the number of negative life experiences that will instantly cease to exist.

> Now this I say, brethren, that flesh and blood cannot inherit the kingdom of God; nor does corruption inherit incorruption. Behold, I tell you a mystery: We shall not all sleep, but we shall all be changed—in a moment, in the twinkling of an eye, at the last trumpet. For the trumpet will sound, and the dead will be raised incorruptible, and we shall be changed. For this corruptible must put on incorruption, and this mortal must put on immortality (1 Corinthians 15:50-53).

The first-century Christians referred to the grave as sleep. They did so because when someone goes to sleep, they also wake up. They believed that someday, the dead bodies of all believers in Christ would wake up and rise from the dead. They also believed that those who are still alive at the time will experience a radical change, during which all the negative things we face in life will vanish more quickly than you can blink. All the pains and problems our physical bodies endure will end in the twinkling of an eye.

Paul said in Romans 8:18 "that the sufferings of this present time are not worthy to be compared with the glory which shall be revealed in us." This reminds us that not only will all the things that burden and bug us disappear, but they will be gone forever!

While we await that moment, we can find comfort in the fact that all the trials and tribulations of life are temporary. In 2 Corinthians 4:17 Paul called them light afflictions (though they sure don't seem light when we experience them!), yet he also gave us a tool by which we can put them in their proper place and perspective by remembering someday they will end faster than you can blink.

Soon and very soon!

DAY 130

THE MENORAH

When the Lord spoke to Moses concerning the construction of the tabernacle and its furnishings, He gave him specific and detailed instructions on how to fashion each item and what materials to use, all of which carried great significance.

> The Lord spoke to Moses, saying: "Speak to the children of Israel, that they bring Me an offering. From everyone who gives it willingly with his heart you shall take My offering. And this is the offering which you shall take from them: gold, silver, and bronze; blue, purple, and scarlet thread, fine linen, and goats' hair; ram skins dyed red, badger skins, and acacia wood; oil for the light, and spices for the anointing oil and for the sweet incense; onyx stones, and stones to be set in the ephod and in the breastplate. And let them make Me a sanctuary, that I may dwell among them. According to all that I show you, that is, the pattern of the tabernacle and the pattern of all its furnishings, just so you shall make it" (Exodus 25:1-9).

The goats' hair, ram skins dyed red, and badger skins were all materials to be used for the outer covering of the tabernacle. The blue, purple, and scarlet thread were to be used on the inside and for the priestly garments. And the furnishings were to be of gold and acacia wood, including the ark of the covenant, the table of showbread, and a lampstand of pure gold, the menorah.

The designs of the menorah, the ark, and the table of showbread were meant to communicate messages to the children of Israel. The menorah was comprised of a center shaft with three branches on each side, making a total of seven lamps. Seven is the number of completeness, and six—which is the number of man—portrays man's incompleteness apart from God—that is, the center shaft of the menorah. The lampstand also reminds us that with the Lord at the center of our lives, we are never alone.

DAY 131

GOD'S HAND ON ISRAEL

On October 6, 1973, Israel was observing Yom Kippur, the holiest day in the Jewish calendar. But the Jewish nation was caught off guard by a surprise attack carried out by Egypt and Syria. About 180 Israeli tanks faced an overwhelming advance of 1,400 Syrian tanks. To the south, along the Suez Canal, fewer than 500 Israeli soldiers were assaulted by 80,000 Egyptians. Despite the overwhelming odds, miraculously, Israel was victorious.

Even with an abundance of clear evidence that Israel is a nation again by the providence and promises of God, here we are again today with Israel under attack by those who hate the Jews. Zechariah 12:3 warned this hatred would continue through the end times: "It shall happen in that day that I will make Jerusalem a very heavy stone for all peoples; all who would heave it away will surely be cut in pieces, though all nations of the earth are gathered against it."

The proof that what we are watching is spiritual in nature is revealed by the fact that the world seems largely indifferent to rape, torture, and murder when such atrocities are done against the Jews. Sadly, many within the church have labeled the Jews as occupiers and see the actions of Palestinian terrorists as justified because of the alleged oppression. Some do this under the banner that proclaims modern Israel is not biblical Israel.

Christians need to remember God's promise in Genesis 12:3: "I will bless those who bless you, and I will curse him who curses you; and in you all the families of the earth shall be blessed." If modern Israel is not biblical Israel, then why is God still protecting them from those who want to annihilate them?

In the famed words of Genesis 12:3, we see a warning followed by a promise. The promise is still true and is manifesting itself today—that is, through Abraham, Isaac, and Jacob came the Holy One of Israel, our Savior, and the world is still blessed by Him. If the promise is still true, the warning is as well.

God protects those who are His, and none can be snatched from His hand!

DAY 132

GOD IS FAITHFUL

In Psalm 37:1-4, David wrote,

> Do not fret because of evildoers, nor be envious of the workers of iniquity. For they shall soon be cut down like the grass, and wither as the green herb. Trust in the Lord, and do good; dwell in the land, and feed on His faithfulness. Delight yourself also in the Lord, and He shall give you the desires of your heart.

In this season of rampant evil, trauma, and turmoil, we need not fret because God is trustworthy—He is faithful. That means at all times, we can bless His name with mouths filled with praise. At all times, we can trust in Him and do good and delight ourselves in Him because He cannot deny His own trustworthiness.

Remember when David went out to fight the champion of the Philistines, Goliath, and King Saul offered David his armor? David said, "I can't use it because I have not tested it." This is not the case with the armor of God. It has been tried and tested down through the ages and has been found to have all the professed capabilities it claims to have. That's because it is God's armor, not man's, and it fits perfectly on every Christian who puts it on.

Ephesians 6:16 mentions a key part of this armor: "Above all, taking the shield of faith with which you will be able to quench all the fiery darts of the wicked one." A shield is of little use in combat when it's lying on the ground. It must be taken up to be effective. What Paul tells us here is that when taken up, or applied, faith in our trustworthy God is able to quench every fiery dart the enemy launches at us.

Remember, the whole armor is God's armor. So when we are under attack or facing the Goliaths of our lives, we're not putting on armor that was fitted and designed for someone else, as happened with David and Saul. God's armor will fit you perfectly!

DAY 133

IT TAKES HUMILITY

You may have heard the saying, "Born once, die twice; born twice, die once." This oft-repeated adage refers to the fact that there is a death that is far worse than the death of the body, which is an appointment that the vast majority of humanity will keep. The second death, however, is not one that anyone must face, but sadly, multitudes will.

Jesus said, "The thief does not come except to steal, and to kill, and to destroy. I have come that they may have life, and that they may have it more abundantly" (John 10:10). And Paul wrote, "If anyone is in Christ, he is a new creation; old things have passed away; behold, all things have become new" (2 Corinthians 5:17).

Abundant life and newness of life are two of the wonderful benefits of being born again. Old things have passed away, making it possible for all things to become new. As born-again Christians, we have a new eternal destiny, but we also have newness of life, and that life is one of abundance. The Greek word translated "abundantly" in John 10:10 actually means "superabundance."

In James 4:10, we are given the exhortation, "Humble yourselves in the sight of the Lord, and He will lift you up." Humbling ourselves before God should be easy once we understand who He is. In His typically loving and gracious manner, He lifts up those who humble themselves before Him and blesses them superabundantly.

With this in mind, we would do well to remember that God has done more for us that we don't know than we do know. He is always watching over us; He has kept the enemy from destroying us; He has protected us when we didn't know it; He has averted more tragedies that Satan has planned against us than we could ever imagine. A very humbling thought indeed!

DAY 134

IT'S A WAY OF LIFE

Ever since the Tower of Babel, man has been trying to achieve what can only be received.

> Now the whole earth had one language and one speech. And it came to pass, as they journeyed from the east, that they found a plain in the land of Shinar, and they dwelt there. Then they said to one another, "Come, let us make bricks and bake them thoroughly." They had brick for stone, and they had asphalt for mortar. And they said, "Come, let us build ourselves a city, and a tower whose top is in the heavens; let us make a name for ourselves, lest we be scattered abroad over the face of the whole earth" (Genesis 11:1-4).

Today, we live in a world filled with thousands of religions. While all claim to be true and most offer a way to access the afterlife, they all share the same basic defect that was true at the Tower of Babel: Religion makes the observant the primary focus and not God. The desire of the builders of Babel was to make a name for themselves. That is what religion does. It makes people feel better about themselves. They do their duty, they keep the ordinances, they observe the rituals, and thus their names can be listed among the faithful adherents of what they believe. But among the religious is not where we want our name listed.

Revelation 13:8 speaks of antichrist worship during the tribulation: "All who dwell on the earth will worship him, whose names have not been written in the Book of Life of the Lamb slain from the foundation of the world." Religion replaces truth with sincerity, faith with feelings, and relationship with rituals. During the tribulation, those who dwell on the earth will worship the dragon and the beast through the religion of the world's most sinister false prophet. The only way to escape the deception and delusion of false religion is to have your name written in the Lamb's Book of Life.

DAY 135

YOU MUST BE BORN AGAIN

There are a myriad of phrases in the Scriptures where a compact set of words carries great meaning. "Let there be light; and there was light" (Genesis 1:3) comes to mind. "The fool has said in his heart, there is no God" (Psalm 14:1) is another great truth in few words. "I will never leave you nor forsake you" (Hebrews 13:5) is a must on any list of such verses. One statement, however, stands above the rest, and it occurs in a dialogue in the Gospel of John, where Jesus said to Nicodemus, "You must be born again" (John 3:7).

Within those five words is the theme of the whole Bible. "You must" implies man's need or lack. "Be born again" reveals the solution to mankind's need. When Jesus replied to Nicodemus's statement acknowledging that the things Jesus did were proof that God was with Him, Jesus said to him, "Most assuredly, I say to you, unless one is born again, he cannot see the kingdom of God" (John 3:3).

Failing to see this precept, Nicodemus said to Jesus, "How can these things be?" (verse 9). Jesus then replied with the most famous of all statements in the Bible:

> God so loved the world that He gave His only begotten Son, that whoever believes in Him should not perish but have everlasting life (John 3:16).

Maybe you're among those who have wondered, *Am I truly born again?* Look at your life for the answer. Are the things of darkness your first love? Do you have new desires that always lead to right pursuits? If you have been born again, you have experienced something that changes every person's life and eternal destiny, and it is this: The same power that raised Christ from the dead dwells in you. This means you are no longer ruled by the desires of the flesh but live in the power of the Holy Spirit!

DAY 136

THE PROPHETIC GENERATION

History is replete with world-changing events. We think of the American Revolution, the Industrial Age, the Great Depression, two world wars, and even the Cold War as having a rightful place on our list.

All, however, pale in comparison to the rebirth of Israel and the regathering of the Jewish people back into their God-given homeland. Yet in spite of this world-changing and incomparable event, many see no significance to what happened, and view it negatively.

In Matthew 24:32-35, we read,

> Now learn this parable from the fig tree: When its branch has already become tender and puts forth leaves, you know that summer is near. So you also, when you see all these things, know that it is near—at the doors! Assuredly, I say to you, this generation will by no means pass away till all these things take place. Heaven and earth will pass away, but My words will by no means pass away.

Jesus had been teaching about the tribulation and the second coming, which means His parable would be illustrating those same subjects. The fact that the fig tree represents national Israel (Joel 1:7; Hosea 9:10) tells us that Israel is back in the land, and all the events recorded in the Olivet Discourse are about to take place.

Not only do we live in a time that could be added to the above list, but we are about to experience the one that tops the list—the rapture of the church, which must happen before the tribulation begins. People's denial of the rapture and their rejection of the Israel of today as biblical Israel are also indications that summer is near.

Therefore, our Bible confidence should be at an all-time high. We have seen more prophetic fulfillments and precursors to them than any generation before us. We are about to experience an unprecedented world-changing event, and for us, it will be out of this world!

DAY 137

ABRAHAM AND JACOB

While reading the Bible, various genealogies may not be on anyone's list of favorite passages, but they are vitally important. For example: Luke 3 records the genealogy of Jesus all the way back to Adam through David, Jesse, Boaz, and on to Jacob, Isaac, and Abraham, and then finally all the way back to Adam. Genesis 17:18-19 makes it clear God's promise runs through this genealogy: "Abraham said to God, 'Oh, that Ishmael might live before You!' Then God said: 'No, Sarah your wife shall bear you a son, and you shall call his name Isaac; I will establish My covenant with him for an everlasting covenant, and with his descendants after him.'" Earlier, in Genesis 12:3, God said, "I will bless those who bless you, and I will curse him who curses you; and in you all the families of the earth shall be blessed."

Had Jesus been born to a Canaanite family, we would have cause to question whether He was the Messiah, and if He was the Messiah, we would have reason to question the infallibility of Scripture. But the genealogy of Luke 3 assures us that the messianic birth line was as Scripture said it would be. The nations of the earth would be blessed through a descendant of Abraham and Sarah.

The Lord said His everlasting covenant was not with Ishmael, but with Isaac and his descendants. How do we know this is still true? The descendants of Abraham through Isaac and Jacob are back in their national homeland, and that means Israel is about to bear the fruit of coming to know their Messiah at the end of the tribulation—which also means we are nearing the end of the church age.

Genealogies remind us that the entirety of God's Word is true! (Psalm 119:160). If the Messiah truly came through the descendants of Abraham through Isaac and Jacob, then our confidence that the Word of God was divinely inspired stands confirmed.

DAY 138

LIGHT IN A DARK WORLD

You may have seen TV shows about actual events in which the announcer says that certain names were changed to protect the innocent. When it comes to heresies creeping into the church, we could say something similar. While the names of ancient heresies have changed, the goal is still to deceive the innocent.

Such is the case with gnosticism, which has changed names multiple times down through the centuries. Some have even called it Christian gnosticism. But there is nothing Christian about it. Its most recent form is antinomianism, a big word that means "no law." As with ancient gnosticism, there are some today who teach that because we are saved by grace, the actions carried out by our physical bodies are of no consequence, and there are no moral laws for the Christian to live by. But Hebrews 12:14 says otherwise: "Pursue peace with all people, and holiness, without which no one will see the Lord."

Holiness, by definition, is a state of purity. If we are to pursue a state of purity, then impurity exists and must be recognized and defined. Thus, according to Scripture, what we do in the body does matter. We also need to be careful not to slip in the other direction, which is legalism. We are saved by the manifested grace of God, and by God's grace, we can live a life that is representative of His saving grace through our behavior.

We may not hear the term *gnosticism* used much today, but it is alive and well and just as dangerous as ever. What we do in our bodies does not determine our salvation, but it does impact our usability and believability when we teach the freedom that can be found in Christ.

First Peter 2:9 reminds us we have been "called...out of darkness into His marvelous light." Make no mistake—when you come to Christ and are saved by grace through faith, your love of darkness will turn to disdain as you walk in His marvelous light.

DAY 139

REDEEMING THE TIME

There are many things in life that come and go quickly, and others that stay for a season. Fortunes, for some, are gained and lost and later gained again. People will move in and out of our lives as we traverse the seasons of life—friends often change, surroundings and jobs change, and as one thing moves into our lives, another moves out.

But there is one commodity of life that cannot be replaced or renewed once it is gone, and that is time. When a moment of time is gone, it is gone forever. That's why Paul's words in Ephesians 5:15-16 are so important: "See then that you walk circumspectly, not as fools but as wise, redeeming the time, because the days are evil."

The Greek word translated "circumspectly" means "exactly." It can also be translated as "diligently" or "perfectly." The contextual meaning of the word is established by the previous verses:

> You were once darkness, but now you are light in the Lord. Walk as children of light (for the fruit of the Spirit is in all goodness, righteousness, and truth), finding out what is acceptable to the Lord. And have no fellowship with the unfruitful works of darkness, but rather expose them (Ephesians 5:8-11).

As children of the light, we need to watch our steps and walk exactly as the Lord has prescribed—in goodness, righteousness, and truth, and not in fellowship with the unfruitful works of darkness. The Holy Spirit then says a few verses later that we are to redeem the time "because the days are evil."

As the days grow darker in these perilous times, God has a plan for us to follow. It is not simply about how to survive, but also about how to thrive as the birth pangs get stronger in these last days. It is no mistake that you are alive right now, and that for such a time as this, God has a plan and purpose for your life.

DAY 140

LISTEN TO THE SPIRIT

All of us have been given bad advice at some point in our lives, and for some, following that advice has led to poor decisions we end up regretting. These poor decisions can often be avoided by asking for God's input: "Call to Me, and I will answer you, and show you great and mighty things, which you do not know" (Jeremiah 33:3).

That's not to say that all advice is bad, but we should filter all human advice through prayer to the One who always knows the right thing to do and whose counsel is never in error. This includes advice from those—maybe even especially those—who attach "thus says the Lord" to their counsel.

As born-again Christians filled with the Holy Spirit, we have an exclusive advantage over the unregenerate person. We have the Spirit within us, who convicts us and convinces us. One who puts up green lights and red lights on the highway of life. One who never leaves nor forsakes us and who orders the steps of the righteous in Christ.

Proverbs 3:5-8 exhorts us to "trust in the LORD with all your heart, and lean not on your own understanding; in all your ways acknowledge Him, and He shall direct your paths. Do not be wise in your own eyes; fear the LORD and depart from evil. It will be health to your flesh, and strength to your bones."

Think about Saul and David—one man leaned on his own understanding and emotions, and the other acknowledged the Lord in all his ways. One experienced darkness and depression, the other health to his flesh and strength to his bones.

When you are faced with decisions that may appeal to your flesh and others are saying, "Go for it; the Lord is in it," ask the Lord if He is, and He will answer you and show you what you need to know.

DAY 141

JESUS FULFILLED THE LAW

Justification by faith is a phrase most Christians are familiar with, yet some of the specifics of justification aren't clear to them. In reference to our sin, *justification* is often defined as "just as if it never happened." This is a great way to understand the end result of justification by faith, but it skips over the process of getting there.

First Timothy 2:5-6 tells us that "there is one God and one Mediator between God and men, the Man Christ Jesus, who gave Himself a ransom for all, to be testified in due time." God has not arbitrarily acted as though our sin never happened; that would violate His justness. The wages of sin had to be paid, which is death, and in due time, Christ died for the ungodly (Romans 5:6).

In Hebrews 10:5, we read this about Christ: "When He came into the world, He said: 'Sacrifice and offering You did not desire, but a body You have prepared for Me.'" This is the mediator that Paul wrote to Timothy about. A mediator was required to represent both sides of the issue equally. If mediation was going to happen, resulting in the justification by faith of all who believe, a mediator who could equally represent both sides was necessary. God could not represent man because He is God and not a man. No man could represent God because he is man and not God. So God became a man in the person of Christ so mediation could be possible.

As Hebrews 4:15 says, "We do not have a High Priest who cannot sympathize with our weaknesses, but was in all points tempted as we are, yet without sin." Jesus fulfilled the law in sinless perfection, and then presented His life in place of ours to the Father—the just for the unjust, that we might become the righteousness of God through Him.

DAY 142

MAKE HIM YOUR EVERYTHING

Early in the morning on the first day of the week, three days after the most horrific mockery of a trial in human history, it was a woman who discovered that the tomb of Jesus was empty. This happened despite the fact Jesus made it clear to the disciples what the future held for Him:

> Now Jesus, going up to Jerusalem, took the twelve disciples aside on the road and said to them, "Behold, we are going up to Jerusalem, and the Son of Man will be betrayed to the chief priests and to the scribes; and they will condemn Him to death, and deliver Him to the Gentiles to mock and to scourge and to crucify. And the third day He will rise again" (Matthew 20:17-19).

Early that Sunday morning, there was no crowd at the tomb—just three heartbroken women (Mark 16:1) who had come to anoint the body of their beloved friend: Mary, the mother of James the less; Salome, the wife of Zebedee and mother to James and John; and Mary of Magdala, from whom Jesus had cast out seven demons.

When Mary of Magdala found the tomb empty, she ran to tell Peter and John, but Jesus didn't reveal Himself to these two members of His inner circle, nor to the wife of the owner of a successful fishing business who was the mother to the two men Jesus nicknamed "Sons of Thunder" (Mark 3:17). He didn't reveal Himself to the mother of James the less. Instead, He first revealed Himself to Mary of Magdala, whom the disciples did not believe when she said Jesus appeared to her.

Upon His resurrection, Jesus didn't reveal Himself first to the Sanhedrin or the Pharisees or to Roman authorities. He first appeared to a woman with a past, whose words didn't seem to mean much to others, and yet here we are nearly 2,000 years later, and millions know her name and story. Our names are known in heaven too—all because of our relationship with Him!

DAY 143

STAND LIKE DAVID

There are two stories in the Bible that most people are familiar with, including those who have never read the Bible. Those stories are the encounter between David and Goliath, and Daniel in the lions' den. Both are remarkable accounts of men who had faith in the true and living God and trusted Him completely in the face of great adversity. Because of David, people know about Goliath, and because of Daniel, they know about the lions.

What they don't know about are David's brother Eliab, who mocked him, and the governors and satraps (a satrap was a provincial governor) who set a trap for Daniel. It is the faithful individuals the world remembers in these two famous accounts, and not their adversaries.

Proverbs 24:10 tells us, "If you faint in the day of adversity, your strength is small." David didn't faint when he saw Goliath, and Daniel didn't faint when he knew his coworkers had it out for him. We live in a day of adversity today, in which all manners of evil are said against us falsely, but we cannot faint or lose heart. We need to be strong in the Lord and the power of His might.

Romans 8:11 speaks of the power that is ours as believers: "If the Spirit of Him who raised Jesus from the dead dwells in you, He who raised Christ from the dead will also give life to your mortal bodies through His Spirit who dwells in you."

David and Daniel were mere men; it was their faith in God that made them mighty. If you want to leave your mark in this world, let it be because you were found faithful, even in the face of adversity. The ability to do so is already in you. For the same Spirit that raised Christ from the dead dwells in every born-again Christian, giving us the power to face opposition in the strength of the Lord.

Those who faced adversity in God's strength in the ancient past are still known to people today. Let our names be found among theirs in the future.

DAY 144

CORRECTLY IDENTIFYING THE LAST TRUMPET

While some have promoted the idea that the "last trumpet" in 1 Corinthians 15:52 is the same as the last of the seven trumpets in Revelation, if that is so, then not only is there a problem with finding comfort in Paul's words about the trumpet in 1 Thessalonians 4:16-18, there is also a contradiction with other Scripture passages.

One of those passages is Revelation 3:10: "Because you have kept My command to persevere, I also will keep you from the hour of trial which shall come upon the whole world, to test those who dwell on the earth." Notice the Lord doesn't say, "I'll keep you from the bowl judgments during the last part of the tribulation." Rather, He says that those who persevere will be kept from the whole of the tribulation, the hour of trial coming on the earth.

Another problem with seeing the last trumpet in 1 Corinthians 15:52 as the seventh trumpet of Revelation 11 is the events that follow the sounding of that trumpet do not match the events following the trumpets mentioned in 1 Corinthians 15:52 and 1 Thessalonians 4:16.

So the "trumpet of God" in 1 Thessalonians 4:16 is not the seventh trumpet in Revelation 11. Rather, it is the trumpet that signals the end of the church age. The removal of the church is necessary before the Antichrist can rise to power, which will happen at the beginning of the tribulation.

For those who argue that Christians have always faced tribulation and therefore will not escape the great tribulation, the answer is simple: The great tribulation is the outpouring of God's wrath, whereas our current tribulations are caused by Satan and man. They are two completely different things.

Dear saints, take comfort in the fact that this ever-darkening world indicates that the unknown day and hour when the dead in Christ will rise and those who are alive in Christ will meet the Lord in the air to be with Him forever might be today!

DAY 145

RULING WITH CHRIST IN HIS KINGDOM

At the end of the tribulation, why will we come back to earth after having already been in heaven? Because God's plan for the future includes the earthly rule of Jesus Christ. In Psalm 132:11-12, the Lord promised King David, "I will set upon your throne the fruit of your body...forevermore." Isaiah 9:6 says that someday, the government of the world "will be upon His shoulder." And all believers who are in heaven during the tribulation will return with Christ to rule and reign with Him in His kingdom.

The parables of the talents and the minas may very well point to how God will judge and reward believers in preparation for their roles in the millennium. In Matthew 25:14-30, in the parable of the talents, those who did more with what the Lord gave them received more. Those who did nothing with what they were given had it taken away and were cast into outer darkness. In Luke 19:11-27, in the parable of the minas, those who multiplied what was entrusted to them were rewarded, and those who did nothing met the same fate as those who did nothing with the talents they were given. In this case, the faithful were made rulers over cities.

That we will rule and reign with Christ during the millennium is fact. It's possible our level of responsibility, or the number of cities we rule over, will be determined by what we did with what the Lord entrusted to us before we died or were raptured. This is speculation, to be sure, but it is calculated speculation because we do know that when we stand before the bema seat of Christ (2 Corinthians 5:10), we will be rewarded for what we did for His glory and kingdom while on earth (1 Corinthians 3:12-15). Whatever responsibility we are given during the millennium, it will be glorious, and we will perform our service as "kings and priests to His God and Father" (Revelation 1:6).

DAY 146

UNCHANGING TRUTH

We have recently become all too familiar with the phrase "trust the science" from people in places of power or authority. Yet these same people tell us to accept that a person can be whatever they think they are in spite of the scientific facts about them. When those who instruct us to "trust what they say" do things that prove they are not trustworthy, trust is the last thing we should extend to them.

Thankfully, for us as Christians, the basis of our trust is a source with a perfect track record—the Bible. It has never been inaccurate or asked us to believe in something contradictory to evidence. Not once has it been misleading or proven itself untrustworthy. Psalm 119:160 declares, "The entirety of Your word is truth, and every one of Your righteous judgments endures forever."

Today, truth is often defined by a person's feelings and emotions, and it is good to know that we have a book of facts that records the past, directs us through the present, and foretells the future. This living, powerful book has told us that Christians do not have an appointment with God's wrath (1 Thessalonians 5:9), and that someday God's wrath is coming upon the whole world (Revelation 16:1).

We do not know the day or the hour of our removal from this world, but we do know that the tribulation will come at a time when the world is crying out for "peace and safety" (1 Thessalonians 5:3). This phrase is interesting because "peace" can mean an exemption from war, but it also refers to harmony between individuals. The word "safety" means "security from enemies and dangers."

We live in a time when people are crying out for harmony between individuals and acceptance of all beliefs that will bring security from enemies and dangers. For the "peace and safety" crowd, one of the enemies and dangers is the Christian faith, which is based on objective truth. We must hold fast to God's unchanging truths until He comes!

DAY 147

BLESSED ARE THE PURE IN HEART

You may have heard the saying, "The heart of the human problem is the problem of the human heart." While the original source of this truism is unknown, it is rooted in biblical truth.

Matthew 15:19-20 tells us that "out of the heart proceed evil thoughts, murders, adulteries, fornications, thefts, false witness, blasphemies. These are the things which defile a man, but to eat with unwashed hands does not defile a man."

Jesus had just rebuked the scribes and Pharisees for elevating their traditions to equal status with the commandments of God. He was responding to their question as to why His disciples did not wash their hands in the manner prescribed by their man-made rules.

He responded, "It's not the failure to wash one's hands properly that defiles a man, but rather, the heart of man itself, from which evil thoughts and their companions proceed."

In Matthew 15:19, the word translated "heart" is the Greek term *kardia*, the root for our English word *cardio*. The word certainly applies to the cardiovascular system of the human body, but it also refers to the soul or mind, the seat of passion and desire. That is confirmed in Jeremiah 17:9-10, which says, "The heart is deceitful above all things, and desperately wicked; who can know it? I, the Lord, search the heart, I test the mind, even to give every man according to his ways, according to the fruit of his doings."

If the Lord tests all of our hearts, and our heart condition is found to be desperately wicked, how, then, do we arrive at the place where we can experience the blessings of being "pure in heart," which Jesus spoke of in the Beatitudes in Matthew 5?

David gave us the answer in the Psalms: "Create in me a clean heart, O God, and renew a steadfast spirit within me" (51:10).

God is still in the heart-cleansing business today. Make sure He has done that for you!

DAY 148

EXTRABIBLICAL REVELATION

We hear a lot today about the legitimacy of extrabiblical revelation, and there are strong emotional responses from those who stand on both sides of the issue. The only way to make our way through the emotions and opinions on the matter is to look to the Word of God.

Let's do that by looking at Acts 16:6-10:

> Now when they had gone through Phrygia and the region of Galatia, they were forbidden by the Holy Spirit to preach the word in Asia. After they had come to Mysia, they tried to go into Bithynia, but the Spirit did not permit them. So passing by Mysia, they came down to Troas. And a vision appeared to Paul in the night. A man of Macedonia stood and pleaded with him, saying, "Come over to Macedonia and help us." Now after he had seen the vision, immediately we sought to go to Macedonia, concluding that the Lord had called us to preach the gospel to them.

This one incident gives us many answers to the hotly debated issue of extrabiblical revelations. Paul and company were forbidden by the Spirit to preach the Word in Asia. Why? We do not know. How? We do not know, other than the Holy Spirit being the agent of communication. The end result was that God the Holy Spirit was speaking to Paul about something that would never be found in the Scriptures. This brings to mind Proverbs 3:5-6: "Trust in the LORD with all your heart, and lean not on your own understanding; in all your ways acknowledge Him, and He shall direct your paths."

The Bible doesn't say, "Jim Elliot, I am going to call you to go to Ecuador in 1950." It doesn't say, "Billy Graham, I am going to launch you into international evangelism in 1949 in Los Angeles." Obviously, the Holy Spirit spoke to these men, just as He spoke to Paul and directed his path.

Yes, God speaks to us outside of His Word, but never in conflict, contradiction, or addition to His Word.

DAY 149

THE POWER OF THE GOSPEL

In the first century, as is true today, there were cultural colloquialisms that most people were familiar with. At times we will hear people say that it is raining cats and dogs, meaning that it's raining hard. In Paul's day, someone might use the phrase "To act the Corinthian," which would mean to be a person who was acting carnal, driven by the desires of their flesh.

With that as our context, let's read Acts 18:5-6:

> When Silas and Timothy had come from Macedonia, Paul was compelled by the Spirit, and testified to the Jews that Jesus is the Christ. But when they opposed him and blasphemed, he shook his garments and said to them, "Your blood be upon your own heads; I am clean. From now on I will go to the Gentiles."

Paul had a long history of run-ins with his own countrymen, whom he loved, and in Corinth, things started off the same way they had in other cities. The Jews opposed Paul and the Christ that he preached.

Today, there are those who use name-calling and loud voices to intimidate and speak against all things Christian. This is nothing less than a satanic effort to silence those who have the one message that all the world needs to hear.

Satan knows he has no way to stifle the soul-saving power of the gospel, so his efforts are focused on getting the church to be silent about it. He knows full well that when the Word of God is heard, people will come to saving faith—not all people, but some. As Paul was told by the Lord in Corinth, "I have many people in this city" (Acts 18:10).

That is true about your city too—whether it is known by a colloquialism like Sin City, as Las Vegas is known, or as a decadent, liberal city like Tel Aviv in Israel. God has people in your city whom He desires to save, and He wants to use you to reach them!

DAY 150

THE NEW JERUSALEM

In John 14:2-3, we read these wonderful words from Jesus: "In My Father's house are many mansions; if it were not so, I would have told you. I go to prepare a place for you. And if I go and prepare a place for you, I will come again and receive you to Myself; that where I am, there you may be also."

These two verses remind us of a great truth that should bring us much comfort and even a sense of excitement and anticipation. While we have all heard about the New Jerusalem's streets of gold, foundations of precious stones, and gates made of single pearls—all of which are beyond our imagination—there is another aspect of the city we need to remember:

> Now I saw a new heaven and a new earth, for the first heaven and the first earth had passed away. Also there was no more sea. Then I, John, saw the holy city, New Jerusalem, coming down out of heaven from God, prepared as a bride adorned for her husband. And I heard a loud voice from heaven saying, "Behold, the tabernacle of God is with men, and He will dwell with them, and they shall be His people. God Himself will be with them and be their God. And God will wipe away every tear from their eyes; there shall be no more death, nor sorrow, nor crying. There shall be no more pain, for the former things have passed away" (Revelation 21:1-4).

In the face of the evils of the world, remember: One day, we will transition to a life of being with the Lord forever. We will meet Him in the air, come back when He does to the Mount of Olives, see Him fight in the day of battle, rule with Him for 1,000 years, and then at last, we will live free of tears, death, sorrow, crying, and pain for all eternity in a city whose builder and maker is God!

DAY 151

KEEP LOOKING UP

You may have heard the expression "Looking for love in all the wrong places." And it seems as though there are times when we who have found and experienced God's magnificent love end up looking not for love, but help, in all the wrong places.

Psalm 121:1-3 tells us where to look:

> I will lift up my eyes to the hills—from whence comes my help?
> My help comes from the LORD, who made heaven and earth. He will not allow your foot to be moved; He who keeps you will not slumber.

It has been said, "One uplook can change your whole outlook." That is a perfect summary of the verses we just read. Our help comes from the Lord, and sometimes we need to lift our eyes above our circumstances and remember our help may come not from a change of circumstances, but from the maker of heaven and earth changing us.

Now, Proverbs 24:6 does say that "by wise counsel you will wage your own war, and in a multitude of counselors there is safety." So don't think we're saying that other believers and family can never be a help to us. But there are times when only the supernatural can supply what we need. That is why the psalmist was inspired to say that our help comes from "the LORD, who made heaven and earth."

The psalmist adds that the Lord keeps us and does not slumber at the task of doing so. Whenever unknown or troubling outcomes are pending, make sure you're looking for help in the right place—from the Lord who made heaven and earth. Jeremiah 32:17 reminds us that there is "nothing too hard" for the Lord, including the intimidating situations we all face in life. So when troubles seem to be mounting, be sure to keep looking up!

DAY 152

RUN FOR THE PRIZE

In John 14:12, Jesus told His disciples that they would do greater works than they had seen up to that point because He was going to His Father. What would be greater than healing the sick, casting out demons, feeding the masses through miraculous means, and even raising the dead? What was that power, and what would they do with it? Acts 1:8 gives the answer:

> You shall receive power when the Holy Spirit has come upon you; and you shall be witnesses to Me in Jerusalem, and in all Judea and Samaria, and to the end of the earth.

This is the greater work Jesus was referring to—the work of being a witness. All who were healed by Jesus went on to die, all who were fed got hungry again, all who had demons cast from them and who were raised from the dead died later. Their encounters with Jesus' miraculous power changed their lives, but didn't necessarily lead to the saving of their souls.

Many Christians today are longing to see the power of God manifest in miraculous ways, yet sadly, few are doing what leads to God displaying that power, which is being a witness.

Paul likened being a witness to running a race and fighting the good fight of faith. It takes discipline for a runner to train well and deny himself of foods or pleasures or activities that would be detrimental to him on race day. Paul said we don't fight like a shadow boxer beating the air with our fists, but rather, we discipline our body so that we will not be disqualified.

The greatest thing we can do in life is lead other people to Jesus, and He has given us His Spirit to empower us to do so. Sometimes being a witness will be like running a race and exhaust us. Sometimes we will have to fight to do what we are called and empowered to do. But we need to recognize that we are all called to be a witness.

DAY 153

WISDOM FROM ABOVE

James 3:13-17 has this to say about wisdom:

> Who is wise and understanding among you? Let him show by good conduct that his works are done in the meekness of wisdom. But if you have bitter envy and self-seeking in your hearts, do not boast and lie against the truth. This wisdom does not descend from above, but is earthly, sensual, demonic. For where envy and self-seeking exist, confusion and every evil thing are there. But the wisdom that is from above is first pure, then peaceable, gentle, willing to yield, full of mercy and good fruits, without partiality and without hypocrisy.

The exceedingly great and precious promises of God's Word are given for the entire world to read and embrace as true. Yet the only people who do this are those who have received the pure wisdom that comes from above. The word translated "pure" means "perfect" or "sacred." It is the root word from which we get *holy*.

Earthly wisdom, of course, is the polar opposite, and it is clear that most of our world is operating in wisdom that is earthly, sensual, and demonic. We know this because the culture around us is filled with self-seeking, confusion, and every evil thing.

We must not miss the connection between the source of our wisdom and how it manifests itself in our lives. Those operating by earthly wisdom are confused about what a woman is, what gender means, what good and evil are, and much more.

Yet the wisdom that comes from above yields great benefits and clarity in the lives of those who have accessed it. We know there are two genders, we know that males cannot become females, and we know the definitions of right and wrong, evil and good. We can say this because the source of pure wisdom wrote a book that is known as God's Word, the Bible.

DAY 154

WHO IS ON THE LORD'S SIDE?

During the US Civil War, both sides used the motto "God is with us." Noting the conflict, President Abraham Lincoln observed, "My concern is not whether God is on our side; my greatest concern is to be on God's side, for God is always right."[6]

We all hope and long for God to be with us, and His promise to us is to never leave nor forsake us (Hebrews 13:5). The fact that we are temples of the Holy Spirit, who is in us, means we never have to be concerned about being without Him. In the Old Testament, God promised Joshua, "Have I not commanded you? Be strong and of good courage; do not be afraid, nor be dismayed, for the LORD your God is with you wherever you go" (Joshua 1:9).

While these promises to the church and Joshua should be sources of comfort for us, they should also be cause for concern. That's because the Lord is also present when we are in a place we shouldn't be, or when we are thinking or doing what we shouldn't think or do. We want to be sure we avoid "golden calf" incidents because we never want to bring God shame:

> Now when Moses saw that the people were unrestrained (for Aaron had not restrained them, to their shame among their enemies), then Moses stood in the entrance of the camp, and said, "Whoever is on the LORD's side—come to me!" And all the sons of Levi gathered themselves together to him (Exodus 32:25-26).

The word "unrestrained" means "naked" or "bare," and to the people's shame, they danced naked around an idol—even after all that God had done for them, including bringing them out of Egypt. What was their excuse for such abhorrent behavior?

The people were tired of waiting on what God would do next and fell into sin because of it. God moves in His own time, and we shouldn't turn to sinful actions when we get impatient.

DAY 155

SUFFERING AND REPENTANCE

There are some things we will be glad to be rid of when we enter eternity, not the least of which are suffering and trials. Yet consider these passages:

> My brethren, count it all joy when you fall into various trials, knowing that the testing of your faith produces patience (James 1:2-3).

> In this you greatly rejoice, though now for a little while, if need be, you have been grieved by various trials, that the genuineness of your faith, being much more precious than gold that perishes, though it is tested by fire, may be found to praise, honor, and glory at the revelation of Jesus Christ (1 Peter 1:6-7).

Suffering and trials can have a positive impact on our lives, as James and Peter point out. They produce patience and prove the genuineness of our faith. We would all prefer to live without this productive pair of life experiences, but the truth is that they are the only means by which certain results can be accomplished in our lives. After all, you can't learn patience by never having it tested, and you can't show the genuineness of your faith without suffering.

Yet many today question the goodness or even the existence of God because of the suffering and trials they experience. You may be going through some form of trial or suffering, and if it is causing you to question God's goodness or faithfulness, remember, there are things you can learn from what you're facing. The greatest proof of that is Jesus Himself learning obedience through His suffering (Hebrews 5:8), and we should learn the same through ours.

The trial- and suffering-free life is not this one, and the presence of suffering and trials in our lives does not annul God's goodness and kindness to us.

DAY 156

THE WORLD IS READY

We live in a time of unprecedented prophetic fulfillment. When Jesus came the first time, numerous (some say 300) prophecies about His coming were fulfilled, all of which pertained to the Jews and Himself. And today, we live in a time when prophecies are being fulfilled about Israel, the church, false Christs, failing human character, wars and rumors of wars, ethnic tensions, famine, pestilence, geological and atmospheric anomalies, and the building of military coalitions that will invade Israel, among a host of other things.

In light of all this, you would think everyone would be living with the expectation of the soon appearing of our great God and Savior, Jesus Christ. And yet Jesus Himself said of the days in which we live, "Be ready, for the Son of Man is coming at an hour you do not expect" (Matthew 24:44).

With all that is clearly prophetic and the precursors of things that will be fulfilled during the tribulation, you would expect the church to be abuzz with excitement and to have a sense of urgency for people coming to Christ. Yet of the 2.42 billion people who bear the label Christian today, only 6.6 percent believe in the rapture of the church.[7] Matthew 24:36-39 tells us what people will be like:

> Of that day and hour no one knows, not even the angels of heaven, but My Father only. But as the days of Noah were, so also will the coming of the Son of Man be. For as in the days before the flood, they were eating and drinking, marrying and giving in marriage, until the day that Noah entered the ark, and did not know until the flood came and took them all away, so also will the coming of the Son of Man be.

The days in which we now live are like the days before the flood. People are going about their business even though signs of impending judgment abound. That should tell us the hour is late as it pertains to church history, and that Jesus is coming for us soon!

DAY 157

TO THE JEW FIRST

To the church in Rome, Paul wrote, "I am not ashamed of the gospel of Christ, for it is the power of God to salvation for everyone who believes, for the Jew first and also for the Greek" (Romans 1:16).

Here, Paul was quick to establish two points: One, he reminded the Jews within the church of the great privilege of having been blessed as the first to hear the gospel. Second, he said the fact that they had heard the gospel, and the fact that Christ—the One whom the gospel was centered on—shared the same ethnicity with them did not relieve them of the necessity of belief in order to be saved.

Paul said in Romans 1 that the gospel of Christ is the power of God to salvation for everyone who "believes," thus reminding the Jews that no one is saved by their first birth. Then in Romans 2, Paul told the Jews that one expression of belief in Christ is "patient continuance" (verse 7). This phrase comes from a single Greek word that means "constancy" or "steadfastness." Paul told the church in Rome that being steadfast or constant in doing good by seeking to live for the next life during this one was how they should live while awaiting immortal incorruptibility.

Jesus said, "Let your light so shine before men, that they may see your good works and glorify your Father in heaven" (Matthew 5:16). Light is a metaphor for truth, truth manifests itself in life through good works, and good works bring glory to God. This reminds us that good works have nothing to do with legalism or a "works righteousness" salvation. For the Jews and Gentiles, good works are the natural (or even supernatural) response to being saved by grace through faith in Christ.

No one can boast that they are saved because of their good works, but everyone who is saved has good works prepared for them by God to walk in (Ephesians 2:10), with the end result being that God is glorified.

DAY 158

THE MILLENNIUM

There are many issues within eschatology (the study of the last days) that are and have been interpreted differently down through the ages, the millennial reign of Christ being among them. Some say there is no millennium, others say we are in the millennium, and still others say the millennium is a yet-future event. So, as always, the question is, Who or what is right?

The fact there will be a time period of 1,000 years after the second coming and before the Great White Throne judgment is clearly stated six times in Revelation 20:2-7. What happens during that time should be taken literally, as there is no figurative or allegorical meaning that can be derived from those verses. Satan will be bound, the group of people known as the first resurrection will rule and reign with Christ during that time, Satan will be released at the end of the 1,000 years to deceive the nations and gather them to battle against the saints and the beloved city of Jerusalem, and fire will come down and consume the devil and his followers, and they will be cast into the lake of fire to join the beast and false prophet.

Again, these events must be taken literally, for there is nothing about them that can be allegorized into "spiritual life lessons." It is also true that to say there is no millennial reign of Christ on Earth leaves multitudes of scriptures unfulfilled, including Isaiah 9:6: "Unto us a Child is born, unto us a Son is given; and the government will be upon His shoulder. And His name will be called Wonderful, Counselor, Mighty God, Everlasting Father, Prince of Peace."

If there is no literal millennial reign of Christ on Earth, then the Son of God will have never ruled the nations with a rod of iron, and thus the government will have never been on His shoulder. That means the millennium is yet to happen, and like all biblical prophecies, what we read about the millennium will be fulfilled exactly as written.

DAY 159

LIFE AFTER DEATH

We live in a day when, for many, feelings and emotions are the single most important factor in determining what is true or valid. Timeless truths have been rejected because of how people feel about them.

Some people "feel" marriage should not be limited to a man and a woman; others "feel" gender cannot be limited to the categories male and female. Still others "feel" that the existence of a universal moral standard is unfair, and thus any consequences for violating such a standard is unjust.

However, from Genesis to Revelation, God is presented as the righteous Judge of all the earth. This, too, has become unacceptable to many, and for them, the only fair option is to allow each person to "do what is right in their own eyes" without the judgment of others, or God, for their actions. This kind of thinking is catastrophic to any society or country and is the very reason our world is in the condition it is in today.

By the world's logic, if there is no universal standard of right and wrong and everyone has a right to do what they feel or believe, then institutions that define, regulate, or enforce the law are irrelevant and should be eliminated, leaving lawlessness to abound.

But there is no escaping the reality declared by Hebrews 9:27-28: "It is appointed for men to die once, but after this the judgment, so Christ was offered once to bear the sins of many. To those who eagerly wait for Him He will appear a second time, apart from sin, for salvation."

Everyone will live forever; what a person does with Jesus determines how and where. There is life after death, and some will spend it in a place where there is fullness of joy and pleasures forevermore, and others will spend it in a lake that burns with fire.

Today is the day to decide your eternal address if you haven't already.

DAY 160

THE UNKNOWN GOD

There is a global identity crisis happening in our world today, one in which long-known physical and biological identifiers have been replaced with confusion instigated by subjective feelings and thoughts. You can ask people, "What is a woman?," and some are unable to answer the question because these days, biological males can claim to be one.

Sadly, this identity crisis has made its way into the church—not only in the physical and biological realms, but also in the spiritual. It used to be that when you asked someone, "What is a woman?," they would immediately answer, "One of the two human genders whose reproductive organs enable them to bear children." But today, even in many churches, the question is met with silence, or with claims that there are multiple genders.

A similar problem is the way people now answer the question, "What is a Christian?" The standard answer used to be "Someone who is born again." But today, many define a Christian as someone who attends church or believes Jesus existed, or as someone who feels they are one.

First John 2:22-23 offers important clarity on this: "Who is a liar but he who denies that Jesus is the Christ? He is antichrist who denies the Father and the Son. Whoever denies the Son does not have the Father either; he who acknowledges the Son has the Father also."

The truth is that being a Christian is far more than a religious identity or cognitive awareness of the existence of a historical personage. To know Christ is to know and have the same power that raised Him from the dead. To know Him is to expect His glorious appearing, at which time the dead in Christ will be raised and the living saints are transformed.

Every person who acknowledges Jesus is God the Son has the Father also, but whoever denies the Son has neither. What a glorious truth it is that the God of all creation has, through His Son, made a way for us to be reconciled to Him!

DAY 161

WHY ISRAEL IS UNDER CONSTANT ATTACK

In Psalm 2:1-5, we read,

> Why do the nations rage, and the people plot a vain thing? The kings of the earth set themselves, and the rulers take counsel together, against the LORD and against His Anointed, saying, "Let us break their bonds in pieces and cast away their cords from us." He who sits in the heavens shall laugh; the LORD shall hold them in derision. Then He shall speak to them in His wrath, and distress them in His deep displeasure.

Every war against Israel reflects an ages-old rejection of the Lord and His anointed in an effort to break the bonds of God's authority and cast away any obligation to Him. These wars are started by those who say, "'Come, and let us cut them off from being a nation, that the name of Israel may be remembered no more.' For they have consulted together with one consent; they form a confederacy against You" (Psalm 83:4-5).

What the psalmist wrote in Psalm 2 and Asaph prayed in Psalm 83 is what we are seeing today. Satan is trying to incite people against Israel to cut them off from being a nation. We are near the end of the generation that saw the rebirth of Israel in 1948. Hosea 5:15 tells us of what is to come: "I will return again to My place till they acknowledge their offense. Then they will seek My face; in their affliction they will earnestly seek Me."

The events we are watching unfold today in relation to Israel are a glimpse of the antisemitism that will be rampant during the tribulation. Yet this time of affliction will lead the surviving one-third of the Jews to finally see Jesus of Nazareth as their Messiah (Zechariah 13:8-9).

So let us "pray for the peace of Jerusalem" (Psalm 122:6), and pray for the Jews to come to know the only source of true peace, the Prince of Peace, Jesus of Nazareth, who is Christ the Lord.

DAY 162

POWER, LOVE, AND A SOUND MIND

The things God has done for us and given to us are endless. Each day is met with new mercies (Lamentations 3:23), we have sufficient grace to endure any circumstance (2 Corinthians 12:9), He has promised to supply all our needs according to His riches in glory by Christ Jesus (Philippians 4:19), and on and on we could go.

For example, consider Romans 8:33: "Who shall bring a charge against God's elect? It is God who justifies." The word "justifies" means "to render innocent," or "to be freed" God, through Jesus, has rendered a verdict in our case—we are innocent in Christ Jesus and the Son has made us free!

Because we have been justified, there is something else we are free from: "God has not given us a spirit of fear, but of power and of love and of a sound mind" (2 Timothy 1:7). The Greek word translated "fear" can also be translated as "timidity" or "cowardice." That means that in the midst of life's intimidating circumstances, when we're waiting for things to work together for good, when the tribulations of this life come, we do not have to be intimidated by them, even though we want them to end or change.

In John 16:33, Jesus said, "These things I have spoken to you, that in Me you may have peace. In the world you will have tribulation; but be of good cheer, I have overcome the world."

Peace, tribulation, and good cheer might seem like contradictory terms or conflicting simultaneous experiences, but they are in fact the end result of not having been given the spirit of fear but of power, love, and a sound mind.

The weapons formed against us won't prosper, nothing can separate us from His love, and no one can snatch us from His hand! This is a good place to shout, "Amen!"

DAY 163

SPIRIT-FILLED YET HATE OTHERS?, PART 1

One of the most fruitful activities you can do, as it pertains to understanding Scripture, is to study the names of God. He is El Shaddai, God Almighty; He is El Elyon, God Most High; He is Jehovah Jireh, the Lord Who Will Provide; He is Jehovah Tsidkenu, the Lord Our Righteousness. The list goes on and on, and each of the names of God reveals another aspect of His nature and character. What's important to know is this: These are not requirements for Him to meet in order for Him to qualify for the position of God (remember, God is a title that means "Supreme Being"), but these are attributes He possesses because He is God.

The same is true for us as Christians who are indwelt and empowered by the same Spirit who raised Christ from the dead. Because we are called by the Father, saved through the blood of the Son, and indwelt by the Holy Spirit, there are going to be common attributes among us. They are not traits that *enable* us to become Christians; rather, they are shared attributes *because* we are Christians. A careful study of the names of God will tell us what kinds of attributes will be common among Spirit-filled Christians.

Galatians 5:22-26 names some of these attributes and their effect:

> The fruit of the Spirit is love, joy, peace, longsuffering, kindness, goodness, faithfulness, gentleness, self-control. Against such there is no law. And those who are Christ's have crucified the flesh with its passions and desires. If we live in the Spirit, let us also walk in the Spirit. Let us not become conceited, provoking one another, envying one another.

We need to note that "fruit" here is singular. That means all the attributes listed are the fruit, the result of, the presence of the Holy Spirit in our lives. The first in the list is love, which, alongside its companions of faith and hope, is the greatest (1 Corinthians 13:13).

DAY 164

SPIRIT-FILLED YET HATE OTHERS?, PART 2

In Matthew 5:43-48, Jesus taught,

> You have heard that it was said, "You shall love your neighbor and hate your enemy." But I say to you, love your enemies, bless those who curse you, do good to those who hate you, and pray for those who spitefully use you and persecute you, that you may be sons of your Father in heaven; for He makes His sun rise on the evil and on the good, and sends rain on the just and on the unjust. For if you love those who love you, what reward have you? Do not even the tax collectors do the same? And if you greet your brethren only, what do you do more than others? Do not even the tax collectors do so? Therefore you shall be perfect, just as your Father in heaven is perfect.

And in John 13:35, Jesus said, "By this all will know that you are My disciples, if you have love for one another."

The first identifying characteristic of Spirit-filled Christians is love—love for those who hate us, and love for those who are like us. Such love will lead to joy, peace, longsuffering, kindness, goodness, faithfulness, gentleness, and self-control. This tells us that hatred for any group of people based on race or skin color is not consistent with the Christian faith—it is not of the fruit of the Spirit that we all share.

Jesus doesn't hate the Jews, and those who are Christlike will not either. Do not buy into the supposed "Christian" antisemitism today that, among other things, denies that modern Israel is biblical Israel. Christianity and antisemitism are diametrically opposed to one another, as is Christianity and racism of any kind. They are not among the common attributes found in Christians.

The greatest characteristic we are to be known for is love.

DAY 165

THE PURPOSE OF THE BELIEVER

When the Jews commemorate the giving of the law with Shavuot (the Feast of Weeks) and the church celebrates its birth on Pentecost Sunday, both are celebrating a picture of the human condition and the hope of reconciliation to God.

In Romans 8:3-4, Paul wrote, "What the law could not do in that it was weak through the flesh, God did by sending His own Son in the likeness of sinful flesh, on account of sin: He condemned sin in the flesh, that the righteous requirement of the law might be fulfilled in us who do not walk according to the flesh but according to the Spirit."

Shavuot reminds us that God gave to man, through the Jews, a law that revealed their sinfulness and separation from God. Pentecost reminds us that God had a remedy for man's separation from Him in the form of His only begotten Son, who would reconcile man to God through His own blood. As 2 Corinthians 5:18-19 says, "Now all things are of God, who has reconciled us to Himself through Jesus Christ, and has given us the ministry of reconciliation, that is, that God was in Christ reconciling the world to Himself, not imputing their trespasses to them, and has committed to us the word of reconciliation."

Shavuot reminds us that all have sinned and fallen short of the glory of God. Pentecost reminds us that through the death, resurrection, and ascension of Jesus, reconciliation with God has now become possible. And the purpose of the church and every Christian is to tell these truths to others.

James 2:10 makes this clear about man's need for Christ: "Whoever shall keep the whole law, and yet stumble in one point, he is guilty of all." Some have broken all of God's laws, some have broken most of God's laws, and others a few of God's laws, but *all* have broken God's law and must be reconciled to Him by the blood of Christ. Thanks be to God that He sent His Son into the world to do that very thing!

DAY 166

ISRAEL IS THE COMPASS OF PROPHECY

Our world is currently in a state of chaos. There is talk of WWIII on the lips of many, rumors of other wars swirling, talk of new pandemic variants almost weekly, tensions between countries are increasing, goods and supplies are dwindling, and the negatives go on and on.

But we, as Christians, need not fear. The One who knows the end from the beginning has given us this promise: "Let your conduct be without covetousness; be content with such things as you have. For He Himself has said, 'I will never leave you nor forsake you.' So we may boldly say: 'The LORD is my helper; I will not fear. What can man do to me?'" (Hebrews 13:5-6).

No matter whether the stresses we face are international or personal, military or emotional, fear is not our master. God is in control:

> Remember the former things of old, for I am God, and there is no other; I am God, and there is none like Me, declaring the end from the beginning, and from ancient times things that are not yet done, saying, "My counsel shall stand, and I will do all My pleasure" (Isaiah 46:9-10).

The Bible has told us of God's miraculous track record of faithfulness. His Word has told us He can part the Red Sea, He can confuse our enemies, He can turn bitter water into sweet, and He fights battles on our behalf. The Bible has also told us about the future—perilous times will come, the love of many will grow cold, Israel will take center stage on the world scene, and a host of other prophecies in the process of being fulfilled prove that the Word of God is living and powerful because the God of the Word is living and powerful.

You may have heard it said that when you find a Bible that is falling apart, you can be sure it belongs to a Christian who isn't! Make sure that can be said of you and your Bible.

DAY 167

MEET HIM IN THE AIR

Most of us have said the old adage "Watch where you're going" with the intention of helping someone avoid falling or tripping, or doing something that could hurt, or at the least, embarrass them. We would do well to apply this adage spiritually, and the Bible, using different words, admonishes us to do just that. Paul wrote, "Brethren, I do not count myself to have apprehended; but one thing I do, forgetting those things which are behind and reaching forward to those things which are ahead, I press toward the goal for the prize of the upward call of God in Christ Jesus" (Philippians 3:13-14).

We are currently living in a very painful season of human history. Wars and rumors of wars abound, good is called evil and evil is called good, the moral character of mankind has degraded significantly, divorce is rampant, babies are aborted in the womb, cancer and disease are ravaging the bodies of many, and God and His people are belittled and disparaged. It seems as though things could not get any worse.

So what do we do in times such as these? Watch where you're going, keep looking up, and wake up each day with this on your mind:

> The grace of God that brings salvation has appeared to all men, teaching us that, denying ungodliness and worldly lusts, we should live soberly, righteously, and godly in the present age, looking for the blessed hope and glorious appearing of our great God and Savior Jesus Christ, who gave Himself for us, that He might redeem us from every lawless deed and purify for Himself His own special people, zealous for good works (Titus 2:11-14).

The way to handle the pains and problems of this present age is by remembering our blessed hope. The hope that Jesus promised to come again and receive us unto Himself so that we may be with Him could be fulfilled today!

DAY 168

THE BIBLE IS NOT POLITICAL, PART 1

Of all the radical changes we have seen in our world in recent years, one of the most tragic is the death of the belief in absolute truth. Things long known to be true and factual are now viewed through the lens of personal subjectivity. If you think something is true, then that is "your truth."

But consider what Scripture says:

> The entirety of Your word is truth, and every one of Your righteous judgments endures forever (Psalm 119:160).

> In the beginning was the Word, and the Word was with God, and the Word was God (John 1:1).

> Jesus Christ is the same yesterday, today, and forever (Hebrews 13:8).

If the whole of God's Word is true, and Jesus is the Word of God and He doesn't change, then His Word doesn't change either. It is all still true.

The efforts of many today to redefine truth as subjective is done with the intention—whether knowingly or not—to encroach upon the Word of God and bring it under the banner of subjectivism. We can see how effectively this perspective has infiltrated the church because many are now taking a salad-bar approach to God's Word: "I'll believe this but not that; I'll accept this moral mandate but not that."

This makes it all the more important for us to be the salt of the earth and the light of the world (Matthew 5:13-15). Salt and light represent the church's preserving and purifying influence on others, and when the church loses these features, it is trampled underfoot by the world, as we see happening today.

DAY 169

THE BIBLE IS NOT POLITICAL, PART 2

Psalm 119:105 extols the importance of God's Word in our lives, saying, "Your word is a lamp to my feet and a light to my path."

Light is also figurative for the Word of God, the entirety of which is true. It has been said, "As goes the church, so goes the nation." We see this being proven all around the world in an age in which the so-called "people of the book" don't even believe it all to be true. The Bible is not a political book because politics is not a biblical concept. Human government is a biblical concept, but not the corrupt system we see today.

> Let every soul be subject to the governing authorities. For there is no authority except from God, and the authorities that exist are appointed by God. Therefore whoever resists the authority resists the ordinance of God, and those who resist will bring judgment on themselves. For rulers are not a terror to good works, but to evil. Do you want to be unafraid of the authority? Do what is good, and you will have praise from the same. For he is God's minister to you for good. But if you do evil, be afraid; for he does not bear the sword in vain; for he is God's minister, an avenger to execute wrath on him who practices evil (Romans 13:1-4).

Sadly, because of the lack of Christian influence in governments around the world, many governments do not punish evil, but rather, protect it. What the Bible prohibits they promote, and what was once forbidden is now called freedom.

Our world today is held captive by corrupt politicians who deny the truths that were once known to be true. But truth does not change because man says it does; truth is what God says it is. After all, He is the maker of heaven and earth.

We are to abide in God's Word even when the world denies it is true, and even when much of what is called the church doesn't believe it is all true.

DAY 170

THE NATURE OF GOD

It is bewildering how so many people today choose the unbiblical path of anti-semitism when there are so many wonderful truths to learn about the nature and character of God through His relationship with Israel. Deuteronomy 7:6-8 says,

> You are a holy people to the LORD your God; the LORD your God has chosen you to be a people for Himself, a special treasure above all the peoples on the face of the earth. The LORD did not set His love on you nor choose you because you were more in number than any other people, for you were the least of all peoples; but because the LORD loves you, and because He would keep the oath which He swore to your fathers, the LORD has brought you out with a mighty hand, and redeemed you from the house of bondage, from the hand of Pharaoh king of Egypt.

When we read verses in which God makes a statement to Israel that is based on His nature and character, we are free to embrace that aspect of His nature and character as being applicable to us as well. Why? Because He is the Lord and He does not change.

Consider the above passage in Deuteronomy. Israel is called a chosen people and a special treasure among all the peoples of the earth. Now read what 1 Peter 2:9-10 says about us:

> You are a chosen generation, a royal priesthood, a holy nation, His own special people, that you may proclaim the praises of Him who called you out of darkness into His marvelous light; who once were not a people but are now the people of God, who had not obtained mercy but now have obtained mercy.

Yes, Jesus came to the Jews first and chose them first, but His intention was to use them to reach the rest of the world. And when they didn't, He chose the church for the job, in which there is neither Jew nor Greek, nor Gentiles.

DAY 171

THE SUSPENSE IS OVER

Among the many benefits of studying Revelation is that we get a glimpse of what goes on in heaven. We read in Revelation 21 about the New Jerusalem, with its twelve foundations made of precious stones, and its four sides having three gates on each side, with each gate comprised of a single giant pearl. The city is made of gold so pure it is clear like glass, and the light of the city does not come from the sun or moon, but from the Lamb of God Himself.

This is what we will see after the millennium and Great White Throne judgment have been completed. The good news is we won't have to wait until the millennium is over to see these unbelievable and amazing things.

In Revelation 4, we are given an actual description of the throne room of God! We see Him on His throne encircled by an emerald-green rainbow, and there is a sea of glass before the throne. We also see four living creatures who cease not day or night, saying, "Holy, holy, holy, Lord God Almighty, who was and is and is to come!" Twenty-four elders are seated there, and angels are all around.

This scene will amaze our eyes with its brilliance and flashes of lightning, and the room will be filled with the majestic sounds of thunder and voices of praise. The sights and sounds will be overpowering to our senses! We will be told, with the sound of the trumpet of God and the voice of an archangel, to "Come up here," and we will!

Maybe right now, things aren't looking so amazing for you. Maybe you are facing hardships that are difficult to the point of being almost unbearable. Read Revelation 4 and remind yourself that this is where you are headed. You are going to a place free of pain, problems, tears, and sorrows—a place of such great beauty that it cannot be described with words, but must be experienced to be understood.

DAY 172

THE TREE OF LIFE AND JESUS

The world today is trying to convince us that more is better. The more genders the better, the more post-pregnancy options the better, and the more belief systems there are, the better, because the broader the path that one can follow, the better. While all of this may sound appealing and inclusive, it has one major problem: They can't all be true.

Imagine a city in which a green light could mean *go* to some drivers, and *stop* to other drivers, and the determining factor as to what a green light meant was up to each individual. What would be the end result? Chaos and catastrophe, and no one could safely get to where they want to go.

We hear today about people having "their truth." In philosophy, there is a principle known as bivalence, which means that any proposition, theory, or statement of fact is either true or false—it cannot be neither, nor can it be both. Not everyone can be right about their religious beliefs or how to access the eternal realm of heaven.

In John 14:6, Jesus declared, "I am the way, the truth, and the life. No one comes to the Father except through Me."

Again, to say that all paths lead to one destination is the practical equivalent of saying all freeways take you to the same city, or all flights end at the same destination. You need to get on the specific freeway or board the specific flight that coincides with your desired destination. It may be appealing to think that no matter what you believe you'll end up in heaven, but it's not true.

In Revelation 2:7, Jesus promised, "He who has an ear, let him hear what the Spirit says to the churches. To him who overcomes I will give to eat from the tree of life, which is in the midst of the Paradise of God."

Only through Jesus can we access heaven and the tree of life. He alone is *the* way, *the* truth and *the* life!

DAY 173

WHEN ISRAEL WILL BE SAVED

The false doctrine of replacement theology requires that God break an everlasting, unconditional covenant made with both Israel and the land He promised to them. Dual Covenant theology makes the Holy One of Israel a misnomer, for it says Israel can be saved without Jesus.

The truth is that Israel has not been replaced by the church. And for a Jew to be saved, he or she must come to the King of Jews for salvation, just like any Gentile.

In Romans 11:25-27, Paul wrote,

> I do not desire, brethren, that you should be ignorant of this mystery, lest you should be wise in your own opinion, that blindness in part has happened to Israel until the fullness of the Gentiles has come in. And so all Israel will be saved, as it is written: "The Deliverer will come out of Zion, and He will turn away ungodliness from Jacob; for this is My covenant with them, when I take away their sins."

If the church has replaced Israel, then why did Paul talk about God taking away Israel's sins and all Israel being saved? If Dual Covenant theology is true and Jews can be saved by keeping the law or simply being born a Jew, why did Paul refer to a Deliverer out of Zion? (Zion here refers to Jerusalem.)

The lessons we should learn from Israel are that God keeps His word, disciplines those He loves, never loses track of His people, and never meant for Israel to become religious. God desires a relationship with His people and can protect them through anything. These are among the lessons we can learn from God's special relationship with His chosen people.

Does God saving all Israel include unbelieving Jews who reject the Messiah? No. No one is saved because of their nationality. No one can be saved except by the blood of the Lamb of God, who was "slain from the foundation of the world" (Revelation 13:8).

DAY 174

THINGS WILL NOT GET BETTER

The founder of Calvary Chapel, Pastor Chuck Smith, used to say that our view of what is happening in the world is similar to what we see when we watch a parade. We are seated on the curb and can see only what is passing by in front of us. God, however, is seated in majesty on high and can see the entire parade from beginning to end.

What God has foretold about the future will happen just as He said. This is one of the most crucial aspects of correctly understanding and applying Bible prophecy. Prophecies are not simply predictions; rather, they reveal information about what God has already foreseen that we cannot observe from our perspective on the curb. In other words, if God has already revealed the future and had His prophets record it, nothing is going to change it.

A second aspect for us to consider about Bible prophecy is that while figurative language is sometimes used to describe things and events so that all generations may understand them, the only way to interpret that language is literally, not allegorically.

For example, in Revelation 9:7, we read, "The shape of the locusts was like horses prepared for battle." Here, the Holy Spirit gave John a description that describes, as best as possible, something that humans have never seen. Each locust's shape was "like" a battle horse. The language, while figurative, describes something that is literal.

In Isaiah 46:9-10, God said about Himself, "Remember the former things of old, for I am God, and there is no other; I am God, and there is none like Me, declaring the end from the beginning, and from ancient times things that are not yet done, saying, 'My counsel shall stand, and I will do all My pleasure.'"

How incredible it is that we serve a God who can talk about tomorrow with the same certainty we can talk about yesterday! Tell someone about Jesus today, for God has revealed to us what will soon come upon the whole world, and things are not going to get any better.

DAY 175

WHEN ISRAEL IS NO MORE

In the midst of all the mundane and repetitive aspects of life, it is always good to have something to look forward to. When we take into account the tedious and painful things that are also part of life, the benefits of having something to look forward to increase exponentially. That's why Titus 2:11-14 is so encouraging:

> The grace of God that brings salvation has appeared to all men, teaching us that, denying ungodliness and worldly lusts, we should live soberly, righteously, and godly in the present age, looking for the blessed hope and glorious appearing of our great God and Savior Jesus Christ, who gave Himself for us, that He might redeem us from every lawless deed and purify for Himself His own special people, zealous for good works.

Denying ungodliness and living righteously in this present age is not easy to do, and Paul gives us the secret of how to persevere by reminding us we have something to look forward to: "the blessed hope and glorious appearing of our great God and Savior Jesus Christ."

In Zechariah 12:10, the Lord offers this hope to the Jewish people: "I will pour on the house of David and on the inhabitants of Jerusalem the Spirit of grace and supplication; then they will look on Me whom they pierced. Yes, they will mourn for Him as one mourns for his only son, and grieve for Him as one grieves for a firstborn."

While the path to this moment will be beyond difficult, it is a blessed hope for believing Jews. Someday, all the Jews who survive the tribulation will be saved. Then Jews and Gentiles will rule together with the Lord during the millennium.

Afterward, however, all ethnic distinctions will be done away with, for in the New Jerusalem, there will be no Jew or Gentile. There will be no temple and no sun, for we will all live in the glorious light of the Lamb forever and ever. We have all this to look forward to for one reason: Our names are written in the Lamb's Book of Life.

DAY 176

WHAT KIND OF GENERATION ARE YOU?

There are many ways in which Christians are different from the world. We are different spiritually, for we know the one true God and have the Holy Spirit. We are different morally, for our standards are defined by God's Word. And we are different behaviorally, for we love our enemies and do good to those who hate us and pray for those who spitefully use us (Matthew 5:44).

There is another way in which we should be different—one that has become more important than ever: "Do all things without complaining and disputing, that you may become blameless and harmless, children of God without fault in the midst of a crooked and perverse generation, among whom you shine as lights in the world" (Philippians 2:14-15).

We live in an unprecedented time of complaints and disputes. There are extremely vocal groups who demand that you think like them and see everything the way they do regarding gender, sexuality, and other issues. They are behind identity politics and virtue signaling and just about anything else that is dividing our world today. And if you disagree with what they think, they consider you a hateful bigot.

So what are we to do? Matthew 5:16 says, "Let your light so shine before men, that they may see your good works and glorify your Father in heaven."

We, of all people, should be cognizant of the lateness of the hour and the shortness of the time we have to reach others with the light of God's truth and thus the hope of heaven.

Jesus said we are the light of the world, but people can't see the light through us when we act like we're part of the darkness, complaining and disputing with one another. Those who are around us will know we are His disciples by the love we have for one another.

DAY 177

THE HOPE OF THE MESSIAH

Few things impact the life experience of believers and nonbelievers alike, and one of them is hope. In some ways, hope affects both groups similarly, and in other ways, hope has completely different meanings. Hope requires an object, and both groups might at one time or another hope for pizza for dinner, or hope to pass a test, or hope to get a raise.

But Isaiah 40:31 speaks of a hope that is unique to God's own: "Those who wait on the Lord shall renew their strength; they shall mount up with wings like eagles, they shall run and not be weary, they shall walk and not faint."

The word "wait" in this famed passage means "to bind together." It can also mean "to hope for" or "expect." That sheds a little more light on the meaning here so we can better understand that those who bind together or place their hope in the Lord will experience renewed strength, power, vigor, and stamina. This is exclusive to those who wait on the Lord. When the Lord is the object of our hope, everything changes.

In Psalm 31:23-24, we read, "Oh, love the Lord, all you His saints! For the Lord preserves the faithful, and fully repays the proud person. Be of good courage, and He shall strengthen your heart, all you who hope in the Lord." This is one of those places where the little word "all" is huge. All who hope in the Lord will be preserved by the Lord!

Hope was Paul's theme in 1 Thessalonians 4:13-14, where he wrote, "I do not want you to be ignorant, brethren, concerning those who have fallen asleep, lest you sorrow as others who have no hope. For if we believe that Jesus died and rose again, even so God will bring with Him those who sleep in Jesus."

The hope we have in Christ is so powerful it even changes the way we experience the greatest of life's pains, like the death of a loved one. We know sorrow, but not without hope.

Remember, such strength is for "all" who hope in the Lord.

DAY 178

THE LAST TRUMPET

Most students of Bible prophecy understand that there is a trumpet associated with the rapture of the church. Some see this trumpet sounding on the Feast of Trumpets, others believe the rapture trumpet is the last of the seven trumpets in the book of Revelation. One point that will help us determine where the rapture falls in the prophetic timeline is understanding the role of trumpets in the Bible.

First Corinthians 14:6-8 helps to provide insight:

> Brethren, if I come to you speaking with tongues, what shall I profit you unless I speak to you either by revelation, by knowledge, by prophesying, or by teaching? Even things without life, whether flute or harp, when they make a sound, unless they make a distinction in the sounds, how will it be known what is piped or played? For if the trumpet makes an uncertain sound, who will prepare for battle?

Paul uses the flute, harp, and trumpet as illustrations of the importance of tongues being interpreted and makes the point that trumpets are used to signal various messages by the tune that is played.

Those who say the last of the seven trumpets of Revelation marks the prophetic timing of the rapture are saying that only then will the wrath of God begin on the earth, after the church is taken out of the way. Yet when the seventh angel sounds his trumpet, more than four billion people will have died on the earth from the direct wrath of God during the ride of the four horsemen of the Apocalypse. So the seventh trumpet does not mark the time of the rapture.

Trumpets announce many things in Scripture; the one in 1 Thessalonians 4:16 signals the end of the church age. We're not waiting for Rosh Hashanah, nor are we waiting for the seventh trumpet during the tribulation. We are waiting for a day and hour predetermined by God that precedes His wrath on the earth, and that day could be today!

DAY 179

THE BELIEVER'S TESTIMONY, PART 1

The Bible is constantly presenting to us the contrast between believers and the world, and how our lives are to be distinct in every way. For example, Paul wrote, "Come out from among them and be separate, says the Lord. Do not touch what is unclean, and I will receive you" (2 Corinthians 6:17).

We are to live separate from the world; we are sons and daughters of light and of the day who live in a world that is of the night and darkness. This should affect how we live:

> Whoever hears these sayings of Mine, and does them, I will liken him to a wise man who built his house on the rock: and the rain descended, the floods came, and the winds blew and beat on that house; and it did not fall, for it was founded on the rock. "But everyone who hears these sayings of Mine, and does not do them, will be like a foolish man who built his house on the sand: and the rain descended, the floods came, and the winds blew and beat on that house; and it fell. And great was its fall." And so it was, when Jesus had ended these sayings, that the people were astonished at His teaching, for He taught them as one having authority, and not as the scribes (Matthew 7:24-29).

Jesus contrasts the lives of those who hear what He says and do it, to those who hear what He says and do not. One, He says, is wise, and the other is foolish.

During Jesus' earthly ministry, those who heard His teaching contrasted it to that of the scribes and said He taught with authority and not by constantly referring to what this rabbi said or that rabbi said, like the scribes did. Paul highlighted this contrast in Romans 12 by exhorting us not to be conformed to this world, but in contrast, to be transformed by our new mind in Christ!

DAY 180

THE BELIEVER'S TESTIMONY, PART 2

We are called to live separate from the world. This distinction was made clear by the contrast Jesus drew between Himself and the thief, meaning Satan, who is the god of this world: "The thief does not come except to steal, and to kill, and to destroy. I have come that they may have life, and that they may have it more abundantly" (John 10:10).

Jesus came to preach good tidings to the poor, heal the brokenhearted, proclaim liberty to the captives, and open the prison to those who are bound, which is the abundant life (Luke 4:18). He said, "I have come as a light into the world, that whoever believes in Me should not abide in darkness" (John 12:46). Satan, however, comes only to take captives and bind them in the dark prison of brokenheartedness and spiritual blindness.

Though we live *in* a dark world, we are not *of* the dark world, for we do not abide in darkness. Our life experience is one of superabundance, a life empowered by the Holy Spirit to proclaim that the liberty we have found in Christ is available to others, a life that says our heart was broken and God healed it, a life that says there were things that once held us captive but Jesus opened the doors of that prison and set us free.

We can't preach freedom when we ourselves are still bound; whoever believes in Jesus should not abide—meaning live—in darkness.

If the Son has made us free, we should live free indeed. Living free is indeed a great contrast in a world that is bound by darkness. It is part of what makes us stand out; it is why we are called to come out and be separate.

Make the commitment that many sang as a child—"This little light of mine, I'm gonna let it shine"—even in the midst of the darkness of today.

DAY 181

THE KEY TO OUR SALVATION

The Bible is a well-integrated message system written by 40 different authors over a period of 1,500 years. This fact alone is significant proof that the Bible is God-breathed. Forty men, most of whom had never met, living at different times in different places under different governments and social structures, wrote a book that is one consistent message cover to cover. The only way to explain this feat is that someone from outside of time, who can see all of the future and knows all of the past, spoke to these men who held the pens and documented the words.

There is one central person who is the focus of the Bible's message: Jesus. There is one central nation that is communicated to and about throughout the Bible: Israel. There is one message that flows as a thread through the Bible, and that is this:

> The life of the flesh is in the blood, and I have given it to you upon the altar to make atonement for your souls; for it is the blood that makes atonement for the soul (Leviticus 17:11).
>
> According to the law almost all things are purified with blood, and without shedding of blood there is no remission (Hebrews 9:22).

Both Testaments record the necessity of a blood sacrifice to atone for the sins of man. Think about the Passover and how, for 1,500 years, the Jews were reminded by this event that the innocent blood of a lamb had to be shed on their behalf.

This is the Bible's core message—that sin requires a blood sacrifice, and a blood sacrifice implies death. Jesus was the perfect sacrifice, and thus the perfect Passover Lamb, and further blood sacrifices are not needed. The Son of God, as the Lamb of God, sanctified His people by shedding His own blood.

Make sure you are numbered among them!

DAY 182

HOPE, EVEN IN DEATH

It is impossible for us to number all the things that change in our lives because of being a Christian. Knowing Christ has an enormous impact on us. There are very big changes, like going to heaven, and there are "smaller" big changes, like not having a spirit of fear (2 Timothy 1:7). One of the bigger things that changes for us is our understanding of and perspective on death.

Hebrews 2:14-15 says, "Inasmuch then as the children have partaken of flesh and blood, He Himself likewise shared in the same, that through death He might destroy him who had the power of death, that is, the devil, and release those who through fear of death were all their lifetime subject to bondage."

For us as Christians, there is no reason for death to bind us with fear. To lose a loved one is still painful and sorrowful, and grief is the right response even among the godly, but death no longer has its former power. Paul wrote in 1 Thessalonians 4:15-18,

> This we say to you by the word of the Lord, that we who are alive and remain until the coming of the Lord will by no means precede those who are asleep. For the Lord Himself will descend from heaven with a shout, with the voice of an archangel, and with the trumpet of God. And the dead in Christ will rise first. Then we who are alive and remain shall be caught up together with them in the clouds to meet the Lord in the air. And thus we shall always be with the Lord. Therefore comfort one another with these words.

Someday, those who died in Christ will be resurrected, and they, with those who are alive and remaining at the time of the rapture, will put on immortal incorruptibility and live forever in a glorified state with bodies like that of Jesus.

That, too, changed when we came to Christ!

DAY 183

ISRAEL'S COMING WAR

The Bible makes it clear that there are certain signs that will be happening all over the world the closer we get to the return of Jesus for His church. Wars and rumors of wars, ethnic tensions, rampant disease and famines as well as an increase in geological and atmospheric anomalies.

The Bible also makes it clear that the closer we get to the return of Jesus for His church, the more Israel will become the focus of world attention. Zechariah 12:3 says, "It shall happen in that day that I will make Jerusalem a very heavy stone for all peoples; all who would heave it away will surely be cut in pieces, though all nations of the earth are gathered against it."

Much like the global events that will precede the rapture of the church are already in motion, so, too, is the gathering of the world against Jerusalem already underway.

We also know that in the future, a group of nations will invade Israel for economic plunder (Ezekiel 38). Russia, Turkey, and Iran all have troops in Syria on the northern border of Israel, and Sudan and Libya have military alliances with both Russia and Turkey.

Our response to these relatively recent developments is twofold: First, as one song says, we are going to see the King very soon! Second, God sent Noah to warn the world that His judgment was coming; He sent angels to warn Sodom and Gomorrah; He sent prophets to warn Israel; and He told the whole church of the signs that would indicate judgment is coming.

The world may not like to hear about repentance as part of the gospel message, but we are to speak up. Tell someone about Jesus today; He is the only way to escape the judgment that is coming upon the whole world.

DAY 184

RITUALS OR RIGHTEOUSNESS?

One of the most interesting conversations in all the Bible is recorded in John 3. Jesus was addressing Nicodemus, a man He referred to as "the teacher of Israel." When Jesus told Nicodemus that a person cannot see the kingdom of God unless he is born again, Nicodemus replied,

> "How can a man be born when he is old? Can he enter a second time into his mother's womb and be born?" Jesus answered, "Most assuredly, I say to you, unless one is born of water and the Spirit, he cannot enter the kingdom of God. That which is born of the flesh is flesh, and that which is born of the Spirit is spirit. Do not marvel that I said to you, 'You must be born again.' The wind blows where it wishes, and you hear the sound of it, but cannot tell where it comes from and where it goes. So is everyone who is born of the Spirit." Nicodemus answered and said to Him, "How can these things be?" Jesus answered and said to him, "Are you the teacher of Israel, and do not know these things?" (John 3:4-10).

How is it that Nicodemus should have known these things? The answer: from the Old Testament. In Genesis 3:15, God said, "I will put enmity between you and the woman, and between your seed and her Seed; He shall bruise your head, and you shall bruise His heel." And in Isaiah 7:14 is this prophecy: "The Lord Himself will give you a sign: Behold, the virgin shall conceive and bear a Son, and shall call His name Immanuel."

Two points the Bible constantly makes clear are the sinfulness of man and God's provision of a Savior. Yet many today, like the Jews of old, prefer ordinances and practices that make them feel worthy of forgiveness and heaven.

For Jew or Gentile, salvation is a gift of God and cannot be earned by rituals and practices.

DAY 185

BE BOLD!

One question frequently pondered by Christians today is, "Why don't we see God move in ways that the early church saw?" Yet many who ask that also believe God is moving today and that He still heals and does the miraculous. So the question is really this: "Why are we not seeing these things in our circle?" The answer is quite simple: We would see more of what the early church saw if we did more of what the early church did.

Acts 4:31 tells us, "When they had prayed, the place where they were assembled together was shaken; and they were all filled with the Holy Spirit, and they spoke the word of God with boldness."

This is how the church responded when the disciples were told, by the Jewish council, not to teach in the name of Jesus anymore. They gathered to pray, and the Lord emboldened all of them to speak the Word of God. The truth is that today, many simply want to experience the shaking of the building without the prayer and boldness in the Word. The early church didn't gather to see the building shake; they gathered to pray and seek the Lord for power to do His will.

Jim Cymbala, pastor of the Brooklyn Tabernacle in New York, quoted another minister who said, "You can tell how popular a church is by who comes on Sunday morning. You can tell how popular the pastor or evangelist is by who comes on Sunday night. But you can tell how popular Jesus is by who comes to the prayer meeting."[8]

The early church prayed that they would have an impact, not an experience. God's response to that prayer was an outpouring of His Spirit, which resulted in His people speaking the Word of God with boldness. Check your own prayer life for its content. Are you asking God for boldness, or only benefits?

DAY 186

ZIONISM AND ANTISEMITISM

While the church has fallen into the habit of dividing itself into subgroups and categories, charismatics, Pentecostals, evangelicals, etc., there is one label that every Christian should have as an identifying component of their beliefs, and that is *Zionist*. A Zionist, by definition, is a person who believes in the development and protection of the Jewish state known as Israel. To some, a Christian Zionist means a heretic or, at the least, an uninformed Christian.

But consider Zechariah 8:3: "Thus says the Lord: 'I will return to Zion, and dwell in the midst of Jerusalem. Jerusalem shall be called the City of Truth, the Mountain of the Lord of hosts, the Holy Mountain.'"

Zionism is not the blind support of every decision or action Israel takes. Rather, Zionism is the recognition that the nation of Israel must exist, and that Jerusalem must be in the possession of the Jews so that prophecy can be fulfilled. Zionism is neither heresy nor a misunderstanding of Scripture. The Lord said through Zechariah, Jeremiah, Amos, and Isaiah that the Jews would return to their national homeland by His hand. And He told Ezekiel:

> Say to the house of Israel, "Thus says the Lord God: 'I do not do this for your sake, O house of Israel, but for My holy name's sake, which you have profaned among the nations wherever you went. And I will sanctify My great name, which has been profaned among the nations, which you have profaned in their midst; and the nations shall know that I am the Lord,' says the Lord God, 'when I am hallowed in you before their eyes. For I will take you from among the nations, gather you out of all countries, and bring you into your own land'" (Ezekiel 36:22-24).

Antisemitism is not simply to be against the Jews, it is to reject the King of the Jews, who brought them back into the land to receive glory for having done so.

DAY 187

HE WILL JUDGE THE NATIONS

One of the most—if not the most—errant and strangest teachings that has plagued the church throughout its history is that of replacement theology. This promotes the teaching that because Israel rejected Yeshua as Messiah, the Jewish people have been cast off as the chosen people of God. There are more than a few problems with this. Notice what God said in Genesis 17:7-8:

> I will establish My covenant between Me and you and your descendants after you in their generations, for an everlasting covenant, to be God to you and your descendants after you. Also I give to you and your descendants after you the land in which you are a stranger, all the land of Canaan, as an everlasting possession; and I will be their God.

In Genesis 21:10, the Lord told Abraham the descendants He was speaking of were those of Isaac through Jacob, not Ishmael, the son of Abraham and Hagar. God gave them the land through an everlasting covenant, and if the church has replaced Israel and all the promises to the Jews now apply to the church, then today, the land of Israel would be filled with Christians, not Jews. But that's not the case.

Probably the most chilling aspect of replacement theology is the idea that God has cast off the people He chose to make an everlasting covenant with. If He did that to Israel, then who's to say He might not do that to the church? Both are referred to as His chosen people—the Jews through birth, and the church by faith.

Matthew 25:31 tells what will happen "when the Son of Man comes in His glory." The second coming will end the tribulation, and afterward, the sheep and goats will be divided by their treatment of Israel, and God will judge the nations that gathered against Israel at the second coming. In light of God's care for Israel, how can anyone come to the conclusion that He has cast off the Jews and the church has replaced them? He hasn't and won't—blessed be His name!

HE CAME TO SERVE

It seems as though the significance of the moniker we wear as members of the body of Christ is lost on many in the church today. When we tell someone we are a Christian, we are not informing them of our religious affiliation, nor are we identifying ourselves with an organization. Rather, we are saying we are "like Christ," for that is the very definition of the term *Christian*.

Before we wander into despair as we consider what we are like in comparison to what Christ is like, or before we lapse into the unbiblical thinking that Christians can and should arrive at a state of moral perfection in this life, we need to remember what Paul wrote: "Being confident of this very thing, that He who has begun a good work in you will complete it until the day of Jesus Christ" (Philippians 1:6).

This means we will continue to be made more "like Christ" until the time we meet Jesus. First John 3:2 says that eventually, "we shall be like Him." Until then, we should want our lives to reflect Him as much as possible while we are being made more like Him.

What was Christ like? Matthew 20:27-28 says, "Whoever desires to be first among you, let him be your slave—just as the Son of Man did not come to be served, but to serve, and to give His life a ransom for many."

What does this look like in day-to-day life? Galatians 6:2-3 says, "Bear one another's burdens, and so fulfill the law of Christ. For if anyone thinks himself to be something, when he is nothing, he deceives himself."

As Christians, we should be known as burden-bearers, people who can be counted on when others fall apart. We should serve and support others in their distresses, just as the Lord does for us.

DAY 189

RUNNING TOWARD HEAVEN

It has been said that the Christian race is a marathon, not a sprint. This reminds us that the destination or finish line of any race determines how the race is run. A 100-meter sprint cannot be run the way you run a marathon, nor a marathon like a 100-meter sprint.

One key truth we need to remember about this race we call the Christian life is that the finish line is further away than that of a marathon, or even a 50- or 100-mile ultramarathon. The finish line is in heaven! This determines how we should run the race.

As Hebrews 12:1-2 says,

> Since we are surrounded by so great a cloud of witnesses, let us lay aside every weight, and the sin which so easily ensnares us, and let us run with endurance the race that is set before us, looking unto Jesus, the author and finisher of our faith, who for the joy that was set before Him endured the cross, despising the shame, and has sat down at the right hand of the throne of God.

Hebrews 12:1-2 points back to those who ran this race before us and describes them as "so great a cloud of witnesses." Among the names listed in Hebrews 11 are many we are familiar with: Abraham, Moses, David, Samuel, Rahab, Gideon, Samson, and others. This great cloud of witnesses includes people who had lied, doubted, been foolish, and been sexually immoral. Yet they are identified as those who laid aside their weights and sins and kept running.

What's great and unique about the race set before us is that the prize has already been won by the One who ran it perfectly on behalf of imperfect people who make up this great cloud of witnesses. That means people like you and me, who have failed and made poor choices at times. And yet in the end, the prize of heaven is assured by the One who ran the race on our behalf.

DAY 190

CHRISTIANS AND ISRAEL

We live in an unprecedented age during which countless ancient prophecies, or precursors to them, are being fulfilled right before our eyes. While some may be more subtle than others, there is none clearer than the rebirth of the nation of Israel, yet many in the church don't see the significance of this event.

Romans 11:16-18 helps provide clarity on this:

> If the firstfruit is holy, the lump is also holy; and if the root is holy, so are the branches. And if some of the branches were broken off, and you, being a wild olive tree, were grafted in among them, and with them became a partaker of the root and fatness of the olive tree, do not boast against the branches. But if you do boast, remember that you do not support the root, but the root supports you.

The firstfruit, the lump, and the root all point back to the believing patriarchs of Israel. The broken-off branches represent all unbelieving Jews. The cultivated olive tree is Israel, and the wild olive tree grafted in is the predominantly Gentile church. In verse 18, Paul skips over the agrarian and ceremonial metaphors and reaches back to the root—Abraham, Isaac, Jacob, Moses, etc.—and says, "You do not support the root, but the root supports you."

If the root, believing Israel, has been cast off, then who are Christians grafted into? If modern Israel is not biblical Israel, then why are the things prophesied about the people of Israel happening to them? Christians should rejoice in the faithfulness of God to Israel and take heart in the fact that God does not cast off people whom He calls chosen.

Don't let anyone rob you of the majestic mercy and goodness of God toward Israel by saying He has cast off the people or replaced them with the church. They're back in the land to tell us He's coming for us soon, and then not long after, He's coming back for the believing Jews, and we will accompany Him.

DAY 191

LIVE SOBERLY AND RIGHTEOUSLY

We have all heard people who say the Christian life is restrictive and boring. While there are definitely prohibitions within the Christian life, none of them diminish the quality of life for anyone who adheres to them. For example, the Bible says, "Do not be drunk" (Ephesians 5:18); those who follow this will never have a hangover or regret a poor decision made while drunk.

The Bible says sexual intimacy is for married male and female couples only (Hebrews 13:4). No one has ever regretted waiting until marriage to honor this directive, while many have regretted that they didn't.

Ecclesiastes 5:18-20 provides this observation for us:

> Here is what I have seen: It is good and fitting for one to eat and drink, and to enjoy the good of all his labor in which he toils under the sun all the days of his life which God gives him; for it is his heritage. As for every man to whom God has given riches and wealth, and given him power to eat of it, to receive his heritage and rejoice in his labor—this is the gift of God. For he will not dwell unduly on the days of his life, because God keeps him busy with the joy of his heart.

Yes, being a Christian is sometimes hard. And yes, being a Christian will always be countercultural. But boring? Never! Restrictive? Not even close, for it is the freest way to live.

One day, when we wake up, the day will be here when everything has changed forever. This makes living a morally pure life—a life that is sober and watchful, a life that is obedient and reverent—the most exciting life we can experience in this fallen world.

Unlike your plans to take time off or to go on vacation, when you count down the days in anticipation, *every* day is a candidate for the moment when we will be taken up in the twinkling of an eye. Perhaps it will be today!

DAY 192

SALVATION IS FOR ALL, PART 1

One of the greatest literary masterpieces in all of literature is Psalm 119. To be sure, the content is divinely inspired. But the psalm has a special construct we need to recognize—it is what's known as an octad acrostic. Acrostics are specific to the Hebrew portions of the Bible. and there are a few in the Psalms, including Psalms 25; 34; 37; 111; 112; 119; and 145. We also find acrostics in Proverbs 31:10-31 and Lamentations 1–4.

An acrostic makes sequential use of the letters of the alphabet for a poem or story. What makes Psalm 119 unique is that the divinely inspired author used each letter of the Hebrew alphabet 8 times to begin a sentence before moving to the next letter, then that letter 8 times, and so on. The 22 consonants of the Hebrew alphabet repeated 8 times each comprise the 176 verses of Psalm 119.

This masterpiece of construct is also a masterpiece of content. Again and again, Psalm 119 highlights for the reader the importance of God's Word:

> How can a young man cleanse his way? By taking heed according to Your word (Psalm 119:9).

> Your word I have hidden in my heart, that I might not sin against You (verse 11).

> My soul clings to the dust; revive me according to Your word (verse 25).

> Let Your mercies come also to me, O LORD—Your salvation according to Your word (verse 41).

This one chapter alone should convince every Jew and Gentile of the importance of God's Word. It should also remind us that while not every chapter of the Bible is a literary masterpiece in construct, every chapter is a literary masterpiece in content.

What heartache could be spared by heeding God's Word, what errors could be avoided by heeding God's Word, what pain could be averted by heeding God's Word! There is no other book like it.

DAY 193

SALVATION IS FOR ALL, PART 2

The Bible is unlike any book ever penned in history because God wrote it. So it's sad when people interpret and cut-and-paste portions of God's Word to their liking, and simply ignore others. There is no greater example of this than the Old Testament misunderstanding of the meaning of the election of the Jews as God's chosen people:

> Rejoice, O Gentiles, with His people; for He will avenge the blood of His servants, and render vengeance to His adversaries; He will provide atonement for His land and His people (Deuteronomy 32:43).

> "From the rising of the sun, even to its going down, My name shall be great among the Gentiles; in every place incense shall be offered to My name, and a pure offering; for My name shall be great among the nations," says the LORD of hosts (Malachi 1:11).

From the time of Moses in Deuteronomy all the way to the 400 years of silence that followed the ministry of the prophet Malachi, God was telling the Jews He would save the Gentiles.

A study of the Word would have told every rabbi and Jew not to pray, as many did and still do each day, "Baruch atah adonai, eloheinu melech ha-olam, she-loh asani goy." "Blessed are You, Lord our God, king of the universe, who has not made me a Gentile." This is the product of the errant thought that the election of the Jews meant the rejection of the Gentiles. The Jews were supposed to reach the Gentiles, not shun them.

This should remind us today to be careful about assuming certain people groups are disqualified from being saved—not only ethnically, but also ideologically. Right now, the church is growing faster in Iran than most other places. Muslims are becoming Christians by the tens of thousands because God is still "not willing that any should perish but that all should come to repentance" (2 Peter 3:9).

DAY 194

BE RECONCILED

Every time a year comes to an end and a new one begins, we wonder about and hope that it will be *the* year the Lord calls His ambassadors home. Until then, it is important for us to remember our mission as ambassadors for Christ—as those who represent one country and live in another. Titus 2:11-14 has this to say:

> The grace of God that brings salvation has appeared to all men, teaching us that, denying ungodliness and worldly lusts, we should live soberly, righteously, and godly in the present age, looking for the blessed hope and glorious appearing of our great God and Savior Jesus Christ, who gave Himself for us, that He might redeem us from every lawless deed and purify for Himself His own special people, zealous for good works.

Ambassadors may live in and experience the customs and culture of the country in which they temporarily reside, yet they are expected to model the character and dignity of the country they represent. This is true for us as well—we are citizens of heaven living on Earth (Philippians 3:20), and our actions and attitudes are to reflect our home country and King.

We also need to recognize that ambassadors are not simply representatives who reflect their home country's standards, they are also to conduct the business of their home country within the one they have been assigned to.

The ministry (act of service) of those who are ambassadors for Christ is that of pleading, or imploring, for the world to be reconciled to God. We have been committed to this task as a people who represent a kingdom whose citizens are all new creations in Christ, and who have been reconciled to God through Him.

Time is running out to warn people that a catastrophic time will soon come to this world that is unlike any other, and the only way to miss it is to be reconciled to God through Christ.

DAY 195

THE EZEKIEL WAR

Whenever there is a war in Israel, the question is asked: Is this a fulfillment of Bible prophecy? While there are many possible prophetic developments that could come from any conflict in Israel, there is one area in which the answer is a definitive yes! Zechariah 12:1-3 is an example:

> Thus says the LORD, who stretches out the heavens, lays the foundation of the earth, and forms the spirit of man within him: "Behold, I will make Jerusalem a cup of drunkenness to all the surrounding peoples, when they lay siege against Judah and Jerusalem. And it shall happen in that day that I will make Jerusalem a very heavy stone for all peoples; all who would heave it away will surely be cut in pieces, though all nations of the earth are gathered against it."

While this passage will reach its ultimate fulfillment during the tribulation, there is no question that Jerusalem is a heavy stone to the world today. The word implies an intoxicating burden. (Intoxicated, in this context, means "overly consumed.")

Not only do we see the world focused on Jerusalem today, but we also see the coalition of the Ezekiel War (see Ezekiel 38:2-6) forming, with three of the five nations poised to strike Israel from the north. Russia, Turkey, and Iran all have recently had military equipment and personnel on the northern border of Israel in Syria. Libya and Sudan have relationships with Russia and Turkey and share the same religious ideology as Iran.

The Jews are the chosen people of God, Israel is the land God gave to His chosen people, God scattered them among the nations because of their rebellion, and He has gathered the people back into the land for His name's sake and glory (Ezekiel 36:22). He will fight for them, He will get the victory, and thus He will get the glory, and the world will know He is the Lord. The Ezekiel War is coming, and current events are leading up to it.

DAY 196

HOLD FAST

In 1 Thessalonians 4:13-18, Paul says,

> I do not want you to be ignorant, brethren, concerning those who have fallen asleep, lest you sorrow as others who have no hope. For if we believe that Jesus died and rose again, even so God will bring with Him those who sleep in Jesus. For this we say to you by the word of the Lord, that we who are alive and remain until the coming of the Lord will by no means precede those who are asleep. For the Lord Himself will descend from heaven with a shout, with the voice of an archangel, and with the trumpet of God. And the dead in Christ will rise first. Then we who are alive and remain shall be caught up together with them in the clouds to meet the Lord in the air. And thus we shall always be with the Lord. Therefore comfort one another with these words.

Yes! Jesus is coming for us, and we will meet Him, along with the dead in Christ taken up in the air, and we will forever be with the Lord. This "floating meeting" should excite us. Getting *harpazo*-ed (raptured) is going to be incredible—what an experience!

What should rightfully grab our attention are Paul's opening words, which could be paraphrased, "I do not want you to be ignorant of a hope so powerful that it infiltrates even the sorrow of death."

Some years ago, the pandemic made death the global topic of the day. Everyone was thinking about it, some were bound by the fear of it, and many experienced the pain and sorrow caused by it.

But the only group of people who face death with sorrow yet not without hope are Christians, who know that, as Paul said, Jesus is coming to take us home!

DAY 197

THE SEED AND THE BLESSING

In John 14, Jesus informed His disciples of two ways their lives were about to change: One, He was going away; and two, He would send them "another Helper" (verse 16). The Greek word translated "another" means "one of the same kind."

> I will pray the Father, and He will give you another Helper, that He may abide with you forever—the Spirit of truth, whom the world cannot receive, because it neither sees Him nor knows Him; but you know Him, for He dwells with you and will be in you. I will not leave you orphans; I will come to you (John 14:16-18).

After this, Jesus gave specific details about the ministry of the Holy Spirit, who indwells the people who are part of His church: "The Helper, the Holy Spirit, whom the Father will send in My name, He will teach you all things, and bring to your remembrance all things that I said to you" (verse 26).

It is critical for us to remember that the Holy Spirit is the author of Scripture, and that He will never teach us anything that contradicts His written Word. That means the Holy Spirit will never teach anyone that the Jews have no right to the land of Israel. The Holy Spirit will never teach anyone that the Jews are no longer God's chosen people. Both ideas contradict God's written Word, which is authored by the Holy Spirit.

Isaiah 2:1-4 tells us that someday, Jew and Gentile will go up to the house of God in Jerusalem, and He will teach them His ways, and they will walk in His paths. They will beat their spears into pruning hooks and their swords into plowshares, and there will be no wars on the earth because the King of the Jews, who is the head of the church, will rule and reign over the earth from Jerusalem, and we with Him.

DAY 198

WHERE IS YOUR FAITH?

While the body of Christ is diverse in many ways, there is one trait we all share in common—no one likes the storms of life. One day, the disciples were on the Sea of Galilee in a boat with Jesus. He was in their presence; they knew they were not alone.

Mark's Gospel recorded this about the event: "He was in the stern, asleep on a pillow. And they awoke Him and said to Him, 'Teacher, do You not care that we are perishing?'" (4:38).

If there was anything the Twelve should have been sure of, it was that Jesus cared for them. He had called them, taught them, corrected them, sent them out with the power over unclean spirits and diseases, and yet a storm arose, and they were afraid and wondered if He even cared.

This is what a lapse of faith looks like. The storms of life come, and though we have experienced the miracle of salvation, at times we wonder where He is. Does He not see? Does He care about our pain and suffering? Why is He even allowing this?

The most important detail about the disciples' failure of faith appears in the opening statements of both Mark and Luke. Jesus said to them, "Let us cross over to the other side of the lake" (Luke 8:22). Before they ever left the shore, Jesus had declared their destination. If He said, "Let's go to the other side," that was where they would end up. It didn't matter what happened in the middle. Whatever happened during the journey may not have been fun or even a bit frightening, but nothing could change their destination. They were going to the other side!

The same is true for us. Someday, we are going to be where our Lord is, and no storm can change that!

DAY 199

THE CHOICE IS YOURS

While there are many statements, verses, and chapters that seem to make the "retreat theme" list frequently—such as Proverbs 31 for women, or David and Goliath in 1 Samuel 17 for men—there is one that is a pinnacle statement among them all. The declaration came from Joshua and was stated when he gave his farewell address to the nation of Israel before his death.

> Now therefore, fear the LORD, serve Him in sincerity and in truth, and put away the gods which your fathers served on the other side of the River and in Egypt. Serve the LORD! And if it seems evil to you to serve the LORD, choose for yourselves this day whom you will serve, whether the gods which your fathers served that were on the other side of the River, or the gods of the Amorites, in whose land you dwell. But as for me and my house, we will serve the LORD (Joshua 24:14-15).

Joshua expressed the attitude we need to have today—in essence, he said, "You do what you want, and I'll do what God wants." These same two choices are still before us today.

Jesus highlighted this same concept in Luke 16:13: "No servant can serve two masters; for either he will hate the one and love the other, or else he will be loyal to the one and despise the other. You cannot serve God and mammon." "Mammon" is an Aramaic word for riches. The implication here is priorities. What Jesus said in Luke is consistent with His words in the Sermon on the Mount in Matthew 6:33: "Seek first the kingdom of God and His righteousness, and all these things shall be added to you."

In other words, the choice is yours, and you can have only one top priority. You can seek the kingdom first or riches first, but you can't do both. One will become the adversary of the other.

DAY 200

RELATIONSHIP OR RELIGION

In a world of some 8 billion people, there are about 1.1 billion atheists, agnostics, and others who do not identify with any particular religion. About 16 percent of the world's population has no religious affiliation,[9] and some say that percentage is expected to increase in the years to come.

That means 84 percent of the world's population identify with some sort of religious group, and 31.4 percent of them identify as Christian. What that tells us is that if you subtract Jews, Christians, atheists, and agnostics, then 52 percent of the world's religious people practice a nonbiblical religion. The sad truth is that more than half of the world's population is searching for something that cannot be found through religion. As Colossians 2:20-23 says,

> If you died with Christ from the basic principles of the world, why, as though living in the world, do you subject yourselves to regulations—"Do not touch, do not taste, do not handle," which all concern things which perish with the using—according to the commandments and doctrines of men? These things indeed have an appearance of wisdom in self-imposed religion, false humility, and neglect of the body, but are of no value against the indulgence of the flesh.

The Greek word translated "religion" means "worship which one prescribes and devises for himself." The Lord made it clear in Psalm 40:6 that humanly prescribed and devised sacrifices and rituals were not pleasing to Him, and an impersonal, ritualistic relationship was not what He desired with the children of Israel. The same is true for the church.

God's desire is for relationship, not religion. Why settle for ineffective and impersonal practices when the God of the universe wants to talk to you through His Word, empower you through His Spirit, and free you by His truth?

Relationship is far better than religion.

DAY 201

SAVING FAITH

It has become increasingly popular, though grossly inaccurate, among many who claim they are Christians to say there are different paths to God. Aside from the obvious objections we would have on hearing such a proposition, let's consider this claim from the perspective of necessity, starting with 1 John 2:1-2:

> My little children, these things I write to you, so that you may not sin. And if anyone sins, we have an Advocate with the Father, Jesus Christ the righteous. And He Himself is the propitiation for our sins, and not for ours only but also for the whole world.

While the word "propitiation" may not be part of our everyday speech, it is an important word for us to know—it means "atonement," or reparation for wrongs committed. The scope of this atonement for sins is sufficient for the whole world: "As many as received Him, to them He gave the right to become children of God, to those who believe in His name" (John 1:12).

Where is the need for other paths when the one path to God is available for all? Whoever receives Jesus Christ, to them He gave the right to become children of God. This also dispels the popular saying that we are all God's children, which is not true. After all, you don't need to *become* a child of God if you already are one.

The beauty of John 1:12 is captured in the two words "as many." There are no ethnic, cultural, physiological, or national requirements to be among the "as many." If you're tall or short, rich or poor, grumpy or jovial, or your skin tone is light or dark or somewhere in between, no matter what you have done in the past, no matter how many or terrible your sins, you can become part of this community of believers who are children of God.

So why is there any need for other paths?

DAY 202

A WHOLE NEW YOU

It seems as though a day doesn't go by without some ruler or world leader doing or saying something that is unbelievably ridiculous—such as accusing Israel of occupying Palestinian land, or one's gender being a personal decision rather than a biological predetermination. We all tire of the foolishness of this world more and more as things continue to digress. However, there is a change coming, and I'm not talking about the Great Reset advocated by the World Economic Forum, where you'll own nothing yet be completely happy. Rather, the change has to do with born-again Christians actually becoming what they've been made to be in Christ Jesus.

Philippians 3:20-21 describes this, saying, "Our citizenship is in heaven, from which we also eagerly wait for the Savior, the Lord Jesus Christ, who will transform our lowly body that it may be conformed to His glorious body, according to the working by which He is able even to subdue all things to Himself."

In the well-known passage 2 Corinthians 5:17, Paul told us that in Christ, we are new creations, and old things have passed away. While this is obviously true, more specifically, what is new about us is that we are filled with His Spirit, and the outward evidence of that inner change becomes visible to all.

Yet even as new creations, we are still living in aging bodies full of weaknesses and frailties. But that, too, will change someday. A glorious body that is immortal and incorruptible will be ours in the twinkling of an eye. This is true even for those whose bodies experienced the wages of sin—they, too, will receive a glorious body as promised in 1 Thessalonians 4:16-17.

If your body is feeling a bit worn out or the aging process seems to be winning the battle, take heart. The new model can run and not grow weary, and walk and not faint (Isaiah 40:31), and not even time will wear it out.

DAY 203

KINGS AND PRIESTS

In Revelation 1:4-6, we read,

> John, to the seven churches which are in Asia: Grace to you and peace from Him who is and who was and who is to come, and from the seven Spirits who are before His throne, and from Jesus Christ, the faithful witness, the firstborn from the dead, and the ruler over the kings of the earth. To Him who loved us and washed us from our sins in His own blood, and has made us kings and priests to His God and Father, to Him be glory and dominion forever and ever. Amen.

In Scripture, it is common for us to read of events in the past tense even though they haven't happened yet. For example, in Isaiah 53, we read, "He *was* wounded for our transgressions" and the "chastisement for our peace *was* upon Him" (verse 5). Yet the One spoken of here would not be born for another 700 years. This should remind us that what God says is true even when His words have not yet been fulfilled.

Maybe you're not feeling very kingly or priestly, and a king's or a priest's life is about as far different from your life as can be right now. Life can be hard, and often we are treated like anything but a king or a priest. This is why the Bible continually points our minds and emotions to the future.

Jesus encouraged this mindset in John 16:33: "These things I have spoken to you, that in Me you may have peace. In the world you will have tribulation; but be of good cheer, I have overcome the world." Again, we read a statement about the future as if it has already taken place.

Jesus overcame the world on the cross, yet the end result of His finished work has yet to be realized. But this promise will be fulfilled when He returns. Until then, we can be of good cheer because we know that what is promised will surely come to pass!

DAY 204

UNDERSTANDING THE TRIBULATION

Among the many Bible verses that are either misquoted or taken out of context is Jesus' famed statement in John's Gospel: "These things I have spoken to you, that in Me you may have peace. In the world you will have tribulation; but be of good cheer, I have overcome the world" (John 16:33).

The word "tribulation" here means "anguish, burdens, persecutions, and troubles." It does not mean "wrath." Jesus was not saying, as many propose, that the church will go through the great tribulation. We know this because the great tribulation is a time of God's wrath, which we do not have an appointment with (1 Thessalonians 5:9).

The purposes of the great tribulation are well defined in Scripture: to finish the years determined for Daniel's people and the holy city (Daniel 9:24), and to punish a Christ-rejecting and disobedient world (Colossians 3:6).

The Bible also states that there are plans for the church during the great tribulation that are out of this world, quite literally: "We must all appear before the judgment seat of Christ, that each one may receive the things done in the body, according to what he has done, whether good or bad" (2 Corinthians 5:10).

The judgment seat of Christ is in heaven, and in order to stand before it, you have to already be there, and it is a place of rewards, not wrath. In Revelation 19, we read that the bride will return to Earth with the Lord, and to return with Him requires that we already be where He is. Therefore, the church cannot be on Earth during any of the tribulation.

The great tribulation, the time of Jacob's trouble (Jeremiah 30:7), the great and terrible Day of the Lord, is not in the church's future. The Day of the Lord centers on Israel and a Christ-rejecting world. We will be safely in heaven, forever to be with the Lord. In that day, we can greatly rejoice!

DAY 205

GOD'S PROMISE TO THE JEWS

As we watch the seemingly endless threats and attacks on Israel and mourn the devastating loss of life that often comes with them, our minds are filled with thoughts of *How long, O Lord? How much longer will evil bring pain and suffering into this world and impact the lives of Your people?*

We can expect this to continue all the way through the end times. Zechariah 12:3 says, "It shall happen in that day that I will make Jerusalem a very heavy stone for all peoples; all who would heave it away will surely be cut in pieces, though all nations of the earth are gathered against it."

Hamas, Hezbollah, Iran, and others who support efforts to destroy the Jews and the nation of Israel are fighting against God's plan, and they will not prevail. For the Jews to be outside of their national homeland profaned the name of the Lord, so He brought them back for His name's sake; He will not allow them to be destroyed, for His name's sake; and they will not be uprooted from their national homeland, for His name's sake (Ezekiel 36:21-24). As glorious as this truth is and as important as it is to remember, we cannot forget that people are dying at the hands of those intent on evil against God's people and land.

Ignorant and hateful people are blaming the actions of Hamas on Israel, and Muslims around the world are violently protesting Israel's defensive actions in Gaza. Jerusalem is becoming a burdensome stone to the world, and eventually, all the nations of the earth will turn against her. Yet the Holy One of Israel says He will be Israel's defense, and someday the people will see it is true that Christ is their Messiah:

> I will pour on the house of David and on the inhabitants of Jerusalem the Spirit of grace and supplication; then they will look on Me whom they pierced. Yes, they will mourn for Him as one mourns for his only son, and grieve for Him as one grieves for a firstborn (Zechariah 12:10).

Someday, all Israel will be saved.

DAY 206

SHARE THE GOOD NEWS

A sad reality is that most people today are not interested in hearing the gospel. What makes this even worse is that some in the church have decided that changing the message is the way to increase the world's receptivity to what we are saying. Many churches have adopted presenting themselves as an "affirming church," meaning they recognize all sexual preferences as acceptable. Others present a message of self-improvement and prosperity "if" you come to know Christ.

This brings to mind Mark 4:3-9:

> "Listen! Behold, a sower went out to sow. And it happened, as he sowed, that some seed fell by the wayside; and the birds of the air came and devoured it. Some fell on stony ground, where it did not have much earth; and immediately it sprang up because it had no depth of earth. But when the sun was up it was scorched, and because it had no root it withered away. And some seed fell among thorns; and the thorns grew up and choked it, and it yielded no crop. But other seed fell on good ground and yielded a crop that sprang up, increased and produced: some thirtyfold, some sixty, and some a hundred." And He said to them, "He who has ears to hear, let him hear!"

Jesus did not tell the disciples to use wayside seed for those by the wayside, use stony ground seed for the those with no root, use thorny ground seed for those among the thorns, and good ground seed for those of the good ground.

Because the soils clearly represent types of people and their reception to the gospel, what Jesus was saying is that there is one gospel for all people. We don't change the message based on the receptivity of the masses. As Paul told the church in Galatia, there is no other gospel, and only the true gospel has the power to save (Galatians 1:8-9).

DAY 207

JUSTIFIED IN JESUS

One of the great doctrines of the Christian faith is one we don't hear much about in the church today: the doctrine of justification. It travels in the company of other pillars of the Christian faith, and it is a doctrine that should bring joy to our hearts and a steadfastness to our minds. Romans 8:29-30 has this to say: "Whom He foreknew, He also predestined to be conformed to the image of His Son, that He might be the firstborn among many brethren. Moreover whom He predestined, these He also called; whom He called, these He also justified; and whom He justified, these He also glorified."

While much has been taught from these verses, we need to remember that this passage is saying that the destination of predestination is conformity into the image of Christ (Philippians 3:21).

Note also what Paul wrote in Romans 5:1: "Having been justified by faith, we have peace with God through our Lord Jesus Christ." In verse 9, he said, "Much more then, having now been justified by His blood, we shall be saved from wrath through Him."

These two verses tell us that justification is living the free life that Jesus came to bring. We don't have to wonder whether we are good enough to go to heaven, or if we've done enough to be accepted in heaven, or if we're of the right bloodline to enter heaven. Justification says Jesus paid it all!

Sadly, many Christians live without the blessings of understanding that the verdict against them has been rendered, and through Christ, that verdict is, "Innocent of all charges."

Is justification important? It is how you become a citizen of heaven, it is why you can look forward to having a glorified body, it determines where you will spend eternity, and it completely justifies your right to be there. What you couldn't earn, justification gave. What you couldn't be born into in the flesh, justification allows. What you couldn't achieve, you have freely received.

DAY 208

OUR GREATEST HOPE

Generally, there are a myriad of things all humans are born with. For example, we possess senses that help keep us safe, like a sense of caution so that we're safe from lions, tigers, and bears. Neuroscientists have discovered that as the brain develops during the adolescent years, the prefrontal cortex, which is the decision-making center of the brain, develops a mechanism through which impulses are filtered and not instantly acted upon. Psalm 139:13-15 says this about our amazing bodies:

> You formed my inward parts; You covered me in my mother's womb. I will praise You, for I am fearfully and wonderfully made; marvelous are Your works, and that my soul knows very well. My frame was not hidden from You, when I was made in secret, and skillfully wrought in the lowest parts of the earth.

King David records the majesty of creation, which all humanity enjoys. God has designed us fearfully and wonderfully, with incredible capacities for innovation and invention. He has made our bodies with minds capable of learning and doing great things. God has also given free will to all of humanity, and man has used his God-given capacities for great evil.

And yet, in the midst of evil and perilous times, we have this promise because of our faith in the Lord: "God has not given us a spirit of fear, but of power and of love and of a sound mind" (2 Timothy 1:7).

In a world where good is called evil and evil is called good, and where fear and all its companions are rampant, it is only those who have the Spirit of the living God that have the discernment to see where things are headed. We know and need not fear because all this has been foretold. We can make our way through these perilous times not with a spirit of fear, but instead, with love and a sound mind.

DAY 209

SPIRIT OF THE LIVING GOD

In Romans 8:11, Paul wrote, "If the Spirit of Him who raised Jesus from the dead dwells in you, He who raised Christ from the dead will also give life to your mortal bodies through His Spirit who dwells in you."

This is the ultimate game-changer for us—the same power that raised Christ from the dead is in us! That means that even though we will have tribulation in this life, we can rejoice because Christ has overcome the world (John 16:33).

In each of the letters to the seven churches in Revelation 2–3, a promise was made to those who overcome. The Greek word translated "overcomes" means "to get the victory." When the world is overcome with fear, we can have victory over it. And when the world is falling apart, we don't have to. So when tribulation comes our way—meaning afflictions, burdens, troubles, or anguish—we can rejoice. How? By looking beyond the moment and to our eternal destiny.

This world is not our home. We are citizens of heaven, and our future habitation is a city whose builder and maker is God—a city in which righteousness dwells and where death, sickness, and pain are banished forever. This hope is exclusive to the born-again Christian!

Isaiah 46:9-10 says, "Remember the former things of old, for I am God, and there is no other; I am God, and there is none like Me, declaring the end from the beginning, and from ancient times things that are not yet done, saying, 'My counsel shall stand, and I will do all My pleasure.'"

Our God sees the future as clearly as we see the past. He declared in ancient times what the future would hold and revealed the details to us through His Word. This is why we need not fear. His Spirit is why we need not fail, and we can hold fast until the end!

DAY 210

JESUS, THE FINAL REVELATION, PART 1

Few things stir up more debate in the church than the subject of eschatology (the study of the last days). While there is room for civil discussion on some subjects, we also have to recognize there are some truths that are vividly clear and not open to debate.

The Bible gives us more information about the last days, including the great tribulation, than any other time period in human history. This includes information about the church age. In 2 Timothy 3:1, Paul wrote, "Know this, that in the last days perilous times will come." And he added in 2 Timothy 4:3, "The time will come when they will not endure sound doctrine."

Ezekiel 36–37 tells us about the rebirth of the nation of Israel and the return of the Jews to their national homeland. Revelation 6–19 spells out the events of the great tribulation clearly and specifically. We could cite many other examples of information given to us about the last days, but the most important aspect of them all is that they comprise the complete revelation of God concerning the last days. That brings us to these words in Revelation 22:18-19:

> I testify to everyone who hears the words of the prophecy of this book: If anyone adds to these things, God will add to him the plagues that are written in this book; and if anyone takes away from the words of the book of this prophecy, God shall take away his part from the Book of Life, from the holy city, and from the things which are written in this book.

In paraphrase, what the Holy Spirit is saying here through John is that the Lord has told us all we need to know, and no new revelation about the last days will be forthcoming. This is followed by one of the most severe warnings in Scripture about trifling with God's Word. In brief, if you add to God's Word about the last days, you will experience the wrath of God in the last days.

DAY 211

JESUS, THE FINAL REVELATION, PART 2

In spite of the ominous warning about adding to or taking away from God's final revelation regarding the last days, there are those who claim to have special revelation from God about those days. Some say that before Jesus can come back, the church must have dominion over the world, and only then can Jesus return. They are adding to what the Lord has told us will happen before His second coming.

The group known as the New Apostolic Reformation teaches dominion theology, the belief that the church must have dominion over education, religion, family, business, the government and military, arts and entertainment, and the media before Jesus can return. This directly contradicts the book of Revelation and Jesus' own words in the Olivet Discourse (Matthew 24–25).

There are also others who have sought to allegorize some or all of the book of Revelation, denying the literal prophetic message of the book and making it into a series of spiritual life lessons. They take away from the words of the book of prophecy, and the consequences for doing this are dire (Revelation 22:18-19). They need to remember what Jesus said in Luke 6:46: "Why do you call Me 'Lord, Lord,' and not do the things which I say?"

The Bible has nothing more to say about the days in which we live; there are no additional details forthcoming with regard to the last days' scenario. There are no new apostles like the original Twelve. Things will get progressively worse and not better, until they are so bad that the righteous are few in comparison to the unrighteous of the world—just as it was in the days of Noah.

If we were able to ask Jesus face to face what He would say about the New Apostolic Reformation and those who allegorize the book of Revelation, what would He tell us?

Do not go after or follow them.

DAY 212

ISRAEL AND BELIEVERS

What a privileged people we are to live in such a time as this! A time replete with prophetic fulfillments and indications that more fulfillments are on the horizon. Millions of Christians have lived and died throughout church history without the nation of Israel regathered, and without the invading nations of the Ezekiel 38 war working toward becoming a coalition. Yet here we are, watching events foretold thousands of years ago happening right before our eyes.

Yet many people through the ages who never had the opportunity to see the fig tree budding were willing to die for their Lord rather than deny Him. How could they be so faithful and passionate for Him without seeing all of what we see today? We find the answer in Psalm 119:105-107:

> Your word is a lamp to my feet and a light to my path. I have sworn and confirmed that I will keep Your righteous judgments. I am afflicted very much; revive me, O LORD, according to Your word.

Christians who endured times of persecution were able to do so without wavering because they had the Word of God. We have that same Word today, with the distinct advantage of watching it unfold before our eyes. The budding of the fig tree would not mean anything to us if it had not been written in the Word of God beforehand. The wasteland of Israel blooming like a rose in the desert would not be of any significance if it had not been foretold in advance.

The comfort that past generations of believers received—those who had not seen what we see today—came from the Word of God. We, too, can obtain that same comfort as we watch our world unravel around us. We can take the budding of the fig tree as an indication that the church age is wrapping up and that the Lord is preparing to take His bride to the Father's house soon.

As we near the end of the time of the Gentiles and see God's promises to His chosen people being fulfilled, let us take heart.

DAY 213

THE POWER OF HIS RESURRECTION

We live in a time during which equality is the mantra of the day. What a person thinks they are must be accepted by all equally. No one has a right to say this or that is not true because if a person feels or thinks a certain way, that is "their truth."

Yet we are not all equal in every way; we are different by God's design. Men and women are different. People come in all shapes and sizes and have varied abilities and talents. While all humans are of equal value, we are not all the same.

Nor are all religions the same. They are not of equal value, nor is one just as valid as another. One significant difference between the Christian faith and all others is stated in 1 Corinthians 15:16-20:

> If the dead do not rise, then Christ is not risen. And if Christ is not risen, your faith is futile; you are still in your sins! Then also those who have fallen asleep in Christ have perished. If in this life only we have hope in Christ, we are of all men the most pitiable. But now Christ is risen from the dead, and has become the firstfruits of those who have fallen asleep.

The resurrection of Jesus impacts not only our eternal destinies but our everyday lives as well. Because of the resurrection…

- We know there is life after death and thus death has lost its sting.
- We need not wonder if what we believe is true; it's been proven.
- We know God loves us because He demonstrated that love.
- Because death has been conquered, we are more than conquerors in Him.
- The wrath of God is not in our future.
- Jesus said He is coming to take us to where He is, and He will.

DAY 214

THE OLD TESTAMENT IS THE KEY TO THE NEW

There are many verses we could consider as monuments of Scripture, yet there is one we could hang as a banner over them all:

> The word of God is living and powerful, and sharper than any two-edged sword, piercing even to the division of soul and spirit, and of joints and marrow, and is a discerner of the thoughts and intents of the heart (Hebrews 4:12).

While it is true that the Old Testament is filled with history, law, and poetry, we must never forget that it is also replete with unfulfilled prophecies. The Old Testament has the same central figure as the New, and that is the Holy One of Israel, who is also the head of the church, Jesus Christ.

The idea that there is a difference in how God is presented in the two Testaments reveals a complete misunderstanding of the two covenants. The Old revealed man's need for a Savior because of his inability to keep the law or to be saved by good works. The New reveals God's response to man's need of a Savior in the person of Jesus Christ, who alone makes it possible for us to be reconciled to God.

The Old Testament is living and powerful and has much to say about the days in which we now live. So why would anyone want to avoid it or say it is irrelevant? Referring to the Old Testament, Paul wrote in Romans 15:4 that "whatever things were written before were written for our learning, that we through the patience and comfort of the Scriptures might have hope." The Old Testament is a source of learning, comfort, and hope.

Jews who do not place any value in reading the New Testament can come to Jesus by reading the Tanach (the Old Testament) and any book that has the capacity to bring people to saving faith in Jesus can only be described as living and powerful.

DAY 215

GOD OF WONDERS

As Christians, we would do well to visit Job 38–39 every once in a while. In those chapters we find God asking Job—whom God said was "blameless and upright" (Job 1:1)—some probing questions that expose the distinction between man and the God who made all things.

> Where were you when I laid the foundations of the earth? Tell Me, if you have understanding. Who determined its measurements? Surely you know! Or who stretched the line upon it? (Job 38:4-5).
>
> Have you entered the treasury of snow, or have you seen the treasury of hail, which I have reserved for the time of trouble, for the day of battle and war? (verses 22-23).

Here, the Lord establishes His authority as creator and His right as righteous judge over all. This reminds us of the greatness and goodness of our God and that it is He who made us, and not we ourselves.

This should also remind us that He who made us is also He who has saved us: "In Him you also trusted, after you heard the word of truth, the gospel of your salvation; in whom also, having believed, you were sealed with the Holy Spirit of promise, who is the guarantee of our inheritance until the redemption of the purchased possession, to the praise of His glory" (Ephesians 1:13-14).

Even after we have trusted in the Lord, we have seasons during which we may feel dry or wonder about why God has allowed certain things to happen. We worry about what tomorrow holds even though we know we shouldn't (Matthew 6:34).

At such times, we need to remember what the Lord told Job: He is the God of wonders, and if we have trusted our eternity to Him, we can do the same with our tomorrows!

DAY 216

WE WILL BE WITH JESUS FOREVER

Many of us have heard people express concern that heaven will be boring. Some go as far as to say, "Who wants to sit on a puffy white cloud playing a harp forever?" An artist's rendition of a cherub (a chubby baby playing a harp) is hardly the place to draw our conclusion about what heaven will be like.

In John 14:2-3, Jesus said, "In My Father's house are many mansions; if it were not so, I would have told you. I go to prepare a place for you. And if I go and prepare a place for you, I will come again and receive you to Myself; that where I am, there you may be also." This promise is stated again in 1 Thessalonians 4:17: "Then we who are alive and remain shall be caught up together with them in the clouds to meet the Lord in the air. And thus we shall always be with the Lord."

When we are caught up in the rapture, we will forever be with the Lord. We will be with Him in the Father's house, where there are many mansions. We will someday walk with Him on streets of gold and encounter men like Abraham, Jacob, David, and Jonathan, and women like Deborah, Rahab, Mary the mother of Jesus, and Salome the mother of the Sons of Thunder, James and John.

Heaven will hardly be boring!

We will walk on streets of gold, meet the saints of old, return with Jesus to rule and reign with Him for 1,000 years, judge angels (1 Corinthians 6:3), live in a city whose builder and maker is God (Hebrews 11:10), never get sick again, never be sad again, and no one will ever die or shed tears again.

Our future is one of fullness of joy and eternal pleasures (Psalm 16:11), and it will all begin in the twinkling of an eye, when we transition to forever being with the Lord.

DAY 217

FALSE RELIGION

Imagine having the opportunity to go on a family vacation and, rather than taking your actual family along, you bring a photo. That is what religion is like—it is comprised of statues, rituals, and recited prayers to or through saints instead of an actual and personal relationship with God, which is what He wants to have with us. This brings to mind Revelation 22:6-9:

> He said to me, "These words are faithful and true." And the Lord God of the holy prophets sent His angel to show His servants the things which must shortly take place. "Behold, I am coming quickly! Blessed is he who keeps the words of the prophecy of this book." Now I, John, saw and heard these things. And when I heard and saw, I fell down to worship before the feet of the angel who showed me these things. Then he said to me, "See that you do not do that. For I am your fellow servant, and of your brethren the prophets, and of those who keep the words of this book. Worship God."

While there is some debate about who John "fell down to worship," we need to recognize this individual's response: "See that you do not do that." John was redirected to "worship God." As 1 Timothy 2:5 says, "There is one God and one Mediator between God and men, the Man Christ Jesus."

We don't need to pray through saints or Mary; we don't need repetitive words or phrases to communicate to God. There is no human agent who can absolve our sins because there is "one Mediator between God and men," and that is Christ Jesus. Not the Pope, not a priest, not an angel, not a dead saint can help us. To exalt any person or practice to the place of enabling us to access or become acceptable to God is nothing more than false religion.

DAY 218

WHEN WE FALL

We are all familiar with the well-known passage 1 Peter 5:8, in which Peter likens the devil to a roaring lion who seeks to devour us. Yet we often miss one of the most significant elements of this verse. Many have observed that lions are very stealthy when they hunt. They stalk their prey silently, creeping slowly toward their target until they are within striking distance—and then they pounce.

Why was Peter comparing Satan to a roaring lion when lions hunt their prey in silence? There are exceptions to the usual practice—a lion will roar while hunting when it is sick, wounded, or dying. It will also roar out of anger, frustration, or pain.

Yet we have no reason to be fearful. First John 4:4 reminds us, "You are of God, little children, and have overcome them, because He who is in you is greater than he who is in the world."

While Satan would like us to think we are defenseless against him, the opposite is true. Yes, every Christian fails and has their struggles, and we will not arrive at sinless perfection in this life. Yet as born-again, Spirit-filled believers, we have the power to resist the devil and make him flee! His power was broken by the blood Christ shed on the cross. It was there that the great enemy and the bondage caused by the fear of death were destroyed.

Satan's tactics have been exposed, and he is like a sick, wounded, and dying lion who roars in anger and frustration as he hunts. He is still dangerous; a sick and dying lion still has sharp teeth and claws. But when you fall and the devil tries to kick you while you're down, the way to defeat him is to repent and start running the race again. There's nothing he can do to stop you!

DAY 219

JESUS IS GOD

While there are many elements of Scripture that some Christians view differently than others—like the timing of the rapture, or the freewill or predestination debate—there is one teaching above all others that is not a matter of interpretation and is nonnegotiable in relation to saving faith, and that is the deity of Jesus Christ.

Some argue that Jesus never claimed to be God; others say God couldn't have a Son. And still others say that God could not become a man. Yet in Proverbs 30:4, we read, "Who has ascended into heaven, or descended? Who has gathered the wind in His fists? Who has bound the waters in a garment? Who has established all the ends of the earth? What is His name, and what is His Son's name, if you know?"

Isaiah 7:14 tells us, "The LORD Himself will give you a sign: Behold, the virgin shall conceive and bear a Son, and shall call His name Immanuel." Here, the Bible tells us 700 years beforehand that a Son was going to be born of a virgin, and His name would be "God with us." That pretty much settles the argument as to whether or not a God-man was to be expected. And 200 years prior to Isaiah, Solomon wrote in Proverbs 30:4 that God has a Son. The Son born would therefore share His Father's attributes and powers, and thus be His equal.

Note also what John 5:18 says: "The Jews sought all the more to kill Him, because He not only broke the Sabbath, but also said that God was His Father, making Himself equal with God."

Jesus' claim to be equal with the Father was clearly Jesus' declaration that He is God. The scribes and Pharisees knew that and thus sought to kill Him on the charge of blasphemy. To say Jesus never claimed to be God is a grave error; believing He is God is essential to our salvation.

DAY 220

THE DAYS OF NOAH

There are many signs we could examine that remind us our redemption is near. Two of the most significant come from when the disciples asked Jesus about the signs of His coming. Matthew's record of the Olivet Discourse is where we will find them:

> As the days of Noah were, so also will the coming of the Son of Man be (Matthew 24:37).

> You also be ready, for the Son of Man is coming at an hour you do not expect (verse 44).

These two statements give us a significant amount of information about the spiritual climate of the world at the time of the coming of the Son of Man. Matthew 24:38-39 provides one point of clarity for us: "As in the days before the flood, they were eating and drinking, marrying and giving in marriage, until the day that Noah entered the ark, and did not know until the flood came and took them all away, so also will the coming of the Son of Man be."

In the Olivet Discourse, the coming of the Son of Man can only mean the rapture of the church. We know this because of Jesus' statement regarding the days "before the flood," when people were indifferent to the signs of impending judgment. Though Noah was building an ark and preaching, people were doing business as usual, eating, drinking, and marrying until the flood took them all away. In essence, Jesus said they ignored the warnings that God's wrath was about to be poured out on the whole world until it was too late.

This can only be true of the pretribulation period—the coming of the Son of Man cannot refer to the second coming simply because at that point, the wrath of God ends rather than begins.

Jesus is coming soon!

DAY 221

WHERE BELIEVERS GO WHEN THEY DIE

In Ephesians 4:8-10, Paul quotes from Psalm 68:18, where David presents the Lord as the conquering King. Elsewhere in the same psalm, David presents the Lord as One who rides the clouds, shakes the earth, commands the rain, rides on the heaven of heavens, and is worthy of praise. In verse 20, he writes, "Our God is the God of salvation; and to God the Lord belong escapes from death."

This is the context of Paul's quotation of Psalm 68—the Lord conquers death and delivers us from captivity. Romans 8:29-30 tells more of what the Lord does for us: "Whom He foreknew, He also predestined to be conformed to the image of His Son, that He might be the firstborn among many brethren. Moreover whom He predestined, these He also called; whom He called, these He also justified; and whom He justified, these He also glorified."

In Old Testament times, when the righteous died, they went to a place of comfort known as Abraham's bosom (Luke 16:19-31). The reason for this was because Jesus was not yet crucified, resurrected, and ascended as the firstborn from the dead. It was only through His shed blood that man could be justified, and only the justified could be glorified. Abraham's bosom was a holding place for the believing dead until the crucifixion and resurrection.

It is only because of this that Paul could write to the Corinthians and to all Christians, "We are confident, yes, well pleased rather to be absent from the body and to be present with the Lord" (2 Corinthians 5:8).

When Christians die, they go directly into the presence of the Lord. This is true for every believer. There is no such thing as purgatory or a state of limbo between here and eternity. The blood of Jesus paid the penalty for our sin in full, and no one saved by Him needs further purification!

DAY 222

REJECTED BY THE WORLD

Among the many signs that we are living in the last days are some that can be seen among those who profess to belong to the church but don't. In 2 Thessalonians 2:3-4, Paul wrote of a defection from truth. In 2 Timothy 3:5, he spoke of a form of godliness but the denial of the power of the gospel. And in the last chapter of his final epistle, he said,

> The time will come when they will not endure sound doctrine, but according to their own desires, because they have itching ears, they will heap up for themselves teachers; and they will turn their ears away from the truth, and be turned aside to fables (2 Timothy 4:3-4).

The Greek word translated "fables" means "an invention or falsehood," or "a lie." One of the lies that has crept into the church in these last days is that the church needs to be more user-friendly and accepting of what people think and feel. To believe that we need to make the gospel more palatable to the masses is a denial of the power of the gospel.

In Romans 1:16, Paul wrote, "I am not ashamed of the gospel of Christ, for it is the power of God to salvation for everyone who believes, for the Jew first and also for the Greek."

Paul was beaten, stoned, and left for dead, spent a day and night in the deep, suffered shipwreck, was ostracized, backstabbed, lied about, and hated, and yet he did not alter one word of the gospel to make it more pleasing or palatable to those who persecuted him.

Paul understood that being disposed of and rejected by men was the very experience of the One who saved him. In these last days, when speaking truth offends others and is considered hate speech, we need to avoid the temptation to repackage the gospel in a more worldly and thus acceptable form.

DAY 223

LET NOT YOUR HEART BE TROUBLED

While we may not be aware of it, most of us are familiar with Newtonian physics and his third law of motion, which says every action has an equal and opposite reaction. The principle states that when two bodies interact, they apply forces to one another that are equal in magnitude and opposite in direction.

It is interesting to apply that principle spiritually in the scene that unfolds in John 8 between Jesus and the Pharisees. The one element of the third law of motion that does not apply is that the Pharisees' words, though opposite, were not equal to those of Jesus.

Jesus said to them, "I am the light of the world." The Pharisees said, "You bear witness of Yourself, so Your witness is not true" (see John 8:12-13).

Jesus said to them, "You shall know the truth and the truth shall make you free." The Pharisees said, "How can You say we will be free when we have never been in bondage?" (see verses 32-33).

Jesus said to them, "I have come from God and not of Myself." The Pharisees said, "You are a Samaritan and have a demon" (see verses 42, 48).

Jesus said to them, "Abraham rejoiced to see My day." The Pharisees said, "You're not old enough to have seen Abraham, so you couldn't have" (see verses 56-57).

Jesus said, "Before Abraham was, I Am." The Pharisees took up stones to stone Him (see verses 58-59).

Every statement Jesus made to the ultrareligious was met with an opposite reaction. When this happens to us, we must not be troubled and remember it is par for the course in such a time as this.

Jesus never backed down from the truth because it was met with the opposite reaction than it should have been met with. He did not accommodate errant beliefs and the twisting of Scripture because people were more comfortable with what they thought than what He said. He spoke the truth. Peter looked to Jesus' example and said that God is glorified when we are reproached by blasphemers (1 Peter 4:12-14).

DAY 224

RESTORING HOPE

While the lessons from the Emmaus Road encounter with Jesus are many, there is one that is often overlooked. Having appeared first to Mary Magdalene and other women and then to Peter, the resurrected Lord next showed Himself to two disciples we know nothing of apart from His interaction with them in Luke 24:13-20.

These two men were dejected and heading home on the very day of Jesus' resurrection. Jesus joined them, and at first, they did not know it was Him. They told Him of their dashed hopes, and He told them the Scriptures said it would happen this way:

> "O foolish ones, and slow of heart to believe in all that the prophets have spoken! Ought not the Christ to have suffered these things and to enter into His glory?" And beginning at Moses and all the Prophets, He expounded to them in all the Scriptures the things concerning Himself (verses 25-27).

The oft-overlooked lesson in this encounter is that these men had lost hope. Their reason for doing so may have been misguided, and yet Jesus chose to engage these two sad disciples nonetheless. He did not go first to the 11 disciples; He did not appear to the council who condemned Him; He did not appear to Pilate, who tried to wash his hands of any guilt in the matter of Jesus' death. Instead, He appeared to two men who needed their hope restored.

This is what Jesus has done for us—He has given us hope. Hope of His presence today, and hope of an unbelievable future in heaven. This is what King David reminded us of when he wrote, "Cast your burden on the LORD, and He shall sustain you; He shall never permit the righteous to be moved" (Psalm 55:22).

The One who saved you will never leave nor forsake you!

DAY 225

THE KEY TO PROPHECY

You may have heard it said that you can know what God is for by recognizing what Satan is against. If that is true (and it is), then we can clearly know that God is for the nation of Israel: "It shall happen in that day that I will make Jerusalem a very heavy stone for all peoples; all who would heave it away will surely be cut in pieces, though all nations of the earth are gathered against it" (Zechariah 12:3).

Why would Satan continue his efforts to destroy the Jews if, as some people claim, they are no longer the chosen people of God? Why the Nazis? Why were there 17 United Nations resolutions condemning Israel in 2020 while there were only 6 against the rest of the world? Zechariah 14:3 says those who oppose Israel will be opposed by God: "The LORD will go forth and fight against those nations, as He fights in the day of battle."

Zechariah 12–14 uses the phrase "in that day" 16 times, a phrase associated exclusively with the seventieth week of Daniel, which is the great tribulation. Why would God fight for Israel during the seventieth week of Daniel if He has cast them off forever? Why does the Iranian regime want to destroy Israel? Why do the Palestinians want to drive the Jewish people into the sea? Why is antisemitism growing at an alarming rate around the world?

The answer? You can know what God is for by recognizing what Satan is against. He is definitely against Israel. What those who side with Satan don't realize is that the Lord is for Israel, and it will not bode well for all who oppose the Jewish nation.

In Amos 9:15, the Lord said, "I will plant them in their land, and no longer shall they be pulled up from the land I have given them."

There will never be a two-state solution as long as God is for Israel!

DAY 226

JESUS DECLARED HIMSELF TO BE GOD

It is popular among many in our day to say that Jesus never claimed to be God, which is not true. He clearly stated His deity in Revelation and implied it multiple times in the Gospels. In Revelation 1:8, He said, "I am the Alpha and the Omega, the Beginning and the End…who is and who was and who is to come, the Almighty."

Jesus is using titles here that are exclusive to God, which makes this a clear declaration that He is God. Not only did Jesus declare Himself to be God, so too did the Holy Spirit. He said through Isaiah that there would be a child born of a virgin who would be called Immanuel, which means "God with us" (Isaiah 7:14).

In Philippians 2:9-11, we read this: "God…has highly exalted Him and given Him the name which is above every name, that at the name of Jesus every knee should bow, of those in heaven, and of those on earth, and of those under the earth, and that every tongue should confess that Jesus Christ is Lord, to the glory of God the Father."

Here, we have the Father referring to the Son as God. The word translated "Lord" is *kyrios*, which means "Supreme One," or "the One who is Master," or even "the Sovereign"—or in a word, God.

He is the blessed One who comes in the name of the Lord, and as Isaiah 9:6 says, He is "Mighty God." He came into the world through the Hebrew people as the Savior of the world.

Jesus is God! He said so, the Spirit says so, and His Father says so, and therefore, so should we. Don't let anyone tell you that Jesus is only a prophet or teacher, because this diminishes the power of His shed blood for the sins of the world to the blood of just another man.

Jesus is not just a man. He is the God-man, the Savior of the world.

DAY 227

LIVING IN PERILOUS TIMES

There are many blessings we enjoy as born-again Christians, yet we tend to forget some of them when the heat is on or the going gets tough. One of the most important facts for us to remember is the difference between happiness and joy. Happiness is based on circumstances—when things are going well, we are happy. When things are not going well, we are not happy. And if we live only to be happy, we will live a roller-coaster existence.

Joy, however, is more stable. It is not based on circumstances being up or down, good or bad. Joy can be a constant in the life of a believer, as confirmed in 1 Peter 4:12-14:

> Beloved, do not think it strange concerning the fiery trial which is to try you, as though some strange thing happened to you; but rejoice to the extent that you partake of Christ's sufferings, that when His glory is revealed, you may also be glad with exceeding joy. If you are reproached for the name of Christ, blessed are you, for the Spirit of glory and of God rests upon you. On their part He is blasphemed, but on your part He is glorified.

Peter says exceeding joy is possible in the midst of fiery trials or when you are reproached or insulted for the name of Christ, both of which are on the increase in these last days. Joy is still ours to have even during the perilous times that the Bible says would come.

We shouldn't allow the perils of the last days to rob us of our joy. We can and should be unhappy about what is going on around us, but the joy of our salvation need not be affected by it. The world has gone mad, but it is not our home. Good is called evil and evil is called good, yet we are headed to a city in which righteousness dwells whose builder and maker is God.

DAY 228

GOD'S CALL ON YOUR LIFE

Of the many wonderful aspects of having a personal relationship with God, the fact that He wants to use us as instruments of His work is one of the most amazing. Not only does He want to use us, He also initiates opportunities for us to be useable.

The extent to which God is willing to use us is evident in Mark 14:27-31:

> Jesus said to them, "All of you will be made to stumble because of Me this night, for it is written: 'I will strike the Shepherd, and the sheep will be scattered.' But after I have been raised, I will go before you to Galilee." Peter said to Him, "Even if all are made to stumble, yet I will not be." Jesus said to him, "Assuredly, I say to you that today, even this night, before the rooster crows twice, you will deny Me three times." But he spoke more vehemently, "If I have to die with You, I will not deny You!" And they all said likewise.

What happened next is exactly the opposite of what Peter vowed. He not only denied the Lord, he did so three times and accompanied his denials with an oath. Yet afterward, on the shores of the Galilee over breakfast, Jesus lovingly and caringly restored Peter to ministry.

There was no "I told you so" from Jesus. No "What do you have to say for yourself now?" Instead, we read only of what Peter needed most—to be able to tell the Lord he loved Him. So the Lord pressed a question to Peter three times, seemingly canceling out each denial with Peter's three declarations of love. And with each of Peter's replies came a word of restoration and then a recommissioning of the disciple. "Feed My lambs," "tend My sheep," and "feed My sheep" were the Lord's words of restoration to the grieving disciple.

God wants to use you for His glory. That is why you're still here, even when things haven't gone as they should.

DAY 229

THAT OTHERS MAY KNOW HIM

You may have heard people say "The odds are not in your favor" when you face a situation that seems difficult or even impossible to overcome. This statement may be true of a sporting event or a personal achievement goal in which the odds are somewhat predicable or calculable. But when God is part of the equation, the adage is no longer valid. Consider these passages:

> The LORD is on my side; I will not fear. What can man do to me? (Psalm 118:6).

> What then shall we say to these things? If God is for us, who can be against us? (Romans 8:31).

The odds were not on Joseph's side when his brothers turned against him, and yet what they meant for evil, God used for good. The odds were not with Moses when he stood before Pharaoh and sought the release of God's people that they might worship the Lord. The odds certainly were not on the unarmed Israelis' side when they fled from Pharaoh and his pursuing armies. And yet God made Himself known to the Egyptians by defending His people.

Gideon found himself greatly outnumbered by the Midianites, and the odds were against Hananiah, Mishael, and Azariah (Shadrach, Meshach, and Abed-Nego) when they stood in violation of King Nebuchadnezzar's directive. The same was true of Daniel when he defied an edict signed by King Darius. Yet God showed Himself strong on behalf of Gideon and the quartet of Jewish captives in Babylon.

The same was true for the apostles as they stood before the Jewish council, and the same is true for Israel today. For us, at times it may look like the odds are not in our favor. But the Lord is on our side, and what God does in the face of insurmountable odds can help cause others to see His mighty hand at work!

DAY 230

WE ARE AMBASSADORS, PART 1

We often talk about the great blessings of being a Christian, and so we should. Among them are the freedom of having been forgiven all our sins, knowing that a better world awaits us, and the promise that weapons formed against us will not prosper. Our minds naturally gravitate toward blessings like these.

Other blessings we should include in our daily recounting and rejoicing are our responsibilities as Christians to preach the gospel, to be the light of the world, to not walk in darkness, and to deny ourselves and take up our cross and follow Him.

First John 1:5-7 admonishes us,

> This is the message which we have heard from Him and declare to you, that God is light and in Him is no darkness at all. If we say that we have fellowship with Him, and walk in darkness, we lie and do not practice the truth. But if we walk in the light as He is in the light, we have fellowship with one another, and the blood of Jesus Christ His Son cleanses us from all sin.

The word *Christian* means "Christlike," and John is saying we are not like Christ when we walk in darkness. And we are like Christ when we forgive our enemies, do good to those who hate us, and pray for those who spitefully use us, as Jesus said in the Sermon on the Mount.

To say we live in difficult times is a major understatement. To say we always respond properly to the situations we face would not be accurate. We live in a time when lies are promoted and protected as truth, fiction is presented as fact, and good and evil have exchanged definitions. And yet being like Christ never changes, for He is the same yesterday, today, and forever!

DAY 231

WE ARE AMBASSADORS, PART 2

James 1:19-20 gives us this exhortation: "My beloved brethren, let every man be swift to hear, slow to speak, slow to wrath; for the wrath of man does not produce the righteousness of God."

It is much easier to be quick to speak and express wrath in times such as these, yet the outcome usually does not line up with our goal in life, which is to be righteous in God. We need to remember that a day of wrath is coming upon the earth, an unprecedented time of judgment poured out in the form of immeasurable cataclysmic events in quick succession, as reported in Revelation 6–19.

Because we are to be like Christ and He is unwilling that any should perish (2 Peter 3:9), we should have the same compassion as He does. If He, as Luke 6:35 says, is kind to the unthankful and evil, then we should be kind to the unthankful and evil. That doesn't mean we never stand up for our rights, nor does it mean we are silent about injustice. But it does mean that just as Christ endured the cross, so, too, should we endure our sufferings with the joy set before us of seeing people come to Christ.

Our wrath does not manifest the righteousness of God; rather, it manifests our flesh. There are times when righteous anger is justified, as are the corresponding actions, as when Jesus overturned the tables of the money changers and merchandisers. But we also have to remember what made Him angry enough that He made a whip to drive out the vendors—His Father's house was being represented as a den of thieves.

Yes, our world is a mess and upsetting. Yes, our world hates us and says all manner of evil against us falsely for His name's sake. However, none of those things exempt us from being like Christ. In fact, they are prime opportunities to be more like Christ.

DAY 232

SANCTIFIED BY TRUTH

Acts 17:2 tells us that Paul was in Thessaloniki for three Sabbaths before he was run out of town by an angry mob stirred up by Jews who had rejected his message about the suffering Savior. The exact number of days Paul was there is not known, but it was less than a month.

This is important for us to recognize because the content of the letters Paul wrote to the church in Thessaloniki included prophecy, which is a subject greatly avoided and ignored in many churches today.

After Paul left, he gave these instructions to the believers there:

> Do not quench the Spirit. Do not despise prophecies. Test all things; hold fast what is good. Abstain from every form of evil. Now may the God of peace Himself sanctify you completely; and may your whole spirit, soul, and body be preserved blameless at the coming of our Lord Jesus Christ. He who calls you is faithful, who also will do it (1 Thessalonians 5:19-24).

Paul reminded them of what he taught during his three-Sabbath visit. This included words about the rapture, our gathering together to Him, and warnings not to be deceived by those who say the rapture had already happened. He told the Thessaloniki believers that a falling away would precede the rapture, and that only after the rapture could the lawless one, or the Antichrist, rise to power. He also taught them about the tribulation and the second coming.

Here, the word "quench" can mean "to extinguish." It can also mean (and does in this context) "to suppress divine influence." Paul added another admonition to that when he said not to "despise" prophecies, which means "to belittle" or "esteem lightly." Yet here we are today, at the end of church history, and prophecy is esteemed lightly, abstinence is seen as evil, divine influence is quenched, and teachings and teachers are seldom tested against the Word.

For these reasons, we can rightly conclude Jesus must be coming for us soon!

DAY 233

ISRAEL AND THE MILLENNIUM

In a world of uncertainty and hopelessness, what a privileged people we are as those who know God. It is because of our relationship with Him that we not only know what the future holds for the world, we also know what will happen beyond the grave and into eternity.

We know that in the last days, perilous times will come (2 Timothy 3:1), and we know that the last days will be as Noah's days—exceedingly violent, with man's thoughts and intents only evil continually (Genesis 6:11 and 6:5 respectively). We also know that there will be a rejection of sound doctrine and a preference for myths and fables within what is called "the church." We also know that Jerusalem will be the focus of world attention, and that someday, the Jews will see that the Holy One of Israel is none other than Jesus Christ.

> I will return again to My place till they acknowledge their offense. Then they will seek My face; in their affliction they will earnestly seek Me (Hosea 5:15).
>
> I will pour on the house of David and on the inhabitants of Jerusalem the Spirit of grace and supplication; then they will look on Me whom they pierced. Yes, they will mourn for Him as one mourns for his only son, and grieve for Him as one grieves for a firstborn (Zechariah 12:10).

The afflictions of the tribulation and the outpouring of God's Spirit during it will cause the surviving third of the Jews (Zechariah 13:8) to look at Jesus as their Messiah at His second coming and mourn the failure of their ancestors to do so. They, along with believing Gentiles and the glorified church, will enter the millennium and live in a world ruled by the King of kings Himself, the Holy One of Israel, the head of the church, Jesus of Nazareth!

God is not finished with the nation of Israel.

DAY 234

WITHSTANDING TEMPTATION, PART 1

One of the most common comments heard from Christians around the world is how difficult it is to find a Bible-teaching church. While the Bible has stated clearly that this will be part of the last-days scenario (Amos 8:11; 2 Timothy 4:3), it is tragic nonetheless.

The anecdote to this is found in Hebrews 4:12: "The word of God is living and powerful, and sharper than any two-edged sword, piercing even to the division of soul and spirit, and of joints and marrow, and is a discerner of the thoughts and intents of the heart."

The absence of Bible teaching has led to many being without discernment regarding even the most basic moral truths and has left them vulnerable to the temptations of the enemy, who is always ready to exploit those who are spiritually weak in the absence of exposure to the living and powerful Word of God.

When it comes to temptation, 1 Corinthians 10:13 says, "No temptation has overtaken you except such as is common to man; but God is faithful, who will not allow you to be tempted beyond what you are able, but with the temptation will also make the way of escape, that you may be able to bear it."

Scripture is an essential part of resisting temptation. Remember how, when Jesus was tempted for 40 days in the wilderness, Satan tried to use a basic physical need to get Jesus to sin?

> Jesus was led up by the Spirit into the wilderness to be tempted by the devil. And when He had fasted forty days and forty nights, afterward He was hungry. Now when the tempter came to Him, he said, "If You are the Son of God, command that these stones become bread." But He answered and said, "It is written, 'Man shall not live by bread alone, but by every word that proceeds from the mouth of God'" (Matthew 4:1-4).

The way of escape Jesus took was the Word of God. For every temptation He faced, His reply was, "It is written." That should be our response too.

DAY 235

WITHSTANDING TEMPTATION, PART 2

The sad truth is that many pastors don't teach God's Word today because they don't like or agree with what it says, especially the warnings of coming judgment. But, as the psalmist says, it's all true, including what it says about God's righteous judgment: "The entirety of Your word is truth, and every one of Your righteous judgments endures forever" (Psalm 119:160).

Many Christians are having trouble keeping it together during these prophesied perilous times. Though they attend church, they don't hear God's Word taught. Consequently, as they see all the negativity in the world, they live without the expectation of the glorious appearing of our great God and Savior Jesus Christ—again, because the Word isn't taught. Many people end up with misplaced hope, and therefore future disappointment, because what they hear might sound good or make them feel good, but it has no foundation in the Word, and therefore is nothing more than empty promises based on fables and human opinion.

The Word of God, however, is living and powerful, and no one who follows its doctrines and precepts is weakened, misguided, or left hopeless or disappointed.

There is nothing like God's Word! If Jesus used it to combat Satan, then so should we. And as we do, we need to remember the truth the Bible tells us about our enemy: "You are of God, little children, and have overcome them, because He who is in you is greater than he who is in the world" (1 John 4:4).

Why live without power, discernment, wisdom, direction, comfort, correction, or any of the other attributes of the Holy Scriptures when we have access to it every single day whether churches are teaching it or not?

There is a famine of hearing God's Word today, but that doesn't mean we have to starve. Every day, open the book that is unlike any other—and every day will be better than it would have been without it!

DAY 236

HE'S PREPARING A PLACE FOR US

One of the most needed admonitions in the New Testament is one that is often unknown or ignored: "Now I plead with you, brethren, by the name of our Lord Jesus Christ, that you all speak the same thing, and that there be no divisions among you, but that you be perfectly joined together in the same mind and in the same judgment" (1 Corinthians 1:10).

The Bible is not a book that is subject to cultural or geographical adaptations. Rather, it is the one constant in an ever-changing world. While there are some matters in the Bible that can be interpreted differently, there are others that are pointedly clear and need no interpretation.

For example, Jesus is God, the Jews are God's chosen people, the church is the bride of Christ, repentance is the by-product of salvation and not the cause of it, and without faith you cannot please God. The list of teachings that are clear and need no interpretation goes on and on.

It is one thing to attend a church that holds to an interpretation of a text over which there is room for discussion. It is another to attend a church that denies what the Bible clearly teaches and replaces it with fabricated ideas.

Consider John 14:1-3:

> Let not your heart be troubled; you believe in God, believe also in Me. In My Father's house are many mansions; if it were not so, I would have told you. I go to prepare a place for you. And if I go and prepare a place for you, I will come again and receive you to Myself; that where I am, there you may be also.

There is nothing here that is open to different interpretations. Jesus is preparing a place for the church and is coming again to take us to where He is. To say we must prepare the world for Jesus' return is not a varied interpretation of this passage; it is a myth concocted by false teachers.

DAY 237

TRUST IN THE LORD

Like most Hebrew and Greek words in the Bible, the word translated "trust" has multiple meanings and applications. In the Old Testament passage Psalm 37:3, we read, "Trust in the LORD, and do good; dwell in the land, and feed on His faithfulness." The Hebrew word for trust here is *bâṭah*, which means "confident, secure, bold, carefree, and hopeful."

In the New Testament passage 2 Corinthians 1:8-10, Paul wrote,

> We do not want you to be ignorant, brethren, of our trouble which came to us in Asia: that we were burdened beyond measure, above strength, so that we despaired even of life. Yes, we had the sentence of death in ourselves, that we should not trust in ourselves but in God who raises the dead, who delivered us from so great a death, and does deliver us; in whom we trust that He will still deliver us.

Here, there are two Greek words translated "trust." The first, in verse 9, is *peithō*, which means "to rely on inward certainty." Paul has self-confidence in view, saying we should not trust in ourselves. In verse 10, the phrase "in whom we trust" is *elpizō*, which means "to have hope" or "hopeful expectation."

Whether you are reading from the Old or New Testament, the Hebrew or Greek text, the trust that is placed in the Lord and not self produces confident, secure, bold, and hopeful expectation. This is a fitting description of living by faith. While trust and faith have distinct definitions, they are inseparable companions. You will not have faith in someone you don't trust, and you cannot say you trust someone unless you put your faith in them.

Proverbs 3:5-6 calls us to "trust in the LORD with all your heart, and lean not on your own understanding; in all your ways acknowledge Him, and He shall direct your paths."

This promise is still true today!

DAY 238

THE MYSTERY OF SPIRITUAL BLINDNESS

We live in a time when many feel as Elijah did: Where are all God's people? Where are the Bible-believing Christians? Where can I find a Bible-teaching church? Yet as was true in Elijah's day, God has people all over the world who have not bowed to the world system. This encompasses people from every tribe, tongue, and nation, including Israel.

> I say then, has God cast away His people? Certainly not! For I also am an Israelite, of the seed of Abraham, of the tribe of Benjamin. God has not cast away His people whom He foreknew. Or do you not know what the Scripture says of Elijah, how he pleads with God against Israel, saying, "Lord, they have killed Your prophets and torn down Your altars, and I alone am left, and they seek my life"? But what does the divine response say to him? "I have reserved for Myself seven thousand men who have not bowed the knee to Baal." Even so then, at this present time there is a remnant according to the election of grace (Romans 11:1-5).

In Romans 11, Paul's purpose was to remind Gentile Christians that He is at work even with Israel. Yes, blindness has come in part to the Jews through their disobedience (verse 25). Yet in the depth of the riches of the wisdom and knowledge of God, He continues to show mercy on people from all nations who were disobedient.

We need to be mindful of this even today, a time in which the remnant church exists in an unprecedented season of global blindness. God has people who have not bowed the knee to Baal—they have not become idolatrous. We need to remember that God is still saving lost souls at this time, and He is still using His people to reach the lost with the gospel.

DAY 239

GOD USES THE BROKEN

Peter is such a wonderful example of the work God can do in a person's life. Peter had a strong personality; he was quick to speak, and sometimes he was right, and other times he should have kept quiet. Like Peter, we have all said things we wish we could take back, and we have rightfully said what has needed to be said.

Though we each have our own struggles and personalities, God has works prepared beforehand for all of us to walk in (Ephesians 2:10). He can create present ministries from our past failures. He can use strong personalities and the softspoken to reach the lost. He can use great minds and strong backs, and He can use the weak and simple for His glory. Peter reminds us that even with our imperfections, there is room for us in God's kingdom and plan. However, the one human attribute that God will not use is pride.

In James 4:10 we read the command, "Humble yourselves in the sight of the Lord, and He will lift you up." First Peter 5:5 says, "God resists the proud, but gives grace to the humble."

Peter, who was a fisherman, is someone we might classify as a working man. Yet his personal battle was the same as that of a man who was once the most powerful in the world, Nebuchadnezzar (read Daniel 4 for Nebuchadnezzar's story). Both struggled with pride.

Peter was first told by Jesus to follow Him—then as a follower, he thought he had the right to correct the One who had called him. Yet it was God who had called and chosen Peter to fulfill specific plans, and it was God who prepared Peter for those plans. The path of preparation for the fisherman was the same as that of the king of Babylon: brokenness.

As Psalm 51:17 says, "The sacrifices of God are a broken spirit, a broken and a contrite heart—these, O God, You will not despise."

DAY 240

WHO IS JESUS TO YOU?

Second Corinthians 1:20 says, "All the promises of God in Him are Yes, and in Him Amen, to the glory of God through us."

The word "Him" in this passage refers to Jesus, and in Him, all that God has promised to us is realized. In Genesis 3:15, God promised mankind a deliverer; Jesus is that Deliverer. In Genesis 22, God promised through Abraham's figurative offering of Isaac that He would provide Himself a sacrifice; Jesus is that sacrifice. Genesis 49:10 promised the Messiah would come from the tribe of Judah; Jesus did.

The Scriptures said Christ would die, be buried, and rise again on the third day, and He did! We serve a risen Savior, not a dead promise maker. There are multitudes whose claims about life after death cannot be validated because they are still in their graves. In contrast, Jesus is alive! Many believe Jesus existed, but the real question is, Who is He? A man, or the God-man?

In Acts 1:8, Jesus said, "You shall receive power when the Holy Spirit has come upon you; and you shall be witnesses to Me in Jerusalem, and in all Judea and Samaria, and to the end of the earth." Jesus said the Holy Spirit's power to be witnesses would come upon His disciples, and it did. Peter said in Acts 2:39 that this promise of the Spirit is true for "as many as the Lord our God will call."

Our world is filled with followers of empty promises, and delusion fills the minds and hearts of people all over the world. Many are captured by the false hope of a promised afterlife that lays unproven in the grave with its promiser. Others see death as nothing more than the cessation of existence.

There is but One who has proven there is life after death, and before He ascended back to heaven, He gave His followers the power to tell others about Him. There is no hope of eternal life apart from Jesus—just empty and unproven promises.

DAY 241

RIGHTEOUS, NOT RELIGIOUS

Estimates of the number of religions around the world range from 4,500 to more than 10,000, with countless variations within them. The truth is that mankind loves religion. According to dictionary.com, *religion* is defined as: (1) a set of beliefs concerning the cause, nature, and purpose of the universe, especially when considered as the creation of a superhuman agency or agencies, usually involving devotional and ritual observances, and often containing a moral code governing the conduct of human affairs; (2) a specific fundamental set of beliefs and practices generally agreed upon by a number of persons or sects.

The second definition tells us that a supernatural agent is not necessary for a set of beliefs to be considered a religion, only a sharing of those beliefs with others. The first definition includes the same general principle yet adds a superhuman agent or agents to the mix, along with ritual observances and a code of conduct.

No matter which definition is used, the end result is the same—man is the central figure of all religion.

Christianity, however, is different. In John 14:6, Jesus said, "I am the way, the truth, and the life. No one comes to the Father except through Me." He made no mention of religious observances, personal achievement, not even adherence to a moral code. Paul wrote in 1 Timothy 1:15, "This is a faithful saying and worthy of all acceptance, that Christ Jesus came into the world to save sinners, of whom I am chief."

John Newton, a former slave ship operator and the author of the world's most famous hymn, "Amazing Grace," had the same perspective as Paul. Near the end of his life, he was quoted as saying, "I am a great sinner, and Christ is a great Savior."

Newton did not say Christianity is a great religion, but Christ is a great Savior. Jesus died, rose, and ascended to make us righteous, not religious.

DAY 242

GOD'S TIMING

The time of the Gentiles has lasted more than two millennia, beginning with the reign of Nebuchadnezzar and those who followed him. The perilous times during which sound doctrine is not endured is a time specific to the end of the church age. Jesus spoke of a single future generation that would see all that was written in the Olivet Discourse come to pass, then said there is a day and hour when the Son of Man will come. Paul further reduced that day and hour to a moment that will last for the duration of the twinkling of an eye (1 Corinthians 15:52).

If we look at these few time markers from Scripture, we could conclude that they provide for us a countdown in which a flurry of events will happen in quick succession near the end.

We're given another timeline in the book of Revelation, which begins, "The Revelation of Jesus Christ, which God gave Him to show His servants—things which must shortly take place. And He sent and signified it by His angel to His servant John" (1:1). The word translated "shortly" means "in quick succession." The phrase "sent and signified" means "to show by signs and symbols." Thus, Revelation tells us that when time is running out, things will happen quickly.

In Revelation, the church age is represented in chapters 2–3, the seventieth week of Daniel in chapters 6–19, the millennium in chapter 20, then the Great White Throne judgment followed by eternity in chapters 21–22.

Our God is a God of order, and He has a predetermined moment in time that He has ordained for His Son to meet the church in the air, with the dead raised up in Christ. That time is at hand. Yes, the rapture is always imminent, but with the Jewish people back in the land of promise, with the widespread defection from truth that is now happening in the church, and with the perilous times that are upon us, we could say the rapture is more imminent now than ever before.

DAY 243

ROLE MODELS

It has been said, "If you aim at nothing, you are sure to hit it!" That truism is meant to establish the importance of having goals in life, but it says nothing about choosing the right goals. For that, we find these instructive passages in Scripture:

> Imitate me, just as I also imitate Christ (1 Corinthians 11:1).

> You became followers of us and of the Lord, having received the word in much affliction, with joy of the Holy Spirit, so that you became examples to all in Macedonia and Achaia who believe (1 Thessalonians 1:6-7).

The Greek word *mimētēs*, translated as "imitate," can also be translated as "follower," as it is in 1 Thessalonians 1:6. That tells us Paul's goal was to imitate Christ and thus be an example worth following. He did not see this as being exclusive to himself but praised the Thessaloniki Christians for doing the same.

Carrying a ball across a goal line or kicking one into a net or throwing one through a hoop does not make someone a worthy role model. Nor does being able to portray someone else in front of a movie camera or singing into a microphone. The truth is there are far too many people today who are viewed as role models simply because they can do those things.

Paul gave us the formula for choosing a role model: Imitate someone who is following Christ. This gives us a broad field of choices for role models, including those who are now with the Lord. We would do well to follow Paul's efforts to imitate Christ. John, James, Peter, Mary the sister of Lazarus, and Ruth the wife of Boaz are also good choices as imitators of God. While these are all fallible humans, they shared the common attribute of being "imitators of God as dear children" (Ephesians 5:1).

There is the word *mimētēs* again, which highlights the common attribute among those worth imitating—they are followers of God as dear children.

DAY 244

ISRAEL WILL STAND

Modern Israel is one of the greatest proofs that the Bible is the infallible Word of God. Scripture said that God would gather His people back in their homeland, and He did. It said that the nations of the world would gather against Jerusalem, and they are. God also said a coalition of nations would one day invade Israel from the north, and those nations are cooperating together today.

The Jews are still God's chosen people, and someday, they will look upon the One whom they pierced and mourn for Him as one mourns for an only Son (Zechariah 12:10).

The modern state of Israel is biblical Israel. If the Jews had never inhabited their homeland again, the Bible would be in error. If replacement theology is true, the same could be said of the Bible—the prophets were wrong, and the Bible is too. But the Bible is correct and every word of God is true, including those written to and about the modern state of Israel in the last days.

In Genesis 17:6-8, God promised:

> I will make you exceedingly fruitful; and I will make nations of you, and kings shall come from you. And I will establish My covenant between Me and you and your descendants after you in their generations, for an everlasting covenant, to be God to you and your descendants after you. Also I give to you and your descendants after you the land in which you are a stranger, all the land of Canaan, as an everlasting possession; and I will be their God.

God's faithfulness to His word and to Israel means we can trust Him when He said He would give us everlasting life through belief in Jesus, and someday be with Him forever. If everlasting doesn't mean everlasting to Israel, then it can't mean everlasting to us in Scripture passages like John 3:16.

DAY 245

GOD IS A GOD OF WAR

One of the most frequently misquoted and misunderstood verses in the Bible is connected to the most frequently quoted and most famous verse in the Bible:

> God so loved the world that He gave His only begotten Son, that whoever believes in Him should not perish but have everlasting life. For God did not send His Son into the world to condemn the world, but that the world through Him might be saved (John 3:16-17).

John 3:16 is obviously the most well-known verse, and verse 17 is frequently misquoted as saying Jesus did not come to condemn the world. The problem with that claim is context. Those who quote that portion of John 3:17 in an effort to say Jesus never condemns anyone usually fail to keep reading and notice what verse 18 says: "He who believes in Him is not condemned; but he who does not believe is condemned already, because he has not believed in the name of the only begotten Son of God."

John 3:18 interprets John 3:17 and clarifies that Jesus did not come into the world to condemn it because the world was already condemned. That's why He came into the world—to save people from the consequences of man's condemned state apart from Him.

In the book of Revelation, we see the revealing of Jesus Christ in His majesty and glory. The Greek word translated "Revelation" is *apokalypsis* and means "full disclosure," or "take the lid off," or "to enlighten." It is Jesus who will open the seven seals that lead to the seven seal judgments, which will be followed by the seven trumpet and seven bowl judgments of God's undiluted wrath on the earth. And it is Jesus who will return in Revelation 19 to judge and make war. It is Jesus who will make war with those who hate and oppose Him, and He will win!

DAY 246

THE LORD DOES NOT CHANGE

We live in a season of history during which change has almost become an idol. Many people today casually change their marriage partner multiple times. There are some who believe you can change your gender. Many see change as a solution to man's problems—change history, change morality, change the justice system, change the political system, change everything!

That is not to say that all changes are wrong or bad. Change can be good as well. But the danger today is that people are wanting to alter what God has ordained as truth, and the standards He has called us to live by. Proverbs 24:19-22 offers wisdom here:

> Do not fret because of evildoers, nor be envious of the wicked; for there will be no prospect for the evil man; the lamp of the wicked will be put out. My son, fear the LORD and the king; do not associate with those given to change; for their calamity will rise suddenly, and who knows the ruin those two can bring?

Again, there are times where change is good and even necessary. But change for the sake of advancing evil and promoting evildoers is wrong.

Many of the people who want change today want to eliminate the fear of the Lord and the God-ordained role of human government, which is to protect what is good and punish evil (Romans 13:4). They want to be able to do what is right in their own eyes. The word for this kind of world is *lawless*. Second Corinthians 6:14 warns us, "Do not be unequally yoked together with unbelievers. For what fellowship has righteousness with lawlessness? And what communion has light with darkness?"

This is what Proverbs 24:19-22 is telling us—we should not yoke ourselves with efforts to change what God has ordained, or change His definitions of right and wrong. The reason for this instruction is obvious: The Lord doesn't change.

DAY 247

CHRISTIANITY AND JUDAISM

Many Christians today are struggling with what to do during this difficult season of history. In many countries, Christianity is in the crosshairs of society, and long-held Christian beliefs are being demonized. For us to believe what the Bible says about many issues is largely viewed as bigoted. To claim Christianity as the exclusive way to heaven is viewed as hateful, or at least disrespectful, to other religions.

Proverbs 24:10-12 provides these instructive words for us:

> If you faint in the day of adversity, your strength is small. Deliver those who are drawn toward death, and hold back those stumbling to the slaughter. If you say, "Surely we did not know this," does not He who weighs the hearts consider it? He who keeps your soul, does He not know it? And will He not render to each man according to his deeds?

Remember, the church was born in a time of adversity, and yet adversity was the vehicle that caused the church to grow and spread around the world. In the passage above, the recognition of small strength is followed by the admonition to deliver or rescue others. The implication here is that this act would require divine strength—similar to what Peter experienced when he preached to the Jews in Jerusalem on Pentecost: "Let all the house of Israel know assuredly that God has made this Jesus, whom you crucified, both Lord and Christ" (Acts 2:36).

Peter could have thought, *You know, Rome isn't going to like this. They colluded with the Jewish leaders to kill Jesus; they could do the same to me. This is a time when keeping quiet is probably my best option.*

But Peter, now filled with the Holy Spirit, didn't have such thoughts. He knew the only hope for his countrymen was to tell them the truth, and he did. What was the result? About 3,000 were saved that day!

DAY 248

KEEP YOUR EYES ON JESUS

While we don't find the term *focus* used directly in Scripture, the Bible continually reminds us that where we focus our attention is important.

> I will lift up my eyes to the hills—from whence comes my help? My help comes from the LORD, who made heaven and earth (Psalm 121:1-2).

> Since we are surrounded by so great a cloud of witnesses, let us lay aside every weight, and the sin which so easily ensnares us, and let us run with endurance the race that is set before us, looking unto Jesus, the author and finisher of our faith, who for the joy that was set before Him endured the cross, despising the shame, and has sat down at the right hand of the throne of God (Hebrews 12:1-2).

In essence, Psalm 121:1-2 says to keep your eyes on the Lord in spite of your circumstances. Hebrews 12:1-2 tells you to not let difficult circumstances keep you from running the race with endurance.

The old adage "One uplook can change your whole outlook" is timely in this day when our focus is more important than ever. If we focus on the problems and difficulties around us, our emotions and outlook will be impacted negatively. If our attention is on things above, where our help comes from, our emotions and outlook will be influenced positively.

Corrie ten Boom, the wonderful Dutch woman who, along with her family, hid Jews in their home to help them escape the Nazis during World War II, was eventually caught. Corrie and her sister Betsie were sent to Ravensbrück, a women's concentration camp, where her sister would die from starvation. It was from this backdrop that Corrie would write, "If you look at the world, you'll be distressed. If you look within, you'll be depressed. If you look at God, you'll be at rest."[10]

DAY 249

ISRAEL'S SIGNIFICANCE

All of us have sinned since the time of our salvation in Christ, and we should be thankful that we have Israel as an example of God's love and faithfulness even to disobedient and disputing people. The replacement theologian would say, "But the Jews killed Jesus." No, they didn't. Jesus came into the world to die, and the Father so loved the world He gave His Son to the cross to die for your sins and mine. The Jews didn't kill Jesus, nor did the Romans. Rather, sin killed Jesus—your sin and mine. That makes us complicit in His death. Should the Lord cast us away? Look to Israel, and the answer is a resounding no!

Israel has been referred to as God's timepiece. In other words, we can watch the prophetic clock tick as we look at the nation of Israel. This highlights for us that we are living in privileged times as it pertains to Bible prophecy. Previous generations of Christians could only wonder about the things we are now watching. They could only read Zechariah 12:3, which speaks of the world viewing Jerusalem as a burdensome stone. Today when we read about this in Scripture, we are also reading and hearing about it on the news!

We are living at a time when the things that are happening in and to Israel should increase our "God confidence" and our trust in His Word. The regathering of the Jews to their national homeland started the last days' prophetic clock ticking. However, unlike the consistent ticking of a clock every second, Jesus said in Matthew 24:8 that things would happen in a birth-pang-like progression when it is time for Him to come. In other words, the events pointing to the end of the age will become more frequent and intense as we draw close to the unknown day and hour of His coming for us.

Matthew 24:44 says, "Be ready, for the Son of Man is coming at an hour you do not expect." Jesus is coming for His church soon, and what is happening in Israel is proof of that.

Are you ready?

DAY 250

THE END TIMES

We have all watched movies or read books filled with plot twists and surprise turns, and with some characters involved in scheming and conniving, while others play the role of heroes. We have found ourselves rooting for the good guys and wishing for evil to be exposed, and wondering, *How is this going to end?*

Real life can be similar to watching a well-written drama or mystery unfold. However, we do not have to wait until the end to know how things will turn out. In Isaiah 46:9-10, God said,

> Remember the former things of old, for I am God, and there is no other; I am God, and there is none like Me, declaring the end from the beginning, and from ancient times things that are not yet done, saying, "My counsel shall stand, and I will do all My pleasure."

When the disciples asked Jesus to teach them how to pray, He included these words in His model prayer: "Your kingdom come. Your will be done on earth as it is in heaven." We need to take note of the fact that if Jesus said, "Pray like this," then He is telling us that God's kingdom is coming, and that God's will is going to be done on Earth as it is in heaven.

This is crucial for us to remember in a time when the world is looking more and more like a kingdom of evil than one in which God's will is done on Earth. We live in a day when the love of many is growing cold and lawlessness is abounding, and evil characters and their malicious plots are proliferating all around us.

Ultimately, God will do what pleases Him. He has told us through the prophets that the world's condition is temporary, and that darkness will not prevail over the kingdom of light.

DAY 251

THE PARABLE OF THE FIG TREE, PART 1

Our planet is changing in ways and at a pace that are both unexpected and unprecedented. Yet the final destination of our world remains the same, as stated in Revelation 22:1-4:

> Now I saw a new heaven and a new earth, for the first heaven and the first earth had passed away. Also there was no more sea. Then I, John, saw the holy city, New Jerusalem, coming down out of heaven from God, prepared as a bride adorned for her husband. And I heard a loud voice from heaven saying, "Behold, the tabernacle of God is with men, and He will dwell with them, and they shall be His people. God Himself will be with them and be their God. And God will wipe away every tear from their eyes; there shall be no more death, nor sorrow, nor crying. There shall be no more pain, for the former things have passed away."

The march toward the final destination of a new heaven and earth has been underway since the garden of Eden, when there were but two people on the earth. Yet for billions of people since then, the proximity of the foretold end was never in view.

That all changed on May 14, 1948, when God's chosen people, long scattered all over world, had a national homeland once again, and a generation now existed that could see "the Day approaching": "Let us consider one another in order to stir up love and good works, not forsaking the assembling of ourselves together, as is the manner of some, but exhorting one another, and so much the more as you see the Day approaching" (Hebrews 10:24-25).

On June 7, 1967, when Jerusalem was reunified with the capture of East Jerusalem and the Temple Mount, the approaching Day could be seen more clearly. And the admonition to not forsake gathering implies a great need for unity and readiness in the church of the last days.

DAY 252

THE PARABLE OF THE FIG TREE, PART 2

Ezekiel 38–39 tells us about a coming day when several nations—named by Ezekiel—will gather on Israel's northern border for an invasion. That day is now seen with greater clarity than ever before.

We have seen the Abraham Accords agreed upon and signed by some Arab nations. The Bible prophesies that some of these countries will protest the invasion of Israel, and with what we see happening in the Middle East, that day is coming more into focus than in any previous generation.

We have watched the US lose its position as the world's only superpower as nations everywhere saw the catastrophic withdrawal of US troops from Afghanistan and the subsequent immediate takeover of the country by the Taliban. The US became a paper tiger in the eyes of many, and a weakened US may explain the reason for the absence of the US in last-days' prophecies.

Matthew 24:32-34 says, "Now learn this parable from the fig tree: When its branch has already become tender and puts forth leaves, you know that summer is near. So you also, when you see all these things, know that it is near—at the doors! Assuredly, I say to you, this generation will by no means pass away till all these things take place."

Israel is likened to a fruitless fig tree in Jeremiah 8:13. Hosea 9:10 and Joel 1:7 both use the idiom of a fig tree to describe Israel. Jesus mentioned fig tree branches becoming tender and putting forth leaves to indicate that the tree is about to bear fruit.

We know from Romans 11:26 that "all Israel" will be saved at the second coming of Christ, and we could well say that with all that is going on in Israel today, and with a resurgence of interest in Judaism by even the most secular Jews in Israel, the season for figs can be seen in the distance.

That tells the church but one thing: Jesus is coming for us soon!

DAY 253

THE GOSPEL

Among the many truths Jesus taught, one of the most frequently overlooked statements is one of the most amazing. In John 14:12, He said, "Most assuredly, I say to you, he who believes in Me, the works that I do he will do also; and greater works than these he will do, because I go to My Father."

Jesus miraculously healed the sick, raised the dead, gave sight to the blind, cast out demons, and fed the hungry. Yet in John 14, He said that not only will those who believe in Him do the same, but they will do greater works because Jesus was returning to His Father. What "greater works" was Jesus talking about?

We find the answer in Acts 1:8, where Jesus said, "You shall receive power when the Holy Spirit has come upon you; and you shall be witnesses to Me in Jerusalem, and in all Judea and Samaria, and to the end of the earth."

We see this promised power manifested immediately in Peter, the very disciple who denied the Lord three times after vowing that he would never do so. A mere 50 days after that last Passover meal with Jesus in the upper room, the Helper, the Holy Spirit, was using Peter's preaching to save thousands.

This is the greater work Jesus was speaking of—leading people to Christ through the power to be witnesses. This promise is given to all Christians today.

As wonderful as Jesus' miracles were—raising the dead, giving sight to the blind, and feeding the masses—the greater work is to lead people to Jesus for the saving of their souls, as Peter did immediately upon being empowered to be a witness.

This is part of the "good works...prepared beforehand that we should walk in them" as mentioned in Ephesians 2:10. If you want to see the mighty works of God, tell someone about Jesus today!

DAY 254

YOUR LIFE IN THIS WORLD

Mankind has long had an unceasing love of religion, whether people know it or not. While religion has the typical spiritual meaning we readily understand, religion is also defined as "a pursuit or interest to which someone ascribes supreme importance."[11] By this definition, atheism is a religion, and so is Darwinian evolution. Any pursuit or interest that has a governing set of principles that are important to believe or practice is, by definition, a religion.

Why does mankind have this love affair with religion? The definition in and of itself tells us: a pursuit or interest to which someone ascribes supreme importance. The key word in this definition is *someone*. This is the reason for man's love of religion—it places man as the central figure of it all. Do this, and the reward is that. Achieve this, and the benefits are these. Observe this and practice that, and become worthy of a reward for your efforts.

This is why many have described Christianity as a relationship and not a religion. Yet today, many who say they are Christians try to make Christianity into a religion through additives to the finished work of Christ on the cross, which Hebrews 10:29 warns against:

> Of how much worse punishment, do you suppose, will he be thought worthy who has trampled the Son of God underfoot, counted the blood of the covenant by which he was sanctified a common thing, and insulted the Spirit of grace?

This is a strong word of caution to the "works righteousness" crowd who believe that certain efforts are the means by which we can deserve what God says is a free gift. This thinking makes our good works equal to the blood of Jesus. In other words, Jesus' blood is not sufficient to save; works must be added, self-abuse and depravation must be added, water baptism must be added, or even the great tribulation must be added or you're not saved. This is an insult to the Spirit of grace.

DAY 255

FROM DEAD TO ALIVE

In Revelation 19:6, we read these glorious words written by the apostle John: "I heard, as it were, the voice of a great multitude, as the sound of many waters and as the sound of mighty thunderings, saying, 'Alleluia! For the Lord God Omnipotent reigns!'"

The word "Omnipotent" here means "absolute authority." By definition, the word means "unlimited power." The truth is you must have unlimited power in order to be the absolute authority over all creation. God is all-powerful; He is omnipresent, or present everywhere; He is omniscient, or He knows everything. Because God is omnipotent, Jeremiah could write these familiar words: "Ah, Lord GOD! Behold, You have made the heavens and the earth by Your great power and outstretched arm. There is nothing too hard for You" (Jeremiah 32:17).

This is a fact we need to carry into every situation we face in life—there is nothing too hard for God. There is no circumstance He cannot deliver us from, and there is no circumstance He cannot sustain us through. There is nothing too hard for Him! First Corinthians 15:21-26 says,

> Since by man came death, by Man also came the resurrection of the dead. For as in Adam all die, even so in Christ all shall be made alive. But each one in his own order: Christ the firstfruits, afterward those who are Christ's at His coming. Then comes the end, when He delivers the kingdom to God the Father, when He puts an end to all rule and all authority and power. For He must reign till He has put all enemies under His feet. The last enemy that will be destroyed is death.

In order to make dead men live and end all systems of earthly rule and authority, and to put all enemies under His subjection and destroy even the great enemy of death, unlimited power and absolute authority are required. And this is who and what our magnificent God is!

What a mighty God we serve!!

DAY 256

WISDOM FROM ABOVE

C.H. Spurgeon wrote a commentary on the Psalms titled *The Treasury of David*. While David was not the sole author of the Psalms, his life and writings within that book are a treasure trove of spiritual and practical lessons. Romans 15:4 affirms the value of the Old Testament by saying, "Whatever things were written before were written for our learning, that we through the patience and comfort of the Scriptures might have hope."

There is much we can learn from the man whom God called "a man after My own heart" (Acts 13:22). Some are good and others not so good. But the end result of reading the things "written before" is that doing so gives us hope. With that in mind, let's read 1 Samuel 18:12-16:

> Now Saul was afraid of David, because the Lord was with him, but had departed from Saul. Therefore Saul removed him from his presence, and made him his captain over a thousand; and he went out and came in before the people. And David behaved wisely in all his ways, and the Lord was with him. Therefore, when Saul saw that he behaved very wisely, he was afraid of him. But all Israel and Judah loved David, because he went out and came in before them.

David did not ask to be king; God chose him. The people's choice for king, Saul, did not like David, who was more loyal to him than even some of those closest to him. Saul's jealousy toward David led him to want to destroy the man after God's own heart.

Many rulers today seek the destruction of the influence of godly people. Like David, we need to behave wisely in the face of growing animosity. When we are attacked, we need to be wise and not resort to works of the flesh. When Satan tries to divide us from within, we need to walk wisely in the pure wisdom that comes from above (James 3:17), which is unpolluted by fleshly desires.

DAY 257

HANG ON TO GOD'S WORD

You may have heard the saying, "When the devil realized he couldn't destroy the church, he joined it." While the sentiment is obviously fictitious, there is an element of truth in it. No, Satan is not a member of the church, but there are those who do his bidding who are. Some do this knowingly and others unwittingly, but the end result is the same—apostasy in the church.

Not all apostasy is in the form of heretical doctrines like denying the Trinity, or rejecting the substitutionary atonement of Jesus' blood for our sins, or saying Jesus was just a man with the "God Spirit" and not God in human flesh. And some of the greatest apostasy in our day comes not from committing heresy, but omitting truth. With that in mind, let's read Psalm 138:2: "I will worship toward Your holy temple, and praise Your name for Your lovingkindness and Your truth; for You have magnified Your word above all Your name."

In recent years, one troubling statement being made in churches is that the Trinity is comprised of God the Father, God the Son, and God the Holy Spirit, not the Holy Bible. The implication is that we should not hold the Bible in too high of esteem, as though it were divine. Yet the psalmist said the Word of God is "magnified" even "above all [His] name." In addition, Jesus told Satan that man should live by every word from God (Matthew 4:4). And Jesus is presented as "the Word" in John 1:1, making Him and the Word inseparable.

A person's word establishes the credibility of their name. When the name of a known thief is mentioned, what thoughts are people likely to think? This is why the psalmist said what he did about God's Word. What you read in the Bible establishes God's credibility. If a church doesn't teach God's Word, how can you learn about His nature and character? You can't.

DAY 258

WHAT MATTERS MOST

You've probably heard the saying, "The definition of insanity is doing the same thing over and over yet expecting a different result." This does a lot to explain the world in which we now live, a world that seems to have lost its mind on every level. It also reminds us that as Christians, we have been given a "sound mind" (2 Timothy 1:7) even in a season during which many people have lost theirs.

The reason today's society is in such a hopeless state is because people keep doing the wrong things over and over and expecting things to get better. They keep looking for hope and happiness in ways and through things that cannot produce them.

Hebrews 11:24-26 points us to a better way:

> By faith Moses, when he became of age, refused to be called the son of Pharaoh's daughter, choosing rather to suffer affliction with the people of God than to enjoy the passing pleasures of sin, esteeming the reproach of Christ greater riches than the treasures in Egypt; for he looked to the reward.

Like Moses, we should understand that the riches and rewards found in Christ are far better than the momentary pleasures of life, especially the sinful ones. Yet the world keeps telling us, "Do this, and you'll be happy." "Get this, and your life will be better." "Go here, and life will be fuller." Yet happiness eludes them, and the world is full of fear and hopelessness.

In 1 Corinthians 15:19, Paul wrote, "If in this life only we have hope in Christ, we are of all men the most pitiable." If our hope is in things that are unproven, unlikely, and even impossible, then that hope will lead to disappointment and a pitiable existence. But if our hope is in the resurrected Lord, our existence will be far from pitiable. Rather, it will be one of cheerful endurance, godly character, and immoveable and steadfast hope.

DAY 259

ARE YOU READY FOR THE RAPTURE?

Those who claim that the rapture is a recent invention of the overactive imagination of some Christians aren't paying attention to what Paul said to the church at Thessaloniki in 1 Thessalonians 4:13-18. There, Paul wrote that there is coming a moment in time when dead believers in Christ and those alive at that same moment will be taken up to meet Jesus in the air and forever be with Him. Paul then said to "comfort one another with these words" (verse 18).

If Paul was talking about the second coming, there would be little comfort in knowing we are going through the tribulation. And we must also consider what 1 Corinthians 15:50-52 says:

> Now this I say, brethren, that flesh and blood cannot inherit the kingdom of God; nor does corruption inherit incorruption. Behold, I tell you a mystery: We shall not all sleep, but we shall all be changed—in a moment, in the twinkling of an eye, at the last trumpet. For the trumpet will sound, and the dead will be raised incorruptible, and we shall be changed.

Here, Paul said not everyone is going to die. The early Christians used the term *sleep* to refer to believers' bodies in the grave because they knew God would resurrect those bodies one day. Paul also said that in the twinkling of an eye, living mortals would be changed into immortals.

Some believers will bypass death and become immortal—and then what? Will they stay here? No; the Bible clearly teaches the rapture of the church prior to the tribulation—a fact supported by the absence of any mention of the church in Revelation 6–18, during which time the tribulation will be in full swing.

In Matthew 24:44, Jesus gives the exhortation, "Therefore you also be ready, for the Son of Man is coming at an hour you do not expect." The doctrine of the rapture is as old as the New Testament. The question is not, Is this a new doctrine? The question is, Are you ready for the rapture?

SALVATION HAS COME

One of the most incredible aspects of being a Christian is packaged succinctly in one short yet profound verse:

> If anyone is in Christ, he is a new creation; old things have passed away; behold, all things have become new (2 Corinthians 5:17).

This reminds us that as born-again believers, our sins have been removed from us as far as the east is from the west (Psalm 103:12), and God remembers them no more. It also reminds us that as new creations in Christ, we can also "walk in newness of life" (Romans 6:4).

For centuries, mankind was divided into two groups: Jews and Gentiles. Yet when Christ came, lived, died, rose from the dead, then ascended into heaven, He created one new man from the two. This truth needs to be heard in our world today. In Christ we are one; there are no ethnic groups in the church because we are all part of the one new man. The church is a new race of people from every sociological and geographical part of the world. We may have different cultural backgrounds, but we are one. We may speak different languages and have different skin colors, but we are one.

If there is one group from whom the Jews should experience love and hear the truth about their Messiah, the Holy One of Israel, the King of the Jews, it should be the church. The Jews should never hear from the lips of a born-again Christian that God has cast them aside. No Jew is going to be jealous of a predominantly Gentile church that tells them Hashem has cast them off forever.

What the Jews need to hear today is that salvation has come in the blessed One who came in the name of the Lord and died for the sins of the whole world, including theirs!

DAY 261

ALL ISRAEL WILL BE SAVED

While much of Bible prophecy is viewed through various lenses of interpretation, there is one prophecy concerning the last days that needs no interpretation—nor can there be any, except one, which is the literal interpretation: "Thus says the Lord God: 'Surely I will take the children of Israel from among the nations, wherever they have gone, and will gather them from every side and bring them into their own land'" (Ezekiel 37:21).

Israel becoming a nation again was the first major prophetic fulfillment to occur since the time of Jesus. The rebirth of Israel in the Jewish people's national homeland, granted by covenant to them by God, ended nearly two millennia of waiting for verses like Ezekiel 37:21 to be fulfilled.

The last time there was flurry of prophetic fulfillment was after 400 years of prophetic silence until John the Baptist burst onto the scene, saying things like this: "There comes One after me who is mightier than I, whose sandal strap I am not worthy to stoop down and loose. I indeed baptized you with water, but He will baptize you with the Holy Spirit" (Mark 1:7-8).

When Jesus came the first time, there were many prophetic promises fulfilled that announced the Messiah was here. And now, there are many prophecies about to be fulfilled that announce His soon return.

After nearly two millennia of nothing happening in relation to end-times Bible prophecy, suddenly, Israel was reborn in May 1948. Ever since, events have unfolded in an escalated fashion, just as birth pains do when the time of birth draws near.

It's been a long time since there was a flurry of prophetic fulfillments, and the fact that we're seeing a new flurry tells us Jesus is coming again soon. First, for the church before the tribulation, and then later, with the church at His return. At that appointed time, the Lord will save His chosen people Israel.

DAY 262

WE ALL NEED JESUS, PART 1

In 1 Corinthians 15:3-4, Paul wrote, "I delivered to you first of all that which I also received: that Christ died for our sins according to the Scriptures, and that He was buried, and that He rose again the third day according to the Scriptures."

Everything Jesus had done and endured was "according to the Scriptures." Yet those He came to first, the Jews, did not universally receive Him, but as many as did receive Him, He gave the right to become children of God (John 1:12). Many Jews faltered in their acceptance of Jesus because they felt that, as Jews, they already were children of God. What's more, they wanted a conquering King, not a suffering Savior.

This is true of many people today in reverse. Having proven He is the Holy One of Israel and the head of the church, they are not looking to Him for those things. They want forgiveness but not repentance, provision but not commitment, and salvation but not sanctification. They prefer a suffering Savior over a conquering King and Lord. It's almost as though Good Friday is where the story ends for them.

However, Jesus is coming again and will rule the world as King of kings and Lord of lords. He is coming back with all who have been made righteous by His atoning blood. Not with the religious, not with the morally good, and not with those whose good works outweigh their bad. He is coming back with those who have been born again—who saw themselves as sinners in need of a Savior.

Like many Jews and Gentiles today, the teacher of Israel, Nicodemus, did not understand his need to be born again. Jesus told him in John 3:3, "Most assuredly, I say to you, unless one is born again, he cannot see the kingdom of God."

What was true then is still true now. We all need Jesus and to be born again!

DAY 263

WE ALL NEED JESUS, PART 2

On the Day of Pentecost, Peter said in Acts 2:36-39,

> "Therefore let all the house of Israel know assuredly that God has made this Jesus, whom you crucified, both Lord and Christ." Now when they heard this, they were cut to the heart, and said to Peter and the rest of the apostles, "Men and brethren, what shall we do?" Then Peter said to them, "Repent, and let every one of you be baptized in the name of Jesus Christ for the remission of sins; and you shall receive the gift of the Holy Spirit. For the promise is to you and to your children, and to all who are afar off, as many as the Lord our God will call."

Peter reminded the ultrareligious Jews that the Father sent His Son into the world as Lord and Christ, and that they needed to change their minds (repent) about who Jesus was. This implies they were in need of reconciliation with God. Peter added that this method of reconciliation would be true for "all who are afar off, as many as the Lord our God will call." That means what Peter preached then is still true today. Our sins were the reason for Jesus being hung on the cross, and repentance is required for us to be reconciled to God.

As Paul said in 1 Timothy 1:15, "Christ Jesus came into the world to save sinners, of whom I am chief." Paul, as a Jew, well understood his need for a Savior. He had persecuted the church, the bride of Christ, and in his mind, this made him the chief of all sinners. Paul had a correct and healthy perception of self, and God has been saving people who see themselves similarly. As Acts 4:12 says, "Nor is there salvation in any other, for there is no other name under heaven given among men by which we must be saved."

Jesus saves!

DAY 264

OCCUPY TILL HE COMES

In Luke 19:11-13, Jesus gave the parable of the minas, and began by saying, "A certain nobleman went into a far country to receive for himself a kingdom and to return. So he called ten of his servants, delivered to them ten minas, and said to them, 'Do business till I come.'"

This nobleman was hated by his fellow citizens, which portrays Jesus' rejection by His own people, who said, "We will not have this man to reign over us" (verse 14).

When the nobleman returned, he called those whom he had given the minas to and asked for an accounting of what they had done with them. One said he turned his mina into ten more, and the nobleman made him ruler over ten cities. Another made five minas, and the nobleman made him ruler over five cities.

The next one said, "Here is your mina, which I have kept put away in a handkerchief. For I feared you, because you are an austere man" (verses 20-21). The nobleman said, "Take his one mina and give it to the one who has ten" (see verse 24).

Jesus then concluded, "I say to you, that to everyone who has will be given; and from him who does not have, even what he has will be taken away from him" (verse 26).

Here is the point for us today: The men in the parable were given minas by someone the other citizens hated, and were told, "Do business until I come." We have the same commission to do business until the Lord comes, even though we live in a culture that says, "We do not want the God-man to be ruler over us."

God is still saving souls in the midst of this wicked and perverse generation, and He is saving them through the gospel message of the shed blood of Jesus Christ. Don't hide what you have been given—occupy and do business until the Lord comes!

DAY 265

GOD FULFILLS HIS PROMISES

In recent years, the world's attention has been drawn to Israel, and as we continue to pray for the peace of Jerusalem, we must remember that we live in prophetic times. We are seeing God's Word being played out on the world stage like no other time in history. Zechariah 12:1-3 comes to mind:

> The burden of the word of the LORD against Israel. Thus says the LORD, who stretches out the heavens, lays the foundation of the earth, and forms the spirit of man within him: "Behold, I will make Jerusalem a cup of drunkenness to all the surrounding peoples, when they lay siege against Judah and Jerusalem. And it shall happen in that day that I will make Jerusalem a very heavy stone for all peoples; all who would heave it away will surely be cut in pieces, though all nations of the earth are gathered against it."

Zechariah wrote of a day we can now see approaching. A time during which Jerusalem is the focus of all the nations, a time during which the Lord, who stretched out the heavens and laid the foundations of the earth, is going to make Jerusalem a very heavy stone for all peoples. This expression means that Jerusalem will be viewed by the world as a hindrance to the peace and security everyone longs for.

We have all heard the saying, "It is always darkest before the dawn." This truism certainly applies to the day in which we now live. The world is spiraling downward morally and spiritually, as the Bible said it would in the last days. Jerusalem has taken center stage in the geopolitical theater of the world. At the end of the darkest time in Israel's history—the seventieth week of Daniel—the dawn will break, and the Jewish people's eyes will be opened to the One "whom they pierced" (Zechariah 12:10). And they will realize that Jesus of Nazareth is indeed the Holy One of Israel, and they will mourn their grave mistake of rejecting Him.

DAY 266

YESHUA IS THE MESSIAH

In many cultures around the world, great care is given to the selection and preservation of family names. Surnames are held in high esteem by the family, and given names are carefully selected in honor of other family members or for other reasons that make a name endearing.

Yet there is one name that is exclusive in its meaning. It stands above all other names in history and even associates the owner of that name with His Father, who is known universally by the title God, which means "supreme being," whose name is Jehovah.

Acts 4:12 speaks of this exclusive name:

> Nor is there salvation in any other, for there is no other name under heaven given among men by which we must be saved.

This one name that stands alone and above all others is not simply an identifier of a single individual. Rather, it is a name that possesses power, but not in the sense of earthly names of renown like Rothschild, Rockefeller, Bezos, or Musk. This name has soul-saving power!

The name we are referring to is Yehoshua (often abbreviated as Yeshua). Joshua is the English translation of the Hebrew name, and in English, Jesus is the translation of the Greek name *Iesous* (pronounced ee-ay-soos). We find His name frequently paired with His title of Christ, meaning "anointed," thus identifying Him as the Messiah.

The fact that Acts 4:12 says His name stands alone as the name that saves and Philippians 2:10-11 says His name is the one to which every knee will bow and confess that He is Lord tells us that there is but one Savior of the world, and He is the Savior of both Jews and Gentiles, and there is and will be no other!

DAY 267

CHANGES

You may have heard people say that God loves us just as we are, but He loves us too much to leave us that way. How wonderful it is to know that there is room for all types of people in God's kingdom! A quick review of the original 12 disciples reminds us of that. Four fishermen, a tax collector, a religious zealot, and the outspoken and the cautious were among them. And yet, as eclectic as this group was, there was one point they all had in common among them: knowing Jesus changed them (Judas being the exception).

Mark 14:48-50 tells us what happened when Judas betrayed Jesus: "Jesus answered and said to them, 'Have you come out, as against a robber, with swords and clubs to take Me? I was daily with you in the temple teaching, and you did not seize Me. But the Scriptures must be fulfilled.' Then they all forsook Him and fled."

When Jesus was arrested, all the disciples forsook Him. Even after they had heard Jesus teach for three years, even after they had seen His divine power manifested countless times, and even after He told them beforehand that He was going to be betrayed and that they would forsake Him, they fled.

Peter, the most outspoken of them all, denied knowing Jesus not once, but three times. Yet on Pentecost Sunday, there was no denial by Peter but only a bold proclamation that Jesus was both Lord and Christ. What would cause a man who saw and heard so much that would prove Jesus is the Christ, the Son of the Living God, to go from someone who denied Him when the pressure was on, to someone who would proclaim Him when, potentially, his own life was at stake?

The answer is simple: the transformative power of the Holy Spirit. Peter and the others had changed dramatically when God the Holy Spirit gave them the power to be witnesses. The same is true for us when we are transformed by His presence in us.

DAY 268

WORLD EVENTS

The following passages convey to us a sense of urgency about the end times:

> You, Daniel, shut up the words, and seal the book until the time of the end; many shall run to and fro, and knowledge shall increase (Daniel 12:4).

> Let us consider one another in order to stir up love and good works, not forsaking the assembling of ourselves together, as is the manner of some, but exhorting one another, and so much the more as you see the Day approaching (Hebrews 10:24-25).

The Bible states clearly and repeatedly that there will come a point in human history when things will reach their final stage. Since the birth of the church age, the world has been marching slowly toward the last of the last days. We are told there will be a generation that will reach the proverbial "point of no return," and it appears that we are there.

That means we are near to the time when a man described as the lawless one (2 Thessalonians 2:8-9) will rise to power and rule the world. As that day approaches, we would expect to see efforts to establish a global world system, a rise in evil, and a departure from traditional Judeo-Christian values.

We have been hearing about a new world order for some time, but who knew that the key factors in advancing its cause would be climate concerns and a virus? And that the same virus would lead to stores and businesses no longer accepting cash, or that there would be a coin shortage, or that much of the world's commerce would be conducted online, moving us toward a system that can easily be used by the Antichrist to monitor global commerce? Or that the mechanism that would be used to draw the invading forces named in the Ezekiel 38 war would be a civil war in Syria?

Jesus is coming for us soon!

DAY 269

NOT OF THIS WORLD, PART 1

While we may differ on some aspects of the Christian faith, there are also matters that allow no room for debate. One of them is that we are to be nothing like the world:

> If the world hates you, you know that it hated Me before it hated you. If you were of the world, the world would love its own. Yet because you are not of the world, but I chose you out of the world, therefore the world hates you (John 15:18-19).

There are a host of other verses that make it clear that we are not of this world and should be nothing like the world and will even be hated by the world. This makes it strange that some in the church have decided that to reach the world, we need to be more like it. In recent years, we have been introduced to terms like *seeker-sensitive* and *relationship evangelism*. That's because the church has become more concerned about how unbelievers feel about the church rather than how the church treats God's Word.

There are some who say people won't get saved if the message of the church isn't more consistent with what they want to hear. The thinking is that if we offend others, we can't win them. Those who advocate this thinking say we need to remove from our facilities and services anything that seekers don't like so they will feel more comfortable in church. The truth is, if what they hear in church makes them comfortable in their sin, then they haven't heard the Word of God.

As Romans 10:17 says, "Faith comes by hearing, and hearing by the word of God." The faith in view here is saving faith—faith in Christ, the Son of the living God. This faith comes when unbelievers hear the Word of God preached, not when they attend a church that's relatable in worldly ways.

DAY 270

NOT OF THIS WORLD, PART 2

In the parable of the sower, Jesus mentioned various types of soils upon which the seeds landed. Some fell by the wayside, others on stony ground, some among thorns, and others on good soil.

> Now the parable is this: The seed is the word of God. Those by the wayside are the ones who hear; then the devil comes and takes away the word out of their hearts, lest they should believe and be saved. But the ones on the rock are those who, when they hear, receive the word with joy; and these have no root, who believe for a while and in time of temptation fall away. Now the ones that fell among thorns are those who, when they have heard, go out and are choked with cares, riches, and pleasures of life, and bring no fruit to maturity. But the ones that fell on the good ground are those who, having heard the word with a noble and good heart, keep it and bear fruit with patience (Luke 8:11-15).

There were not different seeds for different soils; the seed sown on all the soils was the Word of God. This means there were no amendments or cultural adaptations to the content of the gospel. We do not need to be more like the world to make people "want" to become a Christian.

We are not going to win unbelievers to Christ by being more like them and less like Him. We win souls for God's kingdom by telling people they are sinners, and Christ is the only Savior. He died for their sins that they might live forever with Him, and as many as received Him, He gave the right to become children of God (John 1:12).

We don't need to play secular music and look like a club to reach the world; they already have those things. We need to give them what they don't have, which is Christ and Him crucified!

DAY 271

THE SECOND COMING

We live in a world that is always changing. Some changes are for the better, and others, not so much. Today we are blessed to live in an age of advanced technology in every area from food production to communication to health care. We have also arrived at a season of history during which good is called evil and evil is called good. Biological facts are replaced with choices that conflict with the actual facts that physiology proves to be true.

It is also true that this upside-down and backward season of history is going to change. It is a wonderful time to be alive because we enjoy so many advantages that are exclusive to the modern age. We travel distances in hours that used to take months. Diseases that once almost meant certain death are kept in check by modern medicine. Information that once required days or weeks to travel around the world now moves in seconds. Yes, this is a great time to be alive! Yet this is also one of the darkest times spiritually in human history.

> Know this, that in the last days perilous times will come: For men will be lovers of themselves, lovers of money, boasters, proud, blasphemers, disobedient to parents, unthankful, unholy, unloving, unforgiving, slanderers, without self-control, brutal, despisers of good, traitors, headstrong, haughty, lovers of pleasure rather than lovers of God, having a form of godliness but denying its power. And from such people turn away! (2 Timothy 3:1-5).

While it is true that all of these characteristics have long been present in human society, the apostle Paul presents them here as the dominant traits of the last days. There is one more season of change the world will go through, and it is a time of darkness such as the world has never seen—the seventieth week of Daniel, or the tribulation. At the end of this time of God's wrath, the Light of the world will shine forth brightly at His return.

DAY 272

THE RESTRAINER

Many today are longing for, and seeking to bring about, a utopian society that they believe can be accomplished by the removal of all types of authority, moral restrictions, or boundaries. They believe that when everyone does what is right in their own eyes, the world will be as it should be—that is, as long as everyone agrees with them.

The problem with this kind of thinking is that people want everyone else to believe and do what they say is right and thus makes them "free." What they don't realize is the problem pointed out in Jeremiah 17:9: "The heart is deceitful above all things, and desperately wicked; who can know it?"

The widespread assumption is that when people are not restricted by the boundaries of religious beliefs or government authority, they will be happier, and the world will be a better place. But that is false—the exact opposite is actually true. The biggest problem with this way of thinking is that it assumes mankind is basically good when it is not.

Second Thessalonians 2:6-7 tells us the world will get worse: "Now you know what is restraining, that he may be revealed in his own time. For the mystery of lawlessness is already at work; only He who now restrains will do so until He is taken out of the way."

The word "restrain" means "to hold back," or "hinder the progress of." Today, we see evil men growing worse and worse and the love of many growing cold. The advance of evil and the loveless hearts and actions of people are being held back by the Holy Spirit working through the church. He is also hindering the rise of the Antichrist to power, who is described as "the lawless one" (2 Thessalonians 2:8).

When the lawless one comes and total disorder abounds, the end result will be the worst time ever experienced on Earth, not the best. The good news is that the church must be taken out of the way for this to happen.

DAY 273

GOD'S CONTINUED WORK THROUGH ISRAEL

In a time when people are protesting and tearing down statues and other things that represent the past, we must recognize that unfortunately, there have been some in the church who have been doing something similar for almost 2,000 years.

While the chapter and verse divisions of the Bible were not part of the original writings, there is a point we can make from them. There are 1,189 chapters in the Bible—929 in the Old Testament and 260 in the New. Of the 929 chapters of the Old Testament, 918 are in reference to the nation of Israel. Genesis 1–11 records the creation narrative and limited information about the first 2,000 years of human history. Beginning in Genesis 12, the Old Testament deals, in one way or another, with Abraham's descendants through Isaac and Jacob, whose name was changed to Israel.

Then Romans 11:17-18 confirms God's continued work through Israel from the New Testament era onward: "If some of the branches were broken off, and you, being a wild olive tree, were grafted in among them, and with them became a partaker of the root and fatness of the olive tree, do not boast against the branches. But if you do boast, remember that you do not support the root, but the root supports you."

Here, Paul reminded the Gentiles that the gospel came to the Jew first through the King of the Jews, Jesus. The fact that the majority of Israel rejected their Messiah, which opened the door for the grafting in of the Gentiles, does not mean the grafted-in branches should boast against their roots.

To say the church has replaced Israel, or Christians should "unhitch themselves" from the Old Testament, or modern Israel is not the Israel of the Bible is like toppling statues of figures from a nation's history, or the branches boasting against the roots. The past may not always be pretty, but denying it won't make it go away, and ignoring it can rob us of valuable lessons.

DAY 274

THE GREAT SEPARATION

In John 14:1-4, Jesus said,

> Let not your heart be troubled; you believe in God, believe also in Me. In My Father's house are many mansions; if it were not so, I would have told you. I go to prepare a place for you. And if I go and prepare a place for you, I will come again and receive you to Myself; that where I am, there you may be also. And where I go you know, and the way you know.

To this, Thomas replied, "Lord, we do not know where You are going, and how can we know the way?" Then Jesus said to Thomas, "I am the way, the truth, and the life. No one comes to the Father except through Me" (verses 5-6).

The way to the Father's house is exclusively through Jesus. Only through Jesus can we be separated from our former selves (sanctified). Only through Jesus can we be filled with the Holy Spirit, which guarantees we have a future inheritance in heaven (Ephesians 1:13-14). And only through Jesus can we be spared the second death. It is also only through Jesus that we can be separated from this world and supernaturally transported to His Father's house in the twinkling of an eye.

Every believer who ever lived will see the heavenly scene described in Revelation 4, and all will confess that Jesus Christ is Lord. Those who say, "Woe is me; I am a sinner" in this life will say, "Wow, I'm home!" when they arrive in heaven. Those who don't say, "Woe is me; I am a sinner" now will say "Woe is me" when they stand before the Lord at the Great White Throne judgment.

This is the great separation that will last forever. Those who say Jesus is Lord in this life will be with Him forever; those who say Jesus is Lord at the Great White Throne will never see Him again.

DAY 275

THE TWO WITNESSES

Humans are naturally curious. In past history, there were those who wanted to know what was on the other side of a mountain, or how wide an ocean was. Some ventured into the unknown simply to find out what they didn't know. Much of what we enjoy today is because someone wondered whether there was a better way to do something, or if something was possible at all.

This natural curiosity often spills over into our spiritual lives as well. We want to know more than what we are told in Scripture, which leads some to speculate beyond what is written. That isn't necessarily bad or wrong, but it needs to be done with great caution. One passage many wonder about is Revelation 11:3-6:

> "I will give power to my two witnesses, and they will prophesy one thousand two hundred and sixty days, clothed in sackcloth." These are the two olive trees and the two lampstands standing before the God of the earth. And if anyone wants to harm them, fire proceeds from their mouth and devours their enemies. And if anyone wants to harm them, he must be killed in this manner. These have power to shut heaven, so that no rain falls in the days of their prophecy; and they have power over waters to turn them to blood, and to strike the earth with all plagues, as often as they desire.

These men will have divine power similar to that of Elijah, and James 5:17 tells us that Elijah was just like us. Does that mean we can turn water into blood and strike the earth with plagues whenever we want? No, we are told these powers will be specific to the duration of the two witnesses' ministry.

The power to be witnesses is another matter. We have been promised this power along with supernatural protection for the duration of our ministry here on Earth. We don't know who the two witnesses will be. But we do know what witnesses do—they give testimony of Jesus.

DAY 276

A RENEWED MIND

While there are a myriad of things we can be thankful for that are the direct result of being saved, at the top of the list has to be this:

> You, who once were alienated and enemies in your mind by wicked works, yet now He has reconciled in the body of His flesh through death, to present you holy, and blameless, and above reproach in His sight (Colossians 1:21-22).

We've gone from being enemies of God to being holy, blameless, and above reproach in His eyes because of the suffering, death, and resurrection of Jesus, who has reconciled us to the Father, making us no longer alienated from Him by our sins.

Paul pairs our thoughts and actions as alienated enemies when he links the mind with wicked works. This reminds us that repentance is not only a change of mind, but a change of behavior that reflects a change of mind. As Romans 12:2 says, "Do not be conformed to this world, but be transformed by the renewing of your mind, that you may prove what is that good and acceptable and perfect will of God."

We are not to conform to the things the world readily embraces, and we should not allow the culture to define our morals and character. Nor should we abandon the truth in deference to people's desires. Living this way means the world won't love us, but will hate us all the more for our nonconformity.

We need to remember this is nothing new. It is not abnormal for the transformed, renewed, and reconciled saints to be hated. Remember what Matthew 5:11-12 says: "Blessed are you when they revile and persecute you, and say all kinds of evil against you falsely for My sake. Rejoice and be exceedingly glad, for great is your reward in heaven, for so they persecuted the prophets who were before you."

DAY 277

THE FATHER'S LOVE

There are many wonderful lessons to be gleaned from the story of the prodigal son, and to fully understand this parable, we need to observe how Jesus began this account: "All the tax collectors and the sinners drew near to Him to hear Him. And the Pharisees and scribes complained, saying, 'This Man receives sinners and eats with them'" (Luke 15:1-2).

Jesus then answered the complaint of the self-righteous leaders by pointing out that if one of them had lost a sheep, they would go looking for it and rejoice when it was found. He then told the parable of a woman with ten coins. When she lost one, she searched for it until she found it, then rejoiced because it had been recovered.

Finally, Jesus moved on to the story of the prodigal son, who demanded his inheritance before the customary and culturally acceptable time, which would be when his father died or was no longer able to oversee the family fortune. The father, being a man of grace, gave his son what he demanded.

The son then wasted his father's money on riotous living. Because the speaker (Jesus) was a Jew, and because the scribes and Pharisees were Jews, the father and son in the story would have been Jews as well. And for a Jew to end up feeding pigs would be to say a person had sunk as low as he could possibly go.

The great principle in the parable of the prodigal son is that the kindness the father showed to the wayward son is like the kindness God will show to wayward Israel. Though the people of Israel had sunk as low as they could go when they rejected Jesus, someday, when they look upon the One whom they pierced and mourn for Him as one mourns for an only Son (Zechariah 12:10), they will be received by God in the same way the father received his prodigal son.

DAY 278

JESUS IS COMING WITH THE SAINTS

In 1 Corinthians 15:51-53, Paul wrote this wonderful announcement:

> Behold, I tell you a mystery: We shall not all sleep, but we shall all be changed—in a moment, in the twinkling of an eye, at the last trumpet. For the trumpet will sound, and the dead will be raised incorruptible, and we shall be changed. For this corruptible must put on incorruption, and this mortal must put on immortality.

When Jesus comes again to receive us, we will be changed into immortal, incorrupt beings, but that's not all the good news. There's also this: "Our citizenship is in heaven, from which we also eagerly wait for the Savior, the Lord Jesus Christ, who will transform our lowly body that it may be conformed to His glorious body, according to the working by which He is able even to subdue all things to Himself" (Philippians 3:20-21).

Jesus coming back for us is great news! Putting on immortal incorruptibility and being given glorified bodies is amazing. But there's still more:

> Now I saw heaven opened, and behold, a white horse. And He who sat on him was called Faithful and True, and in righteousness He judges and makes war. His eyes were like a flame of fire, and on His head were many crowns. He had a name written that no one knew except Himself. He was clothed with a robe dipped in blood, and His name is called The Word of God. And the armies in heaven, clothed in fine linen, white and clean, followed Him on white horses (Revelation 19:11-14).

Someday when Jesus returns to take possession of the earth, we will come with Him to rule and reign as kings and priests for 1,000 years. And after that, we will dwell in the new heaven and the new earth forever and ever. Amen!

DAY 279

FULFILL YOUR MINISTRY

Paul wrote this powerful admonishment in 2 Timothy 4:1-5:

> I charge you therefore before God and the Lord Jesus Christ, who will judge the living and the dead at His appearing and His kingdom: Preach the word! Be ready in season and out of season. Convince, rebuke, exhort, with all longsuffering and teaching. For the time will come when they will not endure sound doctrine, but according to their own desires, because they have itching ears, they will heap up for themselves teachers; and they will turn their ears away from the truth, and be turned aside to fables. But you be watchful in all things, endure afflictions, do the work of an evangelist, fulfill your ministry.

The apostle warned that a time will come when the church will turn away from the truth and prefer fables and myths cloaked in spiritual-sounding terms. The heaping up of such teachers tells us this will be the dominant trend in the church of the last days.

We have people in the church today who say they are apostles and are not. There are those who say God's will is health and wealth for all Christians. And there are those who say that because we are saved by grace, there is no need for us to concern ourselves with moral standards. And there are still others who believe God has "cast off" Israel. They say Israel no longer has a place in God's redemptive plan.

We live in a day that, when we fulfill our ministry and take a stand for the sound doctrines of God's Word, we will experience afflictions and hardships that are specific to the last days. Yet no matter what others are doing, and what they say to or about us, we must preach the gospel and hold fast to sound doctrine.

Why? Only biblical truth can set people free.

DAY 280

THE RAPTURE VERSUS THE SECOND COMING, PART 1

Among the many elements Peter described about the last days, he mentioned one in particular that is clearly present with us today—that is, the presence of scoffers: "Knowing this first: that scoffers will come in the last days, walking according to their own lusts, and saying, 'Where is the promise of His coming? For since the fathers fell asleep, all things continue as they were from the beginning of creation'" (2 Peter 3:3-4).

In the last days, people will deny the second coming of Jesus, which is clearly stated in Scripture (Zechariah 14:4; Revelation 19:11-16). Their argument and justification for doing this will be, "Jesus has been gone a long time, and we've been hearing about His return since the church fathers died. But nothing has happened."

The rapture-deniers of our day employ the same practice as those who deny the second coming. They ignore what is clearly stated in Scripture by claiming that neither Jesus nor Paul believed in or taught the rapture of the church. But note what Jesus and Paul said:

> Let not your heart be troubled; you believe in God, believe also in Me. In My Father's house are many mansions; if it were not so, I would have told you. I go to prepare a place for you. And if I go and prepare a place for you, I will come again and receive you to Myself; that where I am, there you may be also (John 14:1-3).

> The Lord Himself will descend from heaven with a shout, with the voice of an archangel, and with the trumpet of God. And the dead in Christ will rise first. Then we who are alive and remain shall be caught up together with them in the clouds to meet the Lord in the air (1 Thessalonians 4:16-17).

If there is no rapture, then what were Jesus and Paul referring to? Not the second coming, because we will already be with Jesus when He returns (Revelation 19:14).

DAY 281

THE RAPTURE VERSUS THE SECOND COMING, PART 2

Speaking about the rapture, Paul wrote, "We who are alive and remain shall be caught up together with them in the clouds to meet the Lord in the air. And thus we shall always be with the Lord. Therefore comfort one another with these words" (1 Thessalonians 4:17-18).

And in John 14:1-3, Jesus said He would come again to "receive" to Himself those who believe in Him that they may be where He is. Like many words in the English language, the Greek word translated "receive" can have multiple meanings. It can mean "to associate with" or "to receive near." However, in the context of what Jesus said, the word can be rightfully translated "to take up." Jesus said He is coming again to "take up" believers to where He is.

Revelation 19:14 identifies those who return with Jesus by their apparel, fine linen that is "white and clean." John 14:1-3 cannot be referring to the second coming, which is described in Revelation 19:11-16, when the saints of God will come down to Earth with Jesus, which requires that they first be taken up to be with Him where He is.

The argument of the rapture-deniers today is that belief in the rapture gives people a false hope and leaves them unprepared for the tribulation. But note this promise in Revelation 3:10: "Because you have kept My command to persevere, I also will keep you from the hour of trial which shall come upon the whole world, to test those who dwell on the earth."

To claim there is no rapture and that we need to prepare for the tribulation is not very comforting, and it is not biblical. Jesus is coming to "take up" His church to where He is, and then He is coming with His church to judge the earth and rule and reign in righteousness for 1,000 years.

The rapture is clearly taught in Scripture, as is the second coming. They are distinct from one another, but equally comforting to consider.

DAY 282

ISRAEL, CHOSEN OF GOD

We live at a time during which Bible prophecy is either being fulfilled or moving rapidly toward fulfillment as in no other point in church history. Wars and rumors of wars abound, famine is wreaking its havoc everywhere, people who falsely claim to be the anointed of Christ are all around us, plagues are sweeping the globe, and earthquakes are increasing in frequency and intensity.

Nowhere is the advance of the prophetic narrative more clear than with regard to the regathering of God's chosen people from around the world.

> Say to the house of Israel, "Thus says the Lord GOD: 'I do not do this for your sake, O house of Israel, but for My holy name's sake, which you have profaned among the nations wherever you went. And I will sanctify My great name, which has been profaned among the nations, which you have profaned in their midst; and the nations shall know that I am the LORD,' says the Lord GOD, 'when I am hallowed in you before their eyes. For I will take you from among the nations, gather you out of all countries, and bring you into your own land'" (Ezekiel 36:22-24).

We have been watching the fulfillment of this with our own eyes. God is bringing His chosen people back into their land just as He prophesied. Yet there are many in the church who say, "Modern Israel is not biblical Israel." Or they refer to the people of Israel as occupiers instead of rightful inhabitants. This is a rejection of sound doctrine. God clearly stated that every day His people were outside of the land given to them by everlasting covenant, His name was being profaned—even though it was He who scattered them among the nations because of their idolatry.

The Lord said it was for His name's sake that He would bring the Jews back into their own land—so that all the nations would know that He is the Lord!

DAY 283

THE POWER OF HOPE

As the world moves in the direction of the reign of the Antichrist and the global order he will establish during the tribulation, it is good to know that while we will see and experience the movement in that direction, we will not be here for the great tribulation and his reign of terror.

In light of the fact that troublesome and dangerous times are upon us, it is important that we remember that Jesus has overcome the world, and that we are in Him. Romans 12:21 says, "Do not be overcome by evil, but overcome evil with good."

The word "overcome" is from the Greek word *nikao*, which means to "subdue," "prevail," or even "get the victory." So when perilous times come, we can "get the victory" by not allowing those times to subdue us emotionally or spiritually.

Hebrews 6:19-20 says, "This hope we have as an anchor of the soul, both sure and steadfast, and which enters the Presence behind the veil, where the forerunner has entered for us, even Jesus, having become High Priest forever according to the order of Melchizedek."

Here, hope is described as an anchor of the soul because the object of our hope is Jesus Christ. That is why this hope can "get the victory" over despair and discouragement and even hopelessness. Titus 2:13 says we are "looking for the blessed hope and glorious appearing of our great God and Savior Jesus Christ."

This world is not our home. Our bodies are temporary. Sickness, pain, and sorrow will someday come to an end. For us, everything will change in the twinkling of an eye. This is our blessed hope. This hope has, as its foundation, the One whom we have trusted to save us and who promised to never leave nor forsake us. Such hope is powerful, and it is available to all!

DAY 284

FIGHT THE GOOD FIGHT

It has been said, "If you don't believe there is a devil, just try opposing him for a while." The Bible makes it clear there is a devil and that he is our adversary (1 Peter 5:8), and that his desire is to destroy us (John 10:10). He doesn't fight fairly, he is merciless in his efforts, and he seeks to exploit our weaknesses and play on our emotions. As 2 Corinthians 10:3-5 says,

> Though we walk in the flesh, we do not war according to the flesh. For the weapons of our warfare are not carnal but mighty in God for pulling down strongholds, casting down arguments and every high thing that exalts itself against the knowledge of God, bringing every thought into captivity to the obedience of Christ.

The weapons Paul describes give us some insight into the enemy's weaponry. The word "arguments" means "reasoning," and in this context, it means "reasoning that is hostile to the Christian faith." This was the tactic Satan employed against Eve. He reasoned that what God had said was unfair and untrue.

Paul's good fight of faith included employing the weapons of our warfare, and we should do the same. When Satan says, "God doesn't care," take that thought captive because the cross proves otherwise. When Satan says, "Go ahead and disobey; you will not surely die," remember that he is the father of lies and a murderer (John 8:44). His only desire is to destroy your effectiveness because he knows he cannot have your soul.

There is a devil, and he is evil. He has demonic beings at his disposal to harass and harm you. But he is no match for God, and the same Spirit who raised Christ from the dead lives in you! (Romans 8:11). Nothing can separate you from the love of God, and no one can snatch you from His hand (Romans 8:35; John 10:29).

DAY 285

JESUS IS COMING AGAIN, PART 1

While there are many direct and implied references to the two comings of Jesus to the earth, one of the most significant proofs of His two comings is what *didn't* happen the first time He came: "I will declare the decree: The LORD has said to Me, 'You are My Son, today I have begotten You. Ask of Me, and I will give You the nations for Your inheritance, and the ends of the earth for Your possession. You shall break them with a rod of iron; You shall dash them to pieces like a potter's vessel'" (Psalm 2:7-9).

When Jesus came in human flesh as "the only begotten of the Father, full of grace and truth" (John 1:14), He did not rule the nations with a rod of iron and dash to pieces those who plotted against Him. Nor did He hold them in derision or speak to them with wrath and deep displeasure.

That leaves only two options: The Bible is inaccurate (which is a frightening and untrue thought), or Jesus is coming to the earth again. The latter is not only the better option, it is a biblical fact.

We can also see the distinctions between the two comings based on what Jesus rides. Zechariah 9:9 says this about His first coming: "Rejoice greatly, O daughter of Zion! Shout, O daughter of Jerusalem! Behold, your King is coming to you; He is just and having salvation, lowly and riding on a donkey, a colt, the foal of a donkey."

Jesus rode a donkey for two reasons: first, to fulfill Zechariah 9:9; and second, in the ancient world, a leader rode on a donkey to signify he had come in peace. Jesus making His triumphal entry while riding a lowly animal signified that He came to bring peace between God and man. But at His second coming, He will arrive on a white horse to conquer His enemies (Revelation 19:11).

DAY 286

JESUS IS COMING AGAIN, PART 2

The fact Jesus didn't fulfill everything prophesied about Himself at His first coming clearly indicates He will come again. However, at His second coming, He will arrive not as a lamb, but as the Lion of the tribe of Judah.

> Now I saw heaven opened, and behold, a white horse. And He who sat on him was called Faithful and True, and in righteousness He judges and makes war. His eyes were like a flame of fire, and on His head were many crowns. He had a name written that no one knew except Himself. He was clothed with a robe dipped in blood, and His name is called The Word of God. And the armies in heaven, clothed in fine linen, white and clean, followed Him on white horses. Now out of His mouth goes a sharp sword, that with it He should strike the nations. And He Himself will rule them with a rod of iron. He Himself treads the winepress of the fierceness and wrath of Almighty God. And He has on His robe and on His thigh a name written: KING OF KINGS AND LORD OF LORDS (Revelation 19:11-16).

There is but one person in the Bible who is referred to as "The Word of God," whose name is unlike any others. Jesus! He is King of kings and Lord of lords. In ancient times, when warriors went into battle, they would wear the crest of their kingdom on their chest and their thigh so that when they fought in close quarters, they could identify friends from foes.

Some may find the language in Revelation 19 strong and aggressive, and prefer Jesus with a lamb around His neck or a child on His lap. But at His second coming, He will bring peace to the earth, and that will be possible only through the defeat of those who rage and plot against Him.

DAY 287

DID GOD ABANDON ISRAEL?

It is a sad reality that so many people miss the prophetic significance of the rebirth of the nation of Israel by denying that modern Israel is biblical Israel. It is also unfortunate that the doctrinal significance of Israel's rebirth is lost on many as well.

Psalm 94:14 tells us, "The LORD will not cast off His people, nor will He forsake His inheritance." Romans 11:1 says, "Has God cast away His people? Certainly not! For I also am an Israelite, of the seed of Abraham, of the tribe of Benjamin."

In the latter passage, Paul was asking, "If God is done with the Jews, then why did He save me?" After all, Paul was a Jew, a descendant of Abraham through Isaac and of the tribe of Benjamin. His answer to his own question was, "Certainly not!," and he offered himself as proof.

It is a mystery that there are some who conclude that the Lord has cast off Israel, His chosen people by birth, but He will not cast off the church, His chosen people by faith. Not only does that not make sense, it also contradicts what Scripture tells us about God's choosing of both groups as His own special people. If a Christian is going to learn anything from the nation of Israel, it should be that God is faithful and does not cast off His people even though He disciplines those whom He loves (Hebrews 12:6).

Some like to argue that God cast off the people of Israel for killing their Messiah, while others argue that it was the Romans who killed Jesus. It's true that the leading Jews arrested and convicted Jesus. It is also true that it was Roman soldiers who beat Him and nailed Him to a cross. But the actual truth is that the One who sent Jesus to the cross was His Father.

Why? "God so loved the world that He gave His only begotten Son, that whoever believes in Him should not perish but have everlasting life" (John 3:16).

DAY 288

THE SOUND OF A TRUMPET

Most of us have spent time pondering what heaven will be like. We read of scenes like those recorded in the book of Revelation, and our minds try to create visuals to accompany the words we read, such as those in Revelation 4:1-3:

> After these things I looked, and behold, a door standing open in heaven. And the first voice which I heard was like a trumpet speaking with me, saying, "Come up here, and I will show you things which must take place after this." Immediately I was in the Spirit; and behold, a throne set in heaven, and One sat on the throne. And He who sat there was like a jasper and a sardius stone in appearance; and there was a rainbow around the throne, in appearance like an emerald.

John then describes elders with golden crowns, living creatures repeating a glorious mantra, lightnings and thunderings and voices, and seven lamps before the One who sits on the throne (verses 4-5).

Someday, we are going to be eyewitnesses to this incredible scene! Jesus made it clear that no one knows the day or the hour. We do need to note, however, that John said, "After these things" (Revelation 4:1). This points back to the church age recorded in Revelation 2–3. At the end of the church age, John saw a door opened in heaven and heard a voice "like a trumpet" telling him, "Come up here, and I will show you things which must take place after this."

Just as our minds are filled with images of the scene we read earlier, so too should we rightly imagine an archangel with the trumpet of God pressed to his lips, waiting for the signal from the One on the throne to sound the trumpet and call us to rise up in the air with the dead in Christ so we can all meet Him. We don't know when the Lord will give that order, but we do know it will surely come to pass. Perhaps today!

DAY 289

TURNING THE WORLD UPSIDE DOWN

We hear a lot about change today. There are people who we call world-changers. There are events and moments in life some would call game-changers. There are even song lyrics asking whether we want to bring about change. As Christians, we have those we would put in the category of world-changers, and some of these people were even viewed by unbelievers as such.

When Paul and Silas arrived in Thessaloniki, an angry mob told the rulers of the city, "These who have turned the world upside down have come here too" (Acts 17:6). Peter and the other apostles had similar accusations leveled at them:

> When they had brought them, they set them before the council. And the high priest asked them, saying, "Did we not strictly command you not to teach in this name? And look, you have filled Jerusalem with your doctrine, and intend to bring this Man's blood on us!" But Peter and the other apostles answered and said: "We ought to obey God rather than men" (Acts 5:27-29).

We read of boldness like this and think, *I want to be like that*. The truth is that you are! Peter was a three-time Christ-denier, and by the power of the Holy Spirit, he became one of the boldest preachers in history. Paul was an enemy of the church—he was anti-Christ, meaning he was against Christ. Yet when Paul met Jesus on the road to Damascus and found out he was persecuting the Lord Himself, he asked, "Lord, what do You want me to do?" (Acts 9:6).

The Lord said to him, "Arise and go into the city, and you will be told what you must do."

This is the question we should ask in prayer every day: "Lord, what can I do to turn my world upside down?"

DAY 290

OUR GOD IS AN AWESOME GOD

What a great and awesome God we serve! He creates galaxies by the billions out of nothing. He commands there to be light, and there is. He sets boundaries for the seas, and they obey. He says to the blind, lame, and diseased, "Be healed," and they are. He proclaims to the captives be free, and they are released. He says to an uninhabited and unfruitful land that it will be fruitful and filled with His people, and it is. What a mighty God we serve!

In Psalm 8:3-9, King David wrote,

> When I consider Your heavens, the work of Your fingers, the moon and the stars, which You have ordained, what is man that You are mindful of him, and the son of man that You visit him? For You have made him a little lower than the angels, and You have crowned him with glory and honor. You have made him to have dominion over the works of Your hands; You have put all things under his feet, all sheep and oxen—even the beasts of the field, the birds of the air, and the fish of the sea that pass through the paths of the seas. O Lord, our Lord, how excellent is Your name in all the earth!

David reminds us of so many wonderful things here that we would all do well to remember. A quick glance to the heavens reminds us of the greatness of our God, who has placed into the hands of mankind all that He has created on Earth. David is amazed that in the midst of such a vast creation, God is mindful of man.

The mindfulness of God over man is nowhere more evident than in His love and faithfulness toward Israel. The people were scattered among the nations for centuries for their national rejection of the Messiah, yet they were promised a return to their homeland, which is now flourishing again under the blessings of God.

DAY 291

SATAN WORSHIP

Of the many things the Bible tells us will move in a birth pang-like progression toward their ultimate fulfillment during the tribulation, one of the hardest for us to fathom is the spread of Satan worship. Revelation 13:4 tells us what people will do: "They worshiped the dragon who gave authority to the beast; and they worshiped the beast, saying, 'Who is like the beast? Who is able to make war with him?'"

The Greek word translated "worship" is interesting—it literally means "to kiss the hand." This refers to paying homage or to holding one in reverence. It can also mean "to prostrate and submit."

Earlier, in Revelation 12:9, we read, "The great dragon was cast out, that serpent of old, called the Devil and Satan, who deceives the whole world; he was cast to the earth, and his angels were cast out with him."

The Holy Spirit, through John the beloved, makes it clear who the dragon is. During the tribulation, people will prostrate themselves before and submit to Satan. We also need to recognize what Satan worship is not. On fictional TV shows, we often see it portrayed as a group of black-robed people standing in a circle and chanting while a human sacrifice is strapped to a table awaiting death via a knife about to be plunged into their chest.

But Satan worship is exactly that: worship. It is to prostrate one's self and pay homage to the devil and kneel before him. It is Satan who wants us to buy into the TV version of Satan worshippers. In reality, Satan worship occurs when people submit to Satan's will. What does Satan's will include? Getting people to agree with abortion, gender fluidity, questioning God's Word, and denying that God is the creator of all things.

Satan worship is widely practiced today in ways we often don't recognize—all in preparation for the coming of the lawless one. All of this tells us that Jesus is coming soon!

DAY 292

SHADOWS OR SUBSTANCE

You may have heard the saying that Christianity is a relationship, not a religion. And you may have heard that religion is man's attempt to reach God, whereas Christ is God reaching out to man. Both sentiments are true and wonderful as stated. But some have taken the relationship aspect of Christianity and turned it into a religion. They have a relationship with Christianity rather than with Christ. They speak Christianese, have Christian decals on their cars, and wear crosses around their necks. Everything about them looks Christian, but it's all outward.

In Matthew 7:21-23, Jesus said,

> Not everyone who says to Me, "Lord, Lord," shall enter the kingdom of heaven, but he who does the will of My Father in heaven. Many will say to Me in that day, "Lord, Lord, have we not prophesied in Your name, cast out demons in Your name, and done many wonders in Your name?" And then I will declare to them, "I never knew you; depart from Me, you who practice lawlessness!"

The group Jesus addressed had a lot of spiritual activity in their lives. They called Him Lord and did wonders in His name, yet Jesus said to them, "I never knew you; depart from Me." Their relationship was not with Him but with activities associated with Him.

At the Last Supper, when Jesus told the Twelve that one of them would betray Him, they didn't all say in unison, "It's Judas; he couldn't do any miracles when You sent us out!" Rather, they didn't know who it was. All 12—including lawless Judas—had cast out demons and healed the sick. Remember also that Jesus said He chose the Twelve and that "one of you is a devil" (John 6:70). He didn't say one was once saved and became a devil.

Judas had a relationship with those who had relationships with Jesus. Make sure the substance of your relationship is with Christ, and not just shadows, or religious activities.

DAY 293

PRO-CHOICE

The Bible constantly reminds us of the importance of the choices we make in life. In his farewell address, Joshua, the great field general who led God's people into the land of promise after Moses made a poor choice and forfeited that privilege (Numbers 20:11), made this famous statement about choice:

> If it seems evil to you to serve the LORD, choose for yourselves this day whom you will serve, whether the gods which your fathers served that were on the other side of the River, or the gods of the Amorites, in whose land you dwell. But as for me and my house, we will serve the LORD (Joshua 24:15).

Every day, we choose to either serve the Lord, ourselves, or the idols of this world. And we, like Joshua, should choose each day to serve the Lord. Joshua's famous statement lends itself to addressing one of the big questions often debated in the church about how one comes to faith in Christ: Is it by their own free-will choice, or does God—in His sovereignty—make that choice?

Joshua said to Israel, "Choose to serve the Lord or false gods." The Lord commanded through Moses, in Deuteronomy 30:15-18, that the people love Him and walk in His ways by keeping His commandments, statutes, and judgments. But if their hearts turned away and they worshipped other gods, they would perish, and He would not prolong their days in the land. God's chosen people, whom He elected in His sovereign will, still had to choose to love and serve Him of their own free will.

Choices are important! We make them every day, including whether or not the Lord is first and above all else. Choose a life of serving the Lord, and you will know blessing. Choose false gods and idols or your efforts and desires, and you will know not blessings, but curses.

DAY 294

GOD HAS NOT FORGOTTEN HIS PEOPLE

One of the great truths of the Bible is that the church is the church and Israel is Israel. Each group has specific promises and practices that were given to them by God. Yet they also share certain things in common. They are both God's chosen people—the Jews by birth, and Christians by faith. They both have a common Father, Savior, and Holy Spirit, and there is only one way that Jews and Gentiles can enter into God's kingdom—through the Holy One of Israel, Jesus of Nazareth, the head of the church. Consider as well these promises:

> Be strong and of good courage, do not fear nor be afraid of them; for the LORD your God, He is the One who goes with you. He will not leave you nor forsake you (Deuteronomy 31:6).

> Let your conduct be without covetousness; be content with such things as you have. For He Himself has said, "I will never leave you nor forsake you." So we may boldly say: "The Lord is my helper; I will not fear. What can man do to me?" (Hebrews 13:5-6).

The Lord told the people of Israel He would never leave nor forsake them, and He gave the same promise to the church. That tells us that while Israel and the church are distinct from one another, all the truths that the Bible declares about God's faithfulness and unchanging nature are true for His chosen people by birth and His chosen people by faith.

The Lord has not cast away His people the Jews, nor will He cast away His predominantly Gentile church. If He told the people of Israel that He would never leave them nor forsake them and they are back in the land, then those who are in the church can have the same confidence that God will be faithful to them. As 2 Timothy 2:13 says, "If we are faithless, He remains faithful; He cannot deny Himself."

DAY 295

THE WORD OF TRUTH

The Bible clearly states that mankind has had an adversary ever since there were only two people on the earth. He is called Satan, the dragon, the father of all lies, the wicked one, the destroyer, and on and on goes the list of titles that refer to his utter wickedness.

In John 10:10, Jesus said, "The thief does not come except to steal, and to kill, and to destroy. I have come that they may have life, and that they may have it more abundantly." Here, Satan is referred to as "the thief" by Jesus Himself. Satan's goal? To steal, kill, and destroy. This tells us that his efforts and tactics lead only to death and destruction.

Satan wants the lost to question God's existence and His role as creator, and therefore, His authority over creation. In the garden of Eden, distraction was the tactic Satan used on Eve.

> Now the serpent was more cunning than any beast of the field which the Lord God had made. And he said to the woman, "Has God indeed said, 'You shall not eat of every tree of the garden'?" And the woman said to the serpent, "We may eat the fruit of the trees of the garden; but of the fruit of the tree which is in the midst of the garden, God has said, 'You shall not eat it, nor shall you touch it, lest you die.'" Then the serpent said to the woman, "You will not surely die. For God knows that in the day you eat of it your eyes will be opened, and you will be like God, knowing good and evil" (Genesis 3:1-5).

Satan was trying to distract Eve from the absolute authority of the word of God by implying it was not exactly true. Many people today say, "The Bible *contains* the words of God," which is what Satan did with Eve. But the Bible *is* the Word of God, and *every* word of it is true!

DAY 296

TODY IS THE DAY OF SALVATION

Here we are today, millennia later, and Satan is still deceiving people through the same tactic he used against Eve. His strategy is described by the familiar adage, "If it ain't broke, don't fix it."

This is the thief's strategy toward the lost. He distracts them from believing God's Word is true by suggesting that God has not been completely honest with them about what His words mean, and that His behavior is not consistent with His words. "How could a God of love allow this?" is how Satan often packages his lies. This has been effective ever since the garden.

What about those who are of the faith—those who believe God is a rewarder of those who diligently seek Him? (Hebrews 11:6). Can Satan steal, kill, and destroy their souls? No!

> I am persuaded that neither death nor life, nor angels nor principalities nor powers, nor things present nor things to come, nor height nor depth, nor any other created thing, shall be able to separate us from the love of God which is in Christ Jesus our Lord (Romans 8:38-39).

No, Satan cannot have your soul if you are born again! His efforts can, however, have an impact on you if you listen to him instead of resisting and being steadfast in the faith (1 Peter 5:9).

If you are reading this and you have not yet been born again, and you have been entangled by the tactics of the enemy, today is the day to become free! Acts 3:19 says, "Repent therefore and be converted, that your sins may be blotted out, so that times of refreshing may come from the presence of the Lord."

There is no better way to live than forgiven, with your sins forgotten and the promise of reward in heaven awaiting you because of your faith and trust in God! If you haven't yet experienced this, you can today. It's only a prayer away, and it's very refreshing.

DAY 297

THE GENERATION THAT WILL NOT PASS

The Bible is filled with figurative language, including wonderful idioms, illustrations, and symbols. They all share the same purpose—to make a comparison between a literal biblical truth or reality and something commonly used or known. When we read an idiom or figurative words in Scripture, we need to recognize that something literal is being communicated. For example:

> Now learn this parable from the fig tree: When its branch has already become tender and puts forth leaves, you know that summer is near. So you also, when you see all these things, know that it is near— at the doors! Assuredly, I say to you, this generation will by no means pass away till all these things take place (Matthew 24:32-34).

Not every use of the phrase *fig tree* is an idiom in Scripture—sometimes it simply refers to a literal fig tree. This is why context is so important when we attempt to interpret a passage. Shortly before Jesus' statement about a fig tree in Matthew 24, we read about an encounter Jesus and the Twelve had with a literal fig tree (Matthew 21:18-22). Yet Jeremiah 8:13, Hosea 9:10, and Joel 1:6-7 all set a precedent by using the fig tree to represent national Israel.

In Matthew 24, Peter, Andrew, James, and John asked Jesus about the last days and the signs of His coming. Jesus answered and described what would happen before and during the tribulation. And the fig tree Jesus and the disciples encountered in Matthew 21 was representative of fruitless Israel and the people's national rejection of their Messiah.

The literal meaning of the idiom in Matthew 24:32-34 is this: When Israel becomes a nation again and the land starts to flourish, know that the tribulation is near, even at the door. The generation that sees the rebirth of the nation of Israel will be the generation during which all the events of the Olivet Discourse will be fulfilled.

THE BLOOD OF CHRIST

In a time when expository Bible teaching is growing rarer—*expository* meaning "to explain or describe"—one of the many casualties is a clear understanding of basic biblical doctrines and precepts. One prime example is clarity about the positional and practical sides of salvation.

Second Corinthians 5:17 speaks about the positional side: "If anyone is in Christ, he is a new creation; old things have passed away; behold, all things have become new." Being "in Christ" is a positional truth. Because of our position "in Him," old things have passed away and all things have become new. Our sin record has been purged, and we—through Christ's body and shed blood—have been reconciled to God and have become "accepted in the Beloved" (Ephesians 1:6).

As new creations in Christ, God knows our every misstep and failure, our every feeling of doubt and despair. And yet, because we are in Christ, we cannot be snatched from His hand or separated from His love. These are wonderful positional truths.

When God looks at you and me, He does so through the blood of Jesus. As new creations in Him, we are washed and cleansed from all unrighteousness. When others look at us, they, too, should see us through the blood of Jesus—not positionally, as the Father sees us, but practically, in all that we think, say, and do.

As Galatians 2:20 says, "I have been crucified with Christ; it is no longer I who live, but Christ lives in me; and the life which I now live in the flesh I live by faith in the Son of God, who loved me and gave Himself for me."

"Crucified with Christ" is positional. Living out Christ by faith in the Son of God is practical. What is our motivation for living by faith in the Son of God? Paul's answer is at the end of that magnificent verse: The Son of God "loves me and gave Himself for me."

DAY 299

MODERN-DAY APOSTLES

We live in an age in which there is an overabundance of claimants to the office of apostle or prophet. Some of them gain huge followings in spite of the fact the Bible makes no mention of such individuals rising up in the last days. Jesus even warned of those who use His name to validate their ministries:

> To the angel of the church of Ephesus write, "These things says He who holds the seven stars in His right hand, who walks in the midst of the seven golden lampstands: 'I know your works, your labor, your patience, and that you cannot bear those who are evil. And you have tested those who say they are apostles and are not, and have found them liars; and you have persevered and have patience, and have labored for My name's sake and have not become weary'" (Revelation 2:1-3).

Jesus commended the church at Ephesus for testing those who claimed to be apostles and finding them to be liars.

Paul wrote, "Of these men who have accompanied us all the time that the Lord Jesus went in and out among us, beginning from the baptism of John to that day when He was taken up from us, one of these must become a witness with us of His resurrection" (Acts 1:21-22). This was the criteria for joining the 11 apostles. Paul would be an exception to the rule, as recorded in 1 Corinthians 15:8: "Last of all [Jesus] was seen by me also, as by one born out of due time."

The biblical requirement for any claimant to the office of apostle is that he must have seen Jesus in His resurrected form, or have been with Him during His earthly ministry. Obviously, none of those who claim to be apostles today meet this criterion.

DAY 300

BELIEVE WITH ALL YOUR HEART

In Acts 8, we read the story of Philip's encounter with an Ethiopian eunuch, whom he helped to understand the meaning of Isaiah 53: "As they went down the road, they came to some water. And the eunuch said, 'See, here is water. What hinders me from being baptized?' Then Philip said, 'If you believe with all your heart, you may.' And he answered and said, 'I believe that Jesus Christ is the Son of God'" (Acts 8:36-37).

There is much to consider in this exchange as we witness the salvation of the eunuch. Doctrinally, we can understand that believing with all your heart means you believe that Jesus is the Son of God. As the Son of God, He would have the same attributes of His Father, and thus—as the Jews understood—this made Jesus equal to God.

First John 4:2-3 affirms this truth: "By this you know the Spirit of God: Every spirit that confesses that Jesus Christ has come in the flesh is of God, and every spirit that does not confess that Jesus Christ has come in the flesh is not of God. And this is the spirit of the Antichrist, which you have heard was coming, and is now already in the world."

Next, we read in Acts 8:38 that the eunuch "commanded the chariot to stand still. And both Philip and the eunuch went down into the water, and he baptized him." From this, we can glean that the eunuch's belief in Jesus immediately manifest itself in obedience.

This brings to mind Hebrews 3:18-19: "To whom did He swear that they would not enter His rest, but to those who did not obey? So we see that they could not enter in because of unbelief."

True belief will always manifest itself in our behaviors. In the same way that gravity influences our behavior, true salvation will manifest itself in our behavior too.

DAY 301

THE CHURCH AND GOD'S KINGDOM ON EARTH

It is always a mystery how different people can read the same Bible passage and arrive at diametrically opposing interpretations of it. One example is John 14:1-3:

> Let not your heart be troubled; you believe in God, believe also in Me. In My Father's house are many mansions; if it were not so, I would have told you. I go to prepare a place for you. And if I go and prepare a place for you, I will come again and receive you to Myself; that where I am, there you may be also.

Jesus said He was going to prepare a place for us, come back to get us, and take us to where He is. Yet some have concluded that before Jesus can come back, we must prepare the world for His return.

But what does Matthew 24:37-39 say? "As the days of Noah were, so also will the coming of the Son of Man be. For as in the days before the flood, they were eating and drinking, marrying and giving in marriage, until the day that Noah entered the ark, and did not know until the flood came and took them all away, so also will the coming of the Son of Man be."

"The days before the flood" is an Old Testament parallel to the days before the tribulation. Noah and his family did not have dominion over the earth. The world was a mess, evil was everywhere, and people were indifferent to the impending signs of coming judgment. "The LORD saw that the wickedness of man was great in the earth, and that every intent of the thoughts of his heart was only evil continually" (Genesis 6:5).

Today, the world is a mess morally and spiritually, and filled with violence perpetrated by people bent on only evil continually. The righteous are relatively few, just as in the days of Noah. That can mean only one thing: Jesus is coming soon!

DAY 302

SALT AND LIGHT

The list of truths about what defines the Christian life and experience is peppered all throughout the New Testament, and it is a lengthy list. Much of that list is summarized in a statement made by Jesus a short way into the Sermon on the Mount:

> You are the salt of the earth; but if the salt loses its flavor, how shall it be seasoned? It is then good for nothing but to be thrown out and trampled underfoot by men. You are the light of the world. A city that is set on a hill cannot be hidden. Nor do they light a lamp and put it under a basket, but on a lampstand, and it gives light to all who are in the house. Let your light so shine before men, that they may see your good works and glorify your Father in heaven (Matthew 5:13-16).

In those days, when salt lost its ability to preserve the meat it was packed around, it would be thrown out onto the roads as a kind of topcoat over stones and dirt, and it would literally be trampled underfoot by men.

Second Thessalonians 2:7-8 reveals the significance of our being salt and light: "The mystery of lawlessness is already at work; only He who now restrains will do so until He is taken out of the way. And then the lawless one will be revealed, whom the Lord will consume with the breath of His mouth and destroy with the brightness of His coming."

"Restrains" means "to hold back or detain." It can also mean "to hinder the progress of." In this case, the progress that is being held back by work of the Holy Spirit through the church is the advance of lawlessness and the rise of the Antichrist to power.

We need to remember that being salt and light is not simply a biblical saying; it is a divine commission and responsibility.

DAY 303

IT'S NOT ABOUT STATUS

Today, we are inundated with information about what makes a person happy, successful, and prosperous. Yet this same information ends up making many people unhappy because they do not meet the world's definitions of success and prosperity.

Many self-help gurus tell us how we can be world-changers, and social media has an elite group of participants known as influencers. We're told we can learn how to be one, too, if we mimic their actions.

Yet the most influential person in human history had none of the things the world claims will make us happy. Born in a stable and laid in a manger, He worked with His hands in the family business. And during His ministry, He had nowhere to lay his head. Yet His name stands above all others even though He met none of the standards that, in our day, make someone a world-changer and influencer. More than anyone else, He changed the lives of people:

> Now it came to pass, afterward, that He went through every city and village, preaching and bringing the glad tidings of the kingdom of God. And the twelve were with Him, and certain women who had been healed of evil spirits and infirmities—Mary called Magdalene, out of whom had come seven demons (Luke 8:1-2).

Mary met none of the criteria of today's "success model." And though she lived almost 2,000 years ago, the town she came from is visited by thousands every year because of her. And what about the disciples? "When they [the Jewish council] saw the boldness of Peter and John, and perceived that they were uneducated and untrained men, they marveled. And they realized that they had been with Jesus" (Acts 4:13).

What matters most in life is not what you have or how much. It's not how many people follow you or how widely known you are. What matters most is whether you know Jesus, and whether others can tell that you do.

DAY 304

BEWARE OF FALSE DOCTRINES

When asked by Peter, Andrew, James, and John about the last days and the signs of His return, Jesus gave a long answer. He prefaced His reply with a warning before He taught what is known as the Olivet Discourse: "Take heed that no one deceives you. For many will come in My name, saying, 'I am the Christ,' and will deceive many" (Matthew 24:4-5).

The Greek word translated "take heed" could also be translated "beware of" or "look out for." Figuratively, it means "to exercise discernment." The context of the disciples' question about the signs related to Jesus' coming, combined with Jesus' answer, tells us that efforts to deceive people will increase exponentially in the last days.

Paul gave a similar warning about the progression toward the last days some 30 years later: "Evil men and impostors will grow worse and worse, deceiving and being deceived" (2 Timothy 3:13).

We can rightfully conclude from these warnings that efforts to deceive in the name of Christ will increase the closer we get to the rapture, which will open the door for the ultimate deceiver to ride onto the world scene.

Deception can sound plausible or even true. Spiritual deception uses familiar terms, names, and concepts, but within the elements of truth are hidden lies that are meant to deceive and lead astray. Paul said that over time, deceivers will get better at what they do, and Jesus said we're to beware and be discerning. So what are we to do when things can sound right yet be wrong?

First Thessalonians 5:19-22 says, "Do not quench the Spirit. Do not despise prophecies. Test all things; hold fast what is good. Abstain from every form of evil." All teachings are to be tested against God's Word. If something doesn't line up, do not believe or follow it.

DAY 305

IS TODAY'S ISRAEL BIBLICAL ISRAEL?

One of the most critical aspects of studying the Word of God and arriving at the proper interpretation of any text is context. Take, for example, this wonderful promise to Israel through the prophet Jeremiah:

> Thus says the LORD, who gives the sun for a light by day, the ordinances of the moon and the stars for a light by night, who disturbs the sea, and its waves roar (the LORD of hosts is His name): "If those ordinances depart from before Me, says the LORD, then the seed of Israel shall also cease from being a nation before Me forever." Thus says the LORD: "If heaven above can be measured, and the foundations of the earth searched out beneath, I will also cast off all the seed of Israel for all that they have done, says the LORD" (Jeremiah 31:35-37).

There are clearly eternal and unconditional elements of this great promise that pertain to God's covenant with His chosen people. In other words, there are no conditions to meet or expiration dates associated with this promise to Israel from God.

How do we know that God has a plan for Israel and the Jews today? The sun, the moon, and the ordinances established at creation bear witness that God is faithful to His Word and that He has not cast off Israel. Nor has He replaced Israel with the church.

Denying that the modern nation of Israel is biblical Israel requires the allegorizing of many scriptures that make sense only when taken literally. The problem with allegorizing is that it makes the reader the determiner of the meaning of God's Word instead of the Holy Spirit.

The golden rule of Bible interpretation says, "When the plain sense of Scripture makes complete sense, seek no other sense." Modern Israel being biblical Israel is the only interpretation that makes sense.

DAY 306

MADE ALIVE

You may have heard the saying, "Born once, die twice; born twice, die once." Of the many proofs within the Bible of its divine inspiration, the fact that the birth-to-death ratio has remained at a constant 1:1 for millennia is yet another affirmation. It proves the Bible's truth claim that all have sinned and fallen short of the glory of God (Romans 3:23).

Romans 5:17-19 says,

> If by the one man's offense death reigned through the one, much more those who receive abundance of grace and of the gift of righteousness will reign in life through the One, Jesus Christ. . .as through one man's offense judgment came to all men, resulting in condemnation, even so through one Man's righteous act the free gift came to all men, resulting in justification of life. For as by one man's disobedience many were made sinners, so also by one Man's obedience many will be made righteous.

The "one man" who introduced death into the world was Adam. Every person ever born was born into the family of Adam, and the 1:1 birth-to-death ratio ever since proves that Adam's sin brought death into the world.

Yet as 1 Corinthians 15:22 says, "As in Adam all die, even so in Christ all shall be made alive." This is the very message Jesus gave to a man He called "the teacher of Israel" (verse 10) in John 3:3: "I say to you, unless one is born again, he cannot see the kingdom of God."

This is the "born twice" portion of the adage from above. All people are born with a soul yet are spiritually dead. They must be born again not physically but spiritually to see the kingdom of God. The good news is that anyone can be made alive through belief in the One who died to save them.

DAY 307

THE DAY APPROACHING

There are countless ways in which the Lord has expressed His wonderful love toward us. He gave His only begotten Son, He has not dealt with us according to our iniquities, His faithfulness is great, His mercies are new every morning, and He has given us all things pertaining to life and godliness are among them.

Yet another important expression of God's love to us is that He has given us His Word, and within His Word, He has told us about the ages to come through Bible prophecy:

> The grace of God that brings salvation has appeared to all men, teaching us that, denying ungodliness and worldly lusts, we should live soberly, righteously, and godly in the present age, looking for the blessed hope and glorious appearing of our great God and Savior Jesus Christ, who gave Himself for us, that He might redeem us from every lawless deed and purify for Himself His own special people, zealous for good works (Titus 2:11-14).

The Greek word translated "looking for" means "to await with confidence." How can you await with confidence something you don't know is coming? It is only through prophecy that we can know a blessed hope based on the glorious appearing of our great God and Savior Jesus Christ. Because we know of this, we can await it with confidence. Without this knowledge, we would have no such hope or expectation.

Hebrews 10:25 also tells us that we can see "the Day" approaching. There are many in the church today who dismiss Bible prophecy and are left with the hope of making the world a better place on their own, which will never happen.

We, however, can await with confidence that Jesus is coming, and the signs all around us indicate this will happen soon.

DAY 308

SCOFFERS AND MOCKERS

The apostle Peter wrote of a time that would come that is now here. There are scoffers who deny that anyone will ever be "caught up" to meet the Lord in the air; they argue that too much time has elapsed for this to be true.

> This they willfully forget: that by the word of God the heavens were of old, and the earth standing out of water and in the water, by which the world that then existed perished, being flooded with water. But the heavens and the earth which are now preserved by the same word, are reserved for fire until the day of judgment and perdition of ungodly men. But, beloved, do not forget this one thing, that with the Lord one day is as a thousand years, and a thousand years as one day. The Lord is not slack concerning His promise, as some count slackness, but is longsuffering toward us, not willing that any should perish but that all should come to repentance (2 Peter 3:5-9).

Peter said the scoffers and rapture-deniers will deliberately forget how long God allowed evil to continue in Noah's day before He flooded the world in His wrath and divine judgment. In that day, the thoughts and intents of man's heart were only evil continually (Genesis 6:5), and the righteous were few. Though God waited patiently, the day and hour finally came when He flooded the world.

Jesus warned that the days before His coming will be "as the days of Noah were" (Matthew 24:37). When our world is filled with evil and there are few righteous on the earth—and the goodness of God is not leading men to repentance because they refuse to receive the truth—Jesus will take up those who are in His church and meet them in the air. And they will forever be with the Lord! Paul said we are to "comfort one another with these words" (1 Thessalonians 4:18).

DAY 309

THE PROMISE KEEPER

Isaiah 7:14 proclaims one of the greatest promises in Scripture: "The Lord Himself will give you a sign: Behold, the virgin shall conceive and bear a Son, and shall call His name Immanuel."

The fellowship between God and man, which was broken in the garden, could not be restored by man. God took it upon Himself to regain that fellowship by sending His own Son to Earth "in the likeness of sinful flesh" (Romans 8:3). The birth of Jesus made Isaiah 7:14 a reality: God, who once walked in the garden with Adam and Eve, came to Earth as a male child so that He could walk with man as his friend once again as Immanuel, God with us.

Colossians 1:15-18 says this:

> He is the image of the invisible God, the firstborn over all creation. For by Him all things were created that are in heaven and that are on earth, visible and invisible, whether thrones or dominions or principalities or powers. All things were created through Him and for Him. And He is before all things, and in Him all things consist. And He is the head of the body, the church, who is the beginning, the firstborn from the dead, that in all things He may have the preeminence.

The word "image" is the Greek term *eikōn* (icon), which, in this context, refers to the physical manifestation of the invisible God. Paul was telling us that the head of the church is God, and God was manifested in physical form in the person of Jesus Christ, God with us.

Second Corinthians 1:20-22 further states, "All the promises of God in Him are Yes, and in Him Amen, to the glory of God through us. Now He who establishes us with you in Christ and has anointed us is God, who also has sealed us and given us the Spirit in our hearts as a guarantee."

Though people break their promises, God is a true Promise Keeper!

DAY 310

NOTHING BUT THE BLOOD, PART 1

While there are but two ordinances for the church to observe, baptism and communion, the feasts of Israel also conveyed great truths to God's people.

Knowing that God is a God of order and structure, as evidenced in creation, we need to look beyond the seven feasts of Israel as simply being divided into spring and fall feasts. In them, the gospel is presented, the church age is implied, and the second coming predicted. We also need to recognize that the seven feasts begin with Passover for a reason that is integral to the message presented by them.

In Exodus 12:12-13, God said,

> I will pass through the land of Egypt on that night, and will strike all the firstborn in the land of Egypt, both man and beast; and against all the gods of Egypt I will execute judgment: I am the LORD. Now the blood shall be a sign for you on the houses where you are. And when I see the blood, I will pass over you; and the plague shall not be on you to destroy you when I strike the land of Egypt.

The message of Passover is that innocent blood is required to allow death to pass over us. The death in view in Exodus was the first death, or the death of the flesh. What Passover, or Pesach, pointed to, however, was the second death passing over us—also by the shedding of innocent blood.

The reason Passover is the first of the seven feasts is because without the shedding of blood, there is no remission of sin (Leviticus 17:11; Hebrews 9:22). And without the remission of sin, we cannot be made kings and priests of God—and without the blood being applied, the second death cannot pass over us.

DAY 311

NOTHING BUT THE BLOOD, PART 2

The feast days of Israel were not simply events to observe every year. They represented, much like baptism and communion, something in relationship to the Lord and what He has done, or was going to do, for us.

Romans 5:19 says, "As by one man's disobedience many were made sinners, so also by one Man's obedience many will be made righteous." Romans 3:23 states, "All have sinned," and Romans 6:23 warns that "the wages of sin is death." So how can we go from being condemned sinners to those who are made righteous? The answer is by applying the blood of Jesus.

Colossians 1:21-22 explains this: "You, who once were alienated and enemies in your mind by wicked works, yet now He has reconciled in the body of His flesh through death, to present you holy, and blameless, and above reproach in His sight."

Jesus fulfilled the Feast of Firstfruits when He rose from the dead because the grave had no right or power to hold Him. The spring feasts of Israel tell us that innocent blood allows for the second death to pass over us, and for many to be made righteous and become firstfruits to the Lord and thus be part of the first resurrection. When the Holy Spirit came, Pentecost was fulfilled, and the church age was born.

The first four feasts happen in the spring. Then after a span of time, the three fall feasts occur. This span of time represents the church age, followed by the seventieth week of Daniel.

Like the spring feasts, though they led to the church age, the fall feasts relate exclusively to Israel. (This, by the way, is further proof that the church will not be present on Earth during the seventieth week of Daniel, or the tribulation.) The fall feasts point to the second coming, the repentance of all Israel, and the millennium. Every one of these will be fulfilled by Jesus.

DAY 312

GOD IS GOOD

Scripture is clear about how we're to act toward our enemies:

> I say to you, love your enemies, bless those who curse you, do good to those who hate you, and pray for those who spitefully use you and persecute you, that you may be sons of your Father in heaven; for He makes His sun rise on the evil and on the good, and sends rain on the just and on the unjust (Matthew 5:44-45).

> Love your enemies, do good, and lend, hoping for nothing in return; and your reward will be great, and you will be sons of the Most High. For He is kind to the unthankful and evil (Luke 6:35).

In this matter, God is our example. His kindness has caused the sun to shine and the rain to fall on the evil and the good. God is perfectly able to send sun and water only on the crops of those who love and serve Him. Yet in His grace and mercy, He also sends sun and water on the crops of those who are unthankful for His blessings and grace. There are many who, in their pride, continue to try to avoid God or invent ways to access heaven without involving Him. In vain, they turn to religion or works of righteousness.

Even so, the Lord remains unwilling that any should perish, but desires that all would come to repentance (2 Peter 3:9). For the Christian, the fact God wants to dwell with us and have fellowship with us reminds us of the important truth that He loved us before we loved Him.

As God's ambassadors, we are called to be like Him and do as He does. He is kind to the unthankful and the evil, and we should be too. As we do this, we will find ourselves in a unique place in a self-centered world. The church is the only entity in history whose sole purpose is to rescue its enemies, just as God did for us.

DAY 313

A GUARANTEED INHERITANCE

As Christians, we have a guaranteed inheritance: "In Him you also trusted, after you heard the word of truth, the gospel of your salvation; in whom also, having believed, you were sealed with the Holy Spirit of promise, who is the guarantee of our inheritance until the redemption of the purchased possession, to the praise of His glory" (Ephesians 1:13-14).

This brings more meaning to the promise in Hebrews 13:5 that the Lord will never leave nor forsake us. What's more, He dwells within us, and we're temples of the Holy Spirit (1 Corinthians 6:19). All this also sheds new light on what David wrote in Psalm 139:7-10:

> Where can I go from Your Spirit? Or where can I flee from Your presence? If I ascend into heaven, You are there; if I make my bed in hell, behold, You are there. If I take the wings of the morning, and dwell in the uttermost parts of the sea, even there Your hand shall lead me, and Your right hand shall hold me.

Because of the Spirit of God within us, when our failures make us feel like hiding from God, He is with us. When we are having a terrible day, He is with us. When we feel like we are all alone on the sea of life, even there He is holding us and leading us. The greatest aspect of these wonderful truths is that God wants to dwell with us. He wants to walk through life with us!

So when the devil is trying to convince you that the Lord is no longer interested in you and has forsaken you, remember this exceedingly great and precious promise:

> I give them eternal life, and they shall never perish; neither shall anyone snatch them out of My hand. My Father, who has given them to Me, is greater than all; and no one is able to snatch them out of My Father's hand (John 10:28-29).

DAY 314

SEEKING HIM

The Bible constantly encourages us to seek the Lord. What exactly does that mean? As is true with most words in Scripture, there are multiple Hebrew and Greek words that translate to the English word "seek."

First Chronicles 16:11 says, "Seek the Lord and His strength; seek His face evermore!" In this verse, the word translated "seek" means "to follow after or frequent." It implies a constancy or consistency of pursuit.

In Psalm 27:4, we read, "One thing I have desired of the Lord, that will I seek: That I may dwell in the house of the Lord all the days of my life, to behold the beauty of the Lord, and to inquire in His temple." Here, the Hebrew word translated "seek" means "to search out through worship or prayer."

Then in Hebrews 11:6 we have this: "Without faith it is impossible to please Him, for he who comes to God must believe that He is, and that He is a rewarder of those who diligently seek Him." The Greek word translated "seek" in this famed Hall of Faith passage of Hebrews 11 means "to seek out for one's self, to beg or to crave." This communicates a hunger and thirst for the Lord and thus His Word and His ways.

These meanings reveal that seeking the Lord is a multifaceted effort on our part. According to 1 Chronicles 16:11, we seek forevermore the Lord and His strength and His face, meaning His nature and attributes. Psalm 27:4 tells us how to do this—to search for Him through worship and prayer. Then Hebrews 11:6 indicates that such seeking is our very sustenance and will keep us from spiritual starvation, for the Lord rewards the diligent seeker with His strength, love, grace, mercy, and all else that we know to be true of Him.

Seek God, and you will find Him to be an ever-present help in time of need.

DAY 315

GIRD UP YOUR MIND

First Peter 1:13-16 gives us this important exhortation:

> Gird up the loins of your mind, be sober, and rest your hope fully upon the grace that is to be brought to you at the revelation of Jesus Christ; as obedient children, not conforming yourselves to the former lusts, as in your ignorance; but as He who called you is holy, you also be holy in all your conduct, because it is written, "Be holy, for I am holy."

To gird up your mind means to bind your thoughts, and in this case, your thoughts are to be bound "upon the grace that is to be brought to you at the revelation of Jesus Christ." To set your minds on things above, as Paul said (Colossians 3:2), is to remind yourself of the cost of your redemption. Peter said we're to live holy lives in response to that knowledge. *Holy* means "moral purity," and this is presented to us in the form of "not conforming yourselves to the former lusts." (Here, "lust" means "to long for forbidden things.")

We cannot earn our way to heaven through good behavior or holy living. But on our way to heaven, we are to seek the Lord and not do things that hinder our reflection of Him. Contrary to what some argue today, holiness is not works. Living morally pure is the result of recognizing the magnitude of what God has done for us. It is not obligation, but rather, adoration. Having received what cannot be earned or deserved, nonconformity to our former passions that revealed our need for a Savior is the only reasonable response.

We do this through worship and prayer, and we're to rid ourselves of things we are told to put off. It is in this way that we can experience the Lord's strength—by seeking Him in a constant pursuit of Him until we see Him face to face in all His glory!

Perhaps today!

DAY 316

WHEN IN ROME, PART 1

The Magna Carta was written by a group of thirteenth-century barons to protect their rights and properties against a tyrannical king. The document addressed many practical matters and specific grievances relevant to the oppressive system under which these barons lived. Clause 39 states,

> No freeman shall be seized, imprisoned, dispossessed, outlawed, exiled or ruined in any way, nor in any way proceeded against, except by the lawful judgment of his peers and the law of the land. To no one will we sell, to no one will we deny or delay right or justice.[12]

The book of Romans reminds and instructs us about living free of the tyrannical rule of the god of this world, Satan. Romans opens with this reminder of who Christ is and who we are in Him:

> Paul, a bondservant of Jesus Christ, called to be an apostle, separated to the gospel of God which He promised before through His prophets in the Holy Scriptures, concerning His Son Jesus Christ our Lord, who was born of the seed of David according to the flesh, and declared to be the Son of God with power according to the Spirit of holiness, by the resurrection from the dead. Through Him we have received grace and apostleship for obedience to the faith among all nations for His name, among whom you also are the called of Jesus Christ (Romans 1:1-6).

At this time, Christians were extremely unpopular in Rome and facing persecution. It was in this political and spiritual climate that Paul said, "I am not ashamed of the gospel of Christ, for it is the power of God to salvation for everyone who believes, for the Jew first and also for the Greek" (Romans 1:16).

When in Rome…

DAY 317

WHEN IN ROME, PART 2

In Romans 12:1-2, Paul wrote,

> I beseech you therefore, brethren, by the mercies of God, that you present your bodies a living sacrifice, holy, acceptable to God, which is your reasonable service. And do not be conformed to this world, but be transformed by the renewing of your mind, that you may prove what is that good and acceptable and perfect will of God.

Paul made it clear that a change of mind leads to a change of life. And this serves as proof of the good and acceptable and perfect will of God. To present our bodies as living sacrifices is to do what is holy and acceptable to God.

The word "God" appears 153 times in Romans, more than in any other New Testament book. This identifies the central theme of the epistle and gives us insight on how to live in this world but not of it, how to live for God and not for the things of the world. While Romans addresses many other aspects of the Christian faith and walk, living for God is the core of them all.

Paul was saying what many need to hear today: No matter what public opinion says about the gospel of Jesus Christ, we should not adapt the message to make it more socially acceptable. We should not be ashamed of the content of the gospel. Paul said this in the face of growing persecution. He knew that the one message that can save Jew or Gentile is the uncompromised gospel of Jesus Christ.

Are you telling the people you encounter each day about the King of the Jews, who came into the world to save sinners? Paul would if he were alive today, and so should we!

DAY 318

PRAYER

Daniel 9 records one of three great prayers in the Old Testament, and interestingly, all three concern elements of the same event, the Babylonian captivity. The other two prayers are found in Ezra 9 and Nehemiah 9. There are multiple lessons we could learn about prayer from a careful study of this triad of prayers, but one lesson in particular that we'll focus on relates to supplication.

Supplication means "earnest prayer," which indicates prayer is not about using spiritual-sounding words or repetitive phrases, or overwhelming God with the sheer volume of our words. In fact, Jesus warned about repetition in Matthew 6:7: "When you pray, do not use vain repetitions as the heathen do. For they think that they will be heard for their many words."

Pray or *prayer* means "to motion toward or ascend to God's will or wishes." These days, there is a movement in the church in which people repeat biblical phrases or passages in the hopes of obtaining the meaning of them "for one's self." But repeating words or phrases found in the Bible hundreds or thousands of times is not earnest prayer. True prayer is about ascending to the will and wishes of God. Or as the old adage goes, Prayer is not about getting our will done in heaven; prayer is about getting God's will done on Earth.

Prayer is simply talking to God with the respect and the honor He is due and ascending to His will and wishes on Earth as is true in heaven. Have you ever noticed that in the model prayer we call the Lord's prayer (Matthew 6:9-13), less than 10 percent is dedicated to personal petition? And the prayer is limited to what is needed for "this day" (verse 11). This includes forgiveness, deliverance from the temptations of the evil one, and an acknowledgment of the greatness of God over heaven and earth, followed by "So be it," or "Amen."

DAY 319

SOWING GOSPEL SEEDS

In Matthew 13:18-23, we find Jesus explaining the meaning of the parable of the soils, which He had just shared with the disciples:

> Therefore hear the parable of the sower: When anyone hears the word of the kingdom, and does not understand it, then the wicked one comes and snatches away what was sown in his heart. This is he who received seed by the wayside. But he who received the seed on stony places, this is he who hears the word and immediately receives it with joy; yet he has no root in himself, but endures only for a while. For when tribulation or persecution arises because of the word, immediately he stumbles. Now he who received seed among the thorns is he who hears the word, and the cares of this world and the deceitfulness of riches choke the word, and he becomes unfruitful. But he who received seed on the good ground is he who hears the word and understands it, who indeed bears fruit and produces: some a hundredfold, some sixty, some thirty.

In this parable, Jesus does not say anything about a sower trying to target good soil. Rather, He simply explains the reality of sowing gospel seeds. We have all thought at times that a specific person wouldn't want to hear the gospel, or we've assumed that the likelihood of someone responding positively is low or nonexistent.

That is why God has limited our responsibility to sowing seeds on all types of soil. We do the sowing, and He does the saving. Sometimes the soil that, in our estimation, is hard turns out to be the good soil. Sometimes the person we think is consumed by the cares of this world is the most receptive to the gospel. And sometimes the soil we think is good is actually the hardest.

Our job is to sow gospel seeds as much as possible. Only God knows how people will respond.

DAY 320

THAT THE WORLD MAY KNOW

In Ezekiel 39:7-8, God proclaims,

> "I will make My holy name known in the midst of My people Israel, and I will not let them profane My holy name anymore. Then the nations shall know that I am the LORD, the Holy One in Israel. Surely it is coming, and it shall be done," says the Lord GOD. "This is the day of which I have spoken."

In Ezekiel 38–39, when the Lord fights for Israel against a group of invading nations, His supernatural protection will make His name known among the Jews, and the nations will know that He is the Lord, the Holy One of Israel (a messianic title). This will not be the first time such a scenario has played out. Remember what happened to the people of Israel in Egypt?

In Exodus 14:4, God said, "I will harden Pharaoh's heart, so that he will pursue them; and I will gain honor over Pharaoh and over all his army, that the Egyptians may know that I am the LORD." In Exodus 29:45-46, the Lord said, "I will dwell among the children of Israel and will be their God. And they shall know that I am the LORD their God, who brought them up out of the land of Egypt, that I may dwell among them. I am the LORD their God."

In Exodus, the Lord protected His people during the plagues that rained down upon the Egyptians. His protective hand on Israel proved to everyone that He was the Lord.

God's faithfulness throughout Israel's history—and the fact that He is the Lord and does not change—helps us to recognize that God glorifies Himself in our times of tribulation. When we face trials, we will see His faithful hand at work, and so will others. And we will come through those times with our hope, joy, and faith intact.

When God's power and strength are displayed on your behalf, let people know that He is the Lord!

DAY 321

LET NO ONE DESPISE YOU

Nothing in life will enable our hope to continue, our joy to remain, and our faith to be steadfast like "the blessed hope and glorious appearing of our great God and Savior Jesus Christ"!

> The grace of God that brings salvation has appeared to all men, teaching us that, denying ungodliness and worldly lusts, we should live soberly, righteously, and godly in the present age, looking for the blessed hope and glorious appearing of our great God and Savior Jesus Christ, who gave Himself for us, that He might redeem us from every lawless deed and purify for Himself His own special people, zealous for good works. Speak these things, exhort, and rebuke with all authority. Let no one despise you (Titus 2:11-15).

Paul tells Titus how we are to live in a world of ungodliness and lusts—we are to be sober, righteous, and godly. He then says who we are living for—our great God and Savior Jesus Christ. He mentions what was done for us that would cause us to live for Christ—we were redeemed from every lawless deed, and He is purifying us. We're to do this "in the present age," which suggests also the age to come, the time when Christ appears.

In Hebrews 9:27-28, we read that "it is appointed for men to die once, but after this the judgment, so Christ was offered once to bear the sins of many. To those who eagerly wait for Him He will appear a second time, apart from sin, for salvation."

It is important to remember that the word translated "salvation," in either Hebrew or Greek, can also be translated "deliverance." Jesus is going to appear a second time, apart from the purpose of dying for our sins, and He will deliver this ungodly and lust-filled world from the grip of Satan and bind him for 1,000 years.

If God said it, that settles it, no matter who despises it.

DAY 322

STAND FAST IN THE LORD

One of the wonderful realities about the church is that Christians come in all shapes and sizes and from all ethnic backgrounds and languages. And yet, through Christ, we are one body, of which Christ is the head. Thus, in the midst of enormous diversity, we have amazing unity because we are all believers in Christ.

There is another aspect of being a part of the body of Christ that is common to us all yet we are not always quick to recognize or embrace it:

> Beloved, do not think it strange concerning the fiery trial which is to try you, as though some strange thing happened to you; but rejoice to the extent that you partake of Christ's sufferings, that when His glory is revealed, you may also be glad with exceeding joy. If you are reproached for the name of Christ, blessed are you, for the Spirit of glory and of God rests upon you. On their part He is blasphemed, but on your part He is glorified (1 Peter 4:12-14).

Christians are not exempt from the fiery trials of life, and when we experience them, they should not cause despair, but rather, rejoicing. How can that be so? Peter answered that question by saying that fiery trials are part of our shared Christlikeness, which is cause for gladness and exceeding joy!

When internal strife arises between Christians, we need to be of one mind in Christ and remember that we share a common cause and are called to the greater good of sharing the gospel. And when we are persecuted because of our desire to live godly, we need to remember that we will not be strangers to such things. Christ Himself suffered such persecution, and as His servants, we can expect the same, and we will be blessed for it.

DAY 323

PREPARING BELIEVERS

Most of us have met a person who exudes quiet and calming confidence—a person who is not ruffled by difficult circumstances or hardship. Such people are easy to be around, and their calming influence is palpable.

First Peter 3:15 encourages us to "sanctify the Lord God in your hearts, and always be ready to give a defense to everyone who asks you a reason for the hope that is in you, with meekness and fear."

The word translated "hope" here means "joyful and confident expectation of eternal salvation." Peter is telling us that we should have such a palpable "joyful and confident expectation of eternal salvation" that other people inquire as to where we got it. In times such as these, we could well say to others, in part, "I have such joy because I know the end of the story. I've read the back of the Book."

Without such knowledge, people are usually fearful and hopeless. And when people live in fear, they are often driven by negative emotions and feelings that do not communicate to others with quiet and calming confidence. In fact, their negativity can lead them to be short-tempered and critical.

In Genesis 18:17-18, God said, "Shall I hide from Abraham what I am doing, since Abraham shall surely become a great and mighty nation, and all the nations of the earth shall be blessed in him?"

God does not want the future to be a complete mystery to us. While we don't know every detail of what is to come, we do know a lot about how God will make things turn out in the end. It is very likely that Abraham would have never guessed that his descendants would become a great and mighty nation through the one and only son he and Sarah would have together. God does things in ways that are frequently surprising, but the end results will always be exactly as He foretold.

DAY 324

THE JUDGE OF ALL THE EARTH

Remember when Abraham negotiated with the Lord over the judgment of Sodom because his nephew Lot lived there? Abraham said to God, "Far be it from You to do such a thing as this, to slay the righteous with the wicked, so that the righteous should be as the wicked; far be it from You! Shall not the Judge of all the earth do right?" (Genesis 18:25).

God is the Judge of all the earth, and His judgments are right and true. We also need to remember that God has not forsaken His people Israel, and as the only ethnic people group who have a covenant with Him as a nation, He will judge the nations and peoples, as He has in the past, for their attacks on His chosen people.

> Behold, in those days and at that time, when I bring back the captives of Judah and Jerusalem, I will also gather all nations, and bring them down to the Valley of Jehoshaphat; and I will enter into judgment with them there on account of My people, My heritage Israel, whom they have scattered among the nations; they have also divided up My land (Joel 3:1-2).

Later, in Zechariah 12:9, God said, "It shall be in that day that I will seek to destroy all the nations that come against Jerusalem."

Abraham was right in his assessment of "the Judge of all the earth," for He will not destroy the righteous with the wicked. He will, however, act in judgment on behalf of His covenant people for His name's sake so that, as in times past, the nations will know that He is the Lord. Joel and Zechariah show us that God will remain consistent in His defense of Israel in the future. Israel is God's way of testing the nations in that their treatment of Israel is reflective of their heart toward Him.

God is never unjust, even in His judgments.

DAY 325

HIS WORD IS TRUTH

In an age during which many people take a salad-bar approach to the contents of the Bible—that is, "I like and accept this part, but do not like or accept that part"—modern Israel being biblical Israel is one of the parts people have not liked. Many have cut Israel out of God's plans and pasted the church in its place.

Yet there are prophecies that have not yet been fulfilled in connection with the regathered Jews in the land of their inheritance, and some of them include God judging the nations who come against the Jews. Israel is not perfect, and the Jewish people have not yet looked upon the one whom they pierced and mourned for Him as one mourns for an only Son (Zechariah 12:10). But the God who made an everlasting covenant with Israel is perfect, and the entirety of His Word is truth. If Scripture can be cut and pasted by humans, then we cannot trust God's promises.

In Genesis 12:3, God said, "I will bless those who bless you, and I will curse him who curses you; and in you all the families of the earth shall be blessed." Through the bloodline of Abraham, Isaac, and Jacob came the Messiah, the Holy One of Israel. And through Him, all the nations of the earth have been blessed with the opportunity to be saved through His redeeming blood. Those who curse Israel will be cursed. The word "curse" means "to slight," or "to make little of." That means we need to be careful about those who slight or make little of God's covenant people, through whom the Savior of the world came.

The Boycott, Divestment and Sanctions (BDS) movement against Israel and all antisemitic activities are to be avoided by the church. Ezekiel 36 makes it clear that God has not replaced or cast off Israel. Rather, for His name's sake, He regathered the people into their homeland. To oppose or deny this is to oppose and deny God's Word.

DAY 326

REPENT AND BE CONVERTED

It has been said that God loves you just as you are, but He loves you too much to leave you that way. This points us to the transformative work God does in our lives when we are saved by grace through faith in Christ. It also implies that being saved by grace is manifested in the form of repentance from sin.

Yet there are some who take issue with connecting repentance and being saved by grace, as though the two are incompatible and one negates the other. But the two elements wonderfully complement each other.

Jesus called five of the seven churches in Revelation 2–3 to repent. In His message to the church in Ephesus, Jesus didn't condemn the people's thinking; rather, He criticized their inactions or lack of works. He didn't say, "Repent and think." He said, "Repent and do." If Jesus called churches of already-saved people to repent, then how can repentance be viewed as "works righteousness," or adding works to being saved by grace?

When the first temple was being dedicated and Solomon prayed, he asked the Lord, "When your people sin against each other and You and experience the consequences for their actions, hear the prayers of Your people when they come to their senses" (see 2 Chronicles 6:22-42). The Lord's answer was, "If My people who are called by My name will humble themselves, and pray and seek My face, and turn from their wicked ways, then I will hear from heaven, and will forgive their sin and heal their land" (2 Chronicles 7:14).

Again, where is the negative aspect of repentance, or turning from one's wicked ways? Is not the end result the forgiveness of sin and the healing of their land?

Finally, Acts 3:19 says, "Repent therefore and be converted, that your sins may be blotted out, so that times of refreshing may come from the presence of the Lord."

Repentance brings times of refreshing from the Lord!

DAY 327

KNOWING GOD

As the apostle Paul stood in the Areopagus in Athens, he noted that the people there were religious. That was evident by the fact the city was filled with an estimated 30,000 idols to various pagan deities. Concerning this, Paul said,

> As I was passing through and considering the objects of your worship, I even found an altar with this inscription: TO THE UNKNOWN GOD. Therefore, the One whom you worship without knowing, Him I proclaim to you: God, who made the world and everything in it, since He is Lord of heaven and earth, does not dwell in temples made with hands. Nor is He worshiped with men's hands, as though He needed anything, since He gives to all life, breath, and all things (Acts 17:23-25).

In his effort to relate to the Athenians, Paul made several important points, including the fact that the God who has made Himself known through His only begotten Son, Jesus Christ, remains unknown by many. Paul's comments also remind us that the God of the Bible is distinct from all other "objects of [human] worship." He identified God as the one "who made the world and everything in it...who does not dwell in temples made with hands." (The Greeks were very fond of building temples to deities.)

John 1:18 tells us, "No one has seen God at any time. The only begotten Son, who is in the bosom of the Father, He has declared Him."

Of the many aspects that distinguish the Christian faith from other religions, a key one is the relationship aspect. It has been well said that Christianity is not a religion, but a relationship. A relationship implies intimate knowledge and not simply an awareness of existence. It speaks of personal interaction and communication.

In other words, knowing God.

DAY 328

JESUS IS LORD

In 1 John 5:9-13, we find these powerful words:

> If we receive the witness of men, the witness of God is greater; for this is the witness of God which He has testified of His Son. He who believes in the Son of God has the witness in himself; he who does not believe God has made Him a liar, because he has not believed the testimony that God has given of His Son. And this is the testimony: that God has given us eternal life, and this life is in His Son. He who has the Son has life; he who does not have the Son of God does not have life. These things I have written to you who believe in the name of the Son of God, that you may know that you have eternal life, and that you may continue to believe in the name of the Son of God.

John reminds us that what we believe about Jesus matters. If Jesus was a mere human who was a prophet or great teacher and not deity equal to yet distinct from the Father, then we do not have eternal life.

God has made Himself known to man and offers the invitation to all to come and end their search for rest for their souls. But the invitation is not without conditions. Jesus is the Savior only of those who see Him as who the Father says He is—the only begotten of the Father, full of grace and truth. Seeing Jesus as anything other than God's uncreated, eternally existent Son who was present and active at creation cannot give you eternal life, and thus, He remains unknown to you.

However, you can change that right now by believing and confessing that Jesus is the Christ, the Son of the living God! As Romans 10:9 says, "If you confess with your mouth the Lord Jesus and believe in your heart that God has raised Him from the dead, you will be saved."

DAY 329

PROVEN THROUGH PROPHECY

Through the ages, there have been many writings and books penned that claim a divine origin or angelic delivery (allegedly proving their supernatural origin). Most of them also declare or propose what awaits man after this life. In response, the questions often posed by earnest seekers of truth are these: How do you know that your book and beliefs are right? What makes your beliefs distinct or even exclusive from all other truth claims? The answer is quite simple and even definitive: If a book or writing claims knowledge about the afterlife, it should also be able to speak accurately about the future in this life.

This is what makes the Bible's claim of being the only book of divine origin a valid assertion. The Bible not only tells us what happens after this life, it foretells the events of the future in this life from the position of the distant past, and even claims its author has the ability to do this:

> Remember the former things of old, for I am God, and there is no other; I am God, and there is none like Me, declaring the end from the beginning, and from ancient times things that are not yet done, saying, "My counsel shall stand, and I will do all My pleasure" (Isaiah 46:9-10).

To claim the ability to declare the end of all things from ancient times requires proof to be believable. Many religious writings and teachings claim to have information regarding the afterlife but offer no concrete proof to back up those proclamations. In contrast, the Bible offers irrefutable proof of its divine origin through fulfilled revelations of future events with specific details about events, places, and even people's names. It has also correctly identified cultural and spiritual trends that will occur in the last days. This proof demands that the Bible be recognized as the only book that qualifies as the infallible and divinely inspired Word of God, proven through prophecy.

DAY 330

THE LIVING WORD

Second Timothy 3:1-5 declares,

> Know this, that in the last days perilous times will come: For men will be lovers of themselves, lovers of money, boasters, proud, blasphemers, disobedient to parents, unthankful, unholy, unloving, unforgiving, slanderers, without self-control, brutal, despisers of good, traitors, headstrong, haughty, lovers of pleasure rather than lovers of God, having a form of godliness but denying its power. And from such people turn away!

The phrase "in the last days" tells us that what follows is predictive and not prescriptive. The Holy Spirit was using Paul to tell a future generation what conditions would be like in the last days. Paul was not giving a directive or prescription on how to turn things around. Rather, he simply said, "Turn away from such people"—that is, do not follow in their ways. Look at what Paul wrote and hold it up to our world today, and see how things the Bible foretold are now being fulfilled.

The Bible also said there would be a generation that would see the rebirth of the nation of Israel, and that generation will not pass away until all things concerning Israel are fulfilled. Here we are today, with a people who were scattered among the nations for nearly two millennia and who did not assimilate into the cultures in which they lived. Today, they are back in the same land, speaking the same language as their forefathers, yet many—if not most—churches today believe that modern Israel is not biblical Israel.

Hebrews 4:12 reminds us that the Bible is living and powerful. And prophecy is the breath, so to speak, of the Bible. Otherwise, it is just History, Law, and Poetry. To fail to teach Bible prophecy is to knock the wind out of the Bible.

The Word of God is living and powerful because it is more than words. What it says will happen will always happen.

DAY 331

BELIEVING IS SEEING

It would be futile to attempt to estimate the number of books that have been written all through the ages. Books of history, poetry, science, medicine, and even those addressing spiritual matters are too numerous to even hazard any guesses. Yet among all the books ever written, there is one that stands alone. It contains poetry and history and even some scientific and medical information within its pages, and yet there is no other book like it.

That book, of course, is the Bible. Imagine reading your favorite book (other than the Bible) every single day, month after month, year after year. The book that was once so alive would eventually seem dead through repetitious reading. But the same cannot be said of the Bible. It is alive, it is powerful, and the depths of its riches and knowledge cannot be exhausted even after it is studied every day for weeks, months, and years. Why? Because of the author. Second Timothy 3:16-17 says,

> All Scripture is given by inspiration of God, and is profitable for doctrine, for reproof, for correction, for instruction in righteousness, that the man of God may be complete, thoroughly equipped for every good work.

The Bible is God-breathed and contains all things pertaining to life and godliness. It directs us and corrects us and prepares us for every good work. Yet even above those wonderful attributes there is one element that is exclusive to the Bible—an element that separates it from all the other books ever written.

James 1:21 tells us that "the implanted word...is able to save your souls." While there are many books that can prepare you for a job or a test, there is only one book that can prepare you for eternity: the living and powerful Word of God.

DAY 332

SLOW TO BELIEVE

Luke 24 records the story of two dejected disciples heading home to Emmaus, completely unaware that the One who was the reason for their discouragement had risen from the dead and had joined them as they walked along the road. Jesus asked why they were so sad, to which they replied, "Have You not known the things which happened there in these days?" (Luke 24:18). When Jesus asked, "What things?," they answered,

> The things concerning Jesus of Nazareth, who was a Prophet mighty in deed and word before God and all the people, and how the chief priests and our rulers delivered Him to be condemned to death, and crucified Him. But we were hoping that it was He who was going to redeem Israel. Indeed, besides all this, today is the third day since these things happened (Luke 24:19-21).

Jesus, who had veiled His identity up to this point, said to them, "'O foolish ones, and slow of heart to believe in all that the prophets have spoken! Ought not the Christ to have suffered these things and to enter into His glory?' And beginning at Moses and all the Prophets, He expounded to them in all the Scriptures the things concerning Himself" (verses 25-27).

The central figure of the Bible is Jesus, and the central message of the Bible is that man needs a Savior. If we look to the Bible to make us rich and prosperous, we will have reduced it to the level of many of the other books written through the ages. In contrast, if we come humbly to the Bible and let it speak for itself and cut to the joints and marrow of our sin problem, "even to the division of soul and spirit" (Hebrews 4:12), we have come to the one book that can save us by the central figure presented in it, Jesus Christ.

Don't be among the slow to believe. Jesus is alive!

DAY 333

BE READY

To say we live in exciting times would be a huge understatement! We are seeing the nations prophesied by Ezekiel working together and preparing themselves for the future invasion of Israel, many of them already in position to the north. We are seeing an unprecedented rise of antisemitism worldwide, as prophesied by Zechariah.

We are watching, with our own eyes, the defection from truth that Paul said would happen in the church when he wrote to Timothy and the church at Thessaloniki. Earthquakes are rising in frequency and increasing in intensity, ethnic tensions are manifesting themselves everywhere, and we live in a constant state of hearing about wars and rumors of wars.

For these reasons, we need to pay close attention to Jesus' words in Matthew 24:44: "Be ready, for the Son of Man is coming at an hour you do not expect."

The primary meaning of the Greek word translated "expect" is "think." The word "hour," in this context, means "season." Thus, we could read this statement as saying, "The Son of Man is coming in a season of history when no one expects Him."

The devil has been hard at work to create this atmosphere of un-expectancy by convincing the world that there is no God and thus nothing to look forward to or hope for because this life is all there is. Satan has also been working hard in the church to convince many to deny the coming of the Lord for His church before He pours out His wrath on His enemies. Satan has even caused some to believe that the church is responsible for bringing about the return of Christ by making the world a better place.

All these factors are contributing to a decreased level of expectancy for the imminent return of Jesus to meet His church in the air. This spirit of un-expectancy should increase our expectancy, so be ready—Jesus is coming!

DAY 334

PERILOUS TIMES

In a vivid description of what life will be like in the last days, Paul wrote,

> Know this, that in the last days perilous times will come: For men will be lovers of themselves, lovers of money, boasters, proud, blasphemers, disobedient to parents, unthankful, unholy, unloving, unforgiving, slanderers, without self-control, brutal, despisers of good, traitors, headstrong, haughty, lovers of pleasure rather than lovers of God, having a form of godliness but denying its power. And from such people turn away! (2 Timothy 3:1-5).

This reads like a checklist of modern culture, which begins with people loving self and pleasures rather than God. This love leads to all the other character flaws and moral failures that will make the last days perilous. Paul closed this list with the fact that people will have a "form" of godliness yet deny its power. They will claim to be godly yet deny the principles of the gospel that make it powerful.

In contrast, we read this in Hebrews 6:17-18: "Thus God, determining to show more abundantly to the heirs of promise the immutability of His counsel, confirmed it by an oath, that by two immutable things, in which it is impossible for God to lie, we might have strong consolation, who have fled for refuge to lay hold of the hope set before us."

The words "immutability" and "immutable" mean "unchangeableness" or "unalterable." The Word of God, like the God of the Word, is the same yesterday, today, and forever. How do we know this for sure? Those who trust in Christ, who is the Word (John 1:1), are being saved and their lives are being transformed. And the ancient prophecies of the Bible are being fulfilled undeniably right before our eyes.

The Word of God is living and powerful, and the evidence around us indicates the One from whose mouth comes the sharp two-edged sword is about to return! (Revelation 19:15).

DAY 335

THE CROSS, PART 1

History is replete with symbols and imagery representing everything from kingdoms or countries to historic events, sports teams, families, and more. Yet there is no symbol equal to that of the cross of Christ. Countries have their flags, teams have their mascots and logos, and families have their crests, and they all convey a message about whom or what they represent. The blue-and-white flag with the Star of David takes our minds to the nation of Israel, the Nike swoosh calls to mind a line of athletic shoes and apparel, a scepter speaks of royalty and authority.

First Corinthians 1:18 says, "The message of the cross is foolishness to those who are perishing, but to us who are being saved it is the power of God." To unbelievers, the cross is foolishness, but to us, it communicates the willingness of God to save.

The power of the cross is that God humbled Himself and came in the likeness of a man that He might be able to taste death for everyone. The message of the cross is that through Christ, the great enemy known as death would be conquered as Christ paid the wages of sin in full. And ultimately, the message of the cross is that at the name of Jesus everyone will someday bow and confess that He is Lord (Philippians 2:10).

In Luke 9:23-25, Jesus gave this invitation:

> If anyone desires to come after Me, let him deny himself, and take up his cross daily, and follow Me. For whoever desires to save his life will lose it, but whoever loses his life for My sake will save it. For what profit is it to a man if he gains the whole world, and is himself destroyed or lost?

On the cross, Jesus humbled Himself to save us. As we take up our cross, we, too, should humble ourselves in order to serve Him.

THE CROSS, PART 2

To the apostle Paul, the cross was everything. In 1 Corinthians 1:17, he wrote, "Christ did not send me to baptize, but to preach the gospel, not with wisdom of words, lest the cross of Christ should be made of no effect." For us, preaching the message of the cross should be primary to all that we do as Christians, and it cannot be equated to other practices, including baptism.

Paul said this about the cross in Philippians 3:18-19: "Many walk, of whom I have told you often, and now tell you even weeping, that they are the enemies of the cross of Christ: whose end is destruction, whose god is their belly, and whose glory is in their shame—who set their mind on earthly things." In other words, the cross divides humanity into two groups: friends of God and "enemies of the cross of Christ."

The cross is not merely jewelry or a logo. The cross is a message—a message that can save the human soul, a message that can transform human lives, a message that can heal the brokenhearted, set captives free, turn mourning into dancing, give hope to the hopeless, and fill up that which is lacking. Most important of all, the message of the cross is that man can be reconciled to God.

We often see celebrities and athletes who wear crosses yet have no clue about the message it represents. The Bible clearly states that we are not to make graven images, and it would be a stretch to consider the cross as such. But we also need to make sure we don't merely wear the symbol, but preach the message it represents.

Colossians 1:21-22 speaks of what the cross accomplished: "You, who once were alienated and enemies in your mind by wicked works, yet now He has reconciled in the body of His flesh through death, to present you holy, and blameless, and above reproach in His sight."

Through the cross, we who were enemies of God are made holy and blameless in His sight—not by baptism or the Eucharist, but only by the shed blood of Christ.

DAY 337

RUN WITH ENDURANCE

In Hebrews 12:1-2, we read these well-known words:

> Since we are surrounded by so great a cloud of witnesses, let us lay aside every weight, and the sin which so easily ensnares us, and let us run with endurance the race that is set before us, looking unto Jesus, the author and finisher of our faith, who for the joy that was set before Him endured the cross, despising the shame, and has sat down at the right hand of the throne of God.

This passage says, in essence, that because the people in the Hebrews 11 Hall of Faith are our fellow witnesses, let's seek to live like they did. Let's not be ensnared by the things of this world, whether they be weights or sins. Let us run our race unhindered as we look to Jesus, who, though He despised the shame of the cross, for the joy of saving us endured it, and now sits at the right hand of God's throne.

"Despising the shame" means "to disdain the disgrace." Not all aspects of being a Christian are going to be pleasant. Being hated by all for His name's sake will be among the challenges we face.

We need to run this race without the things that rob us of our endurance. Usually when we think of weights and sins, sexual immorality or addictions come to mind. But oftentimes the things that hinder our endurance are mental and emotional in nature.

First Peter 4:14 says, "If you are reproached for the name of Christ, blessed are you, for the Spirit of glory and of God rests upon you. On their part He is blasphemed, but on your part He is glorified." Yes, you read that right: God is glorified when we are reproached, and His Spirit rests upon us in those times. So keep running—we're almost to the finish line!

DAY 338

NOT EVERYONE...

Through the centuries, many in the church have debated whether a Christian can lose their salvation or depart from it. But there is one thing we know for sure that cannot be debated: the sad reality that there are those who claim to be saved when, in reality, they're not.

> Not everyone who says to Me, "Lord, Lord," shall enter the kingdom of heaven, but he who does the will of My Father in heaven. Many will say to Me in that day, "Lord, Lord, have we not prophesied in Your name, cast out demons in Your name, and done many wonders in Your name?" And then I will declare to them, "I never knew you; depart from Me, you who practice lawlessness!" (Matthew 7:21-23).

This chilling statement at the end of the Sermon on the Mount tells us the following: First, calling Jesus your Lord doesn't mean He is. Second, doing things in His name doesn't mean you're saved. Third, a person who truly knows Jesus will experience personal and moral transformation. Notice that Jesus offers as evidence the absence of any moral standards as proof of not knowing Him. "Lawlessness" here refers to transgression, iniquity, and unrighteousness.

Jesus' words are a timely reminder for the church in our day. There are many Christians who hold to the position that when it comes to our salvation, any mention of personal transformation or turning from sin is adding works to being saved by grace. But notice what Romans 6:4 says: "We were buried with Him through baptism into death, that just as Christ was raised from the dead by the glory of the Father, even so we also should walk in newness of life."

"Newness of life" means no longer living as we used to. This is not works righteousness, as some would accuse; rather, it is His righteousness at work in us, transforming our thinking and giving us new desires. Such change doesn't earn us our salvation; it is the result of our salvation and is the opposite of living in lawlessness.

DAY 339

FAITH AT WORK

Paul wrote in Ephesians 2:8-10, "By grace you have been saved through faith, and that not of yourselves; it is the gift of God, not of works, lest anyone should boast. For we are His workmanship, created in Christ Jesus for good works, which God prepared beforehand that we should walk in them."

When we are saved by God's grace through faith in Him, we become His workmanship. As such, we are new creations in Christ and "re-created" for good works that God Himself prepared for us to walk in—and we should walk in them.

In this context, "walk" is a metaphor for our journey through life. Here, we can see clearly that being saved by grace through faith is not the end, but the beginning of lifelong transformation. And someday, we will see our Lord face to face and be as He is:

> Behold what manner of love the Father has bestowed on us, that we should be called children of God! Therefore the world does not know us, because it did not know Him. Beloved, now we are children of God; and it has not yet been revealed what we shall be, but we know that when He is revealed, we shall be like Him, for we shall see Him as He is. And everyone who has this hope in Him purifies himself, just as He is pure (1 John 3:1-3).

There is a movement today that has convinced many that once we are saved by grace, there is no need to concern yourself with anything else. Personal transformation, newness of life, and no longer living as an unsaved person are all said to be putting ourselves back under the law. Yet John the beloved—who ministered with Jesus for three years—said that everyone who is saved by grace through faith purifies himself, which means to live in moral purity or holiness.

DAY 340

GOD'S FAITHFULNESS

Of the many truths we can learn about God from the nation of Israel, there is none more significant than that of His faithfulness:

> You are a holy people to the LORD your God; the LORD your God has chosen you to be a people for Himself, a special treasure above all the peoples on the face of the earth. The LORD did not set His love on you nor choose you because you were more in number than any other people, for you were the least of all peoples; but because the LORD loves you, and because He would keep the oath which He swore to your fathers, the LORD has brought you out with a mighty hand, and redeemed you from the house of bondage, from the hand of Pharaoh king of Egypt. Therefore know that the LORD your God, He is God, the faithful God who keeps covenant and mercy for a thousand generations with those who love Him and keep His commandments (Deuteronomy 7:6-9).

God is omniscient. He knows all, and His faithfulness is not impeded by our doubts, fears, and failures. The people of Israel murmured after the exodus from Egypt, yet God remained faithful to His promises. They were fearful when the 12 spies returned from their reconnaissance mission into the Promised Land, yet God remained faithful to His word. The people disobeyed God's command to let the land rest every seventh year for 490 years, and even in His discipline of them, God spoke to them through Jeremiah before they were exiled to Babylon and said, "I know the thoughts that I think toward you, says the LORD, thoughts of peace and not of evil, to give you a future and a hope" (Jeremiah 29:11).

When God found it necessary to punish Israel, His thoughts toward the people were not of evil, but of hope. Through Israel, we see that God is faithful even when we're not.

DAY 341

RAPTURE: TRUE OR FALSE?

The rapture is clearly taught in 1 Thessalonians 4:13-18:

> I do not want you to be ignorant, brethren, concerning those who have fallen asleep, lest you sorrow as others who have no hope. For if we believe that Jesus died and rose again, even so God will bring with Him those who sleep in Jesus. For this we say to you by the word of the Lord, that we who are alive and remain until the coming of the Lord will by no means precede those who are asleep. For the Lord Himself will descend from heaven with a shout, with the voice of an archangel, and with the trumpet of God. And the dead in Christ will rise first. Then we who are alive and remain shall be caught up together with them in the clouds to meet the Lord in the air. And thus we shall always be with the Lord. Therefore comfort one another with these words.

The rapture-denier has to answer this question: If the resurrection of the believing dead reunites the soul with a glorified body, how are those who are alive and remain going to get to heaven when the church age ends? Are they all going to die so they can be resurrected? There is no scriptural evidence to support that proposition.

The only plausible answer is that when the bodies of the believing dead are resurrected, Christians who are alive at the time will be raptured. Consider what Philippians 3:20-21 says: "Our citizenship is in heaven, from which we also eagerly wait for the Savior, the Lord Jesus Christ, who will transform our lowly body that it may be conformed to His glorious body, according to the working by which He is able even to subdue all things to Himself."

Don't you have to be alive to eagerly await something—in this case, the Savior? At the rapture, in the twinkling of an eye, our lowly bodies will be instantly transformed into glorious bodies like that of the resurrected Jesus.

DAY 342

BUT WAIT—THERE'S MORE!

We have all experienced what is known as upselling. A salesperson will try to get us to buy more than what we wanted or intended to buy. Some of the pitchmen on television tell us, "But wait—there's more, but only if you act now!" Many of those who are lured by such upselling will end up with more than they wanted and less money than they had.

While the Bible does not try to upsell us or get into our wallets like a TV pitchman, it is true that the longer we walk with the Lord and study His Word, the more that we discover and grow. In that sense, we could say "But wait—there's more" every single day. There is more for us to know about God and His Word, there is more to experience of His love and mercy, and in our day, there is more of His plan to know and to watch unfold before our eyes.

First John 3:2 tells us what the future holds: "Beloved, now we are children of God; and it has not yet been revealed what we shall be, but we know that when He is revealed, we shall be like Him, for we shall see Him as He is."

In times such as these, it is easy to get distracted from the fact that the best is yet to come. In recent years, when lockdowns were widespread and people were sheltering in place, the enemy tried to get us to focus our minds on the difficulties of the moment instead of on God's promises for the future. While we should not make our way through life indifferent to daily needs and caring for our families and others, we do need to keep in mind the temporary status of life as we know it.

This world is not our home, but it seems we are heading there soon!

DAY 343

THE SECOND COMING AND BEYOND

In Zechariah 12:10, God gives this amazing prophecy about the second coming: "I will pour on the house of David and on the inhabitants of Jerusalem the Spirit of grace and supplication; then they will look on Me whom they pierced. Yes, they will mourn for Him as one mourns for his only son, and grieve for Him as one grieves for a firstborn."

When Jesus returns to Jerusalem, the Jewish people—loved and chosen by God—will recognize that Isaiah 7:14 was about Jesus, Micah 5:2 was about Jesus, Isaiah 11:1 was about Jesus, Hosea 11:1 was about Jesus, and Psalms 2, 22, 34, and a host of other chapters included references to Jesus. Most significantly, when Jesus returns, they will recognize that Isaiah 53 was all about Him, and they will mourn the actions of their ancestors as one would the loss of their only son.

In Isaiah 25:8, we find a prophecy that looks beyond the second coming: "He will swallow up death forever, and the Lord GOD will wipe away tears from all faces; the rebuke of His people He will take away from all the earth; for the LORD has spoken." We could go on to talk about what awaits us in the New Jerusalem, including the streets of gold, gates of single pearls, and more, but there is one important fact we need to remember: If you do not know Jesus of Nazareth as your Savior and Lord, you need to act now because time is short. There are no opportunities in the afterlife to be saved. There is no purgatory, no state of limbo, no soul sleep. Upon death, we immediately go to our final and eternal destiny.

If you have not yet experienced the forgiveness of sins through the blood of Jesus Christ and been born again and filled with His Spirit—and come to know that after this life, immortal incorruptibility awaits you—now is the day of salvation. Tomorrow is not guaranteed to anyone; today is the day to call on the Lord and be saved.

DAY 344

IN THE BEGINNING, GOD

While there are many books and teachings that address matters relating to life in the here and now as well as life after death, the Bible alone speaks with authority on these issues. Genesis 1:1 says, "In the beginning God created the heavens and the earth." After this, the matter of life is addressed, the laws of nature are established, the genetics and physiology of humanity are identified as male and female, and the other end of the spectrum is addressed as well—death and eternity.

Genesis 3:1-5 takes us to the time when sin entered the picture:

> Now the serpent was more cunning than any beast of the field which the LORD God had made. And he said to the woman, "Has God indeed said, 'You shall not eat of every tree of the garden'?" And the woman said to the serpent, "We may eat the fruit of the trees of the garden; but of the fruit of the tree which is in the midst of the garden, God has said, 'You shall not eat it, nor shall you touch it, lest you die.'" Then the serpent said to the woman, "You will not surely die. For God knows that in the day you eat of it your eyes will be opened, and you will be like God, knowing good and evil."

In all of God's creation, man had only one prohibition: not to eat of the tree of the knowledge of good and evil. Satan, in the form of a serpent, twisted God's Word and told Eve a half-truth, saying that she would not die. She ate, and Adam ate, and neither died physically at that moment, but both died spiritually and began the slow march to physical death as well. The intimate fellowship they had once enjoyed with God was broken.

But thanks be to God, that relationship can now be restored through the blood Christ shed on the cross for the sins of the whole world, and whosoever calls on the name of the Lord will be saved.

DAY 345

HE IS RISEN!

The apostle Paul made this rather startling yet true statement when he wrote to the Christians in Corinth: "If in this life only we have hope in Christ, we are of all men the most pitiable."

Paul made that statement after he established his argument for Christ's resurrection as proof that someday, we will experience the redemption of our bodies.

> Now if Christ is preached that He has been raised from the dead, how do some among you say that there is no resurrection of the dead? But if there is no resurrection of the dead, then Christ is not risen. And if Christ is not risen, then our preaching is empty and your faith is also empty. Yes, and we are found false witnesses of God, because we have testified of God that He raised up Christ, whom He did not raise up—if in fact the dead do not rise. For if the dead do not rise, then Christ is not risen. And if Christ is not risen, your faith is futile; you are still in your sins! (1 Corinthians 15:12-17).

If our hope in Christ does not assure us of a life beyond this one in bodies capable of eternal existence, how pitiful it would be for us to endure all the hardships and persecutions of life that target those of the Christian faith!

But we have this assurance stated in 1 Corinthians 15:20-21: "Now Christ is risen from the dead, and has become the firstfruits of those who have fallen asleep. For since by man came death, by Man also came the resurrection of the dead."

The resurrection of Christ provides not only irrefutable proof of His deity, but also gives us confidence that the promise of Christlike bodies capable of eternal existence will be fulfilled. We can know this because He is risen and alive forevermore!

DAY 346

HIS SECOND APPEARING

Hebrews 9:27-28 tells us that "it is appointed for men to die once, but after this the judgment, so Christ was offered once to bear the sins of many. To those who eagerly wait for Him He will appear a second time, apart from sin, for salvation."

The fact that Jesus existed is among the most documented historical facts in human history. Authors, both secular and sacred, acknowledge He lived, was born in Bethlehem, and lived in Nazareth. Though opinions vary on who He actually was, very few debate the fact that He existed, and He is the most polarizing figure in human history.

As Christians, we not only know the historical facts of Jesus' first appearing, we also have the hope of His appearing a second time apart from the purpose of dying for our sins. We also know from Revelation 19:14 that when He returns, we will be with Him. For us to descend from heaven with Him requires, as Paul wrote in 1 Corinthians 15:52-54, our being "changed" from mortal to immortal and corruptible to incorruptible.

In addition, Romans 8:29 says that "whom [God] foreknew, He also predestined to be conformed to the image of His Son, that He might be the firstborn among many brethren." Since our conformity into the image of Christ is a promise to all who are born again, how are the believers who are alive prior to Jesus' return going to put on immortal and incorruptible bodies like that of Jesus in order to return with Him when He comes again to rule and reign on the earth?

Jesus will appear a second time, and at that moment, the dead in Christ will rise, and those who are alive and remain will meet Him and them in the air, and forever, we will be with the Lord (1 Thessalonians 4:13-18).

Maybe even today!

DAY 347

FROM SUSPENSE TO ANTICIPATION

While it is true that anticipation has two sides, the side we favor is not the sense that something awful or unknown is on the horizon, but rather, the opposite. For Christians, there is coming an event that the word *wonderful* falls short of describing.

Think about how living every day in anticipation of something "beyond good" possibly happening would impact our outlook. It would change how we view hardships, painful situations, and the normal stresses of life.

To live with this kind of anticipation is not a pipe dream for us. Rather, it is completely possible today and every day that something incredibly amazing could happen. In John 14:1-3, Jesus said,

> Let not your heart be troubled; you believe in God, believe also in Me. In My Father's house are many mansions; if it were not so, I would have told you. I go to prepare a place for you. And if I go and prepare a place for you, I will come again and receive you to Myself; that where I am, there you may be also.

In times of great difficulties, we have all been offered the sage advice "Don't worry" from well-meaning people. Yet such words are frequently offered without the mechanics of how to not worry. Jesus, however, didn't say, "Let not your heart be troubled," then leave the disciples hanging.

Jesus went on to say that He would prepare a place for them—and us. And that He would come again to receive them—and us—to Himself so we can be where He is.

When Jesus said, "Let not your heart be troubled," He backed up His words by saying He would return to get us so we can be where He is. Every day, we can and should live in anticipation of His arrival to meet us in the air.

DAY 348

BEARING WITNESS

Frequently, the last words of a great and godly person before their death are words of great value to consider and ponder. As Jesus hung from the cross, He uttered seven statements worthy of our attention and thus recorded for us in the Gospels.

The apostle Paul qualifies as a great and godly man whose final words would be noteworthy. We have those words, at least the ones that were recorded in print, in the last chapter of 2 Timothy:

> I charge you therefore before God and the Lord Jesus Christ, who will judge the living and the dead at His appearing and His kingdom: Preach the word! Be ready in season and out of season. Convince, rebuke, exhort, with all longsuffering and teaching. For the time will come when they will not endure sound doctrine, but according to their own desires, because they have itching ears, they will heap up for themselves teachers; and they will turn their ears away from the truth, and be turned aside to fables. But you be watchful in all things, endure afflictions, do the work of an evangelist, fulfill your ministry (4:1-5).

The word "charge," and the context in which Paul used it here, is not a common usage of the word today. The Greek word literally means "to testify or bear witness." Figuratively, and within this context, we might read it as Paul "passing the torch of ministry" to Timothy and saying, "I place you under responsibility—before God and the Lord Jesus Christ—to preach the Word." Paul added that this is to be done "in season and out of season," meaning when the fruit is plentiful, and when it is meager.

Paul's last words include the admonishment to "Preach the Word!" because the apostle had seen—as Isaiah 55:11 says—that God's Word does not return void in any season.

DAY 349

THE GREAT COMMISSION

A young woman who had heard the gospel and come to saving faith in Christ was eager to share the good news with others even though she knew next to nothing of the Scriptures. There was only one verse she could quote, and it was the very one that changed her life:

> God so loved the world that He gave His only begotten Son, that whoever believes in Him should not perish but have everlasting life (John 3:16).

This baby Christian stood on the corner of a busy intersection in her city and told this verse to everyone as they passed by. After a while, an antagonistic man began to deride her and demanded, "What about this ridiculous story of Jonah and the whale? You can't possibly believe that!"

The woman replied, "I don't know about that, but what I do know is that 'God so loved the world that He gave His only begotten Son, that whoever believes in Him should not perish but have everlasting life.'" This process repeated itself numerous times as the man hurled the typical Bible-denier accusations at her, and he always received the same reply.

The man finally left exasperated and in a huff. The next day, the woman returned to her passion and post, and after a while, she saw the man approaching her. But something was different this time—tears streamed down his cheeks, and when he was close enough to speak, he told the woman, "I was so angry at you yesterday, but all I could hear all night long was you saying over and over, 'God so loved the world that He gave His only begotten Son, that whoever believes in Him should not perish but have everlasting life.' And I, too, have now given my life to Christ, and He has saved me."

You may not know all the Bible stories, but you do know your story. Today, tell someone what Jesus has done for you!

DAY 350

THE LAST DAYS

Most of us recognize that there are many biblical issues or topics on which there is room for a variety of viewpoints. But the matter of whether we are in the last days is not among them. Even so, some people say, "How do you know we are in the last days? You can't know that for sure."

Such statements directly contradict the Bible's clear statements concerning the last days, including when those days will begin, what they will be like, and the spiritual climate on the earth during that time.

The book of Hebrews begins with these words:

> God, who at various times and in various ways spoke in time past to the fathers by the prophets, has in these last days spoken to us by His Son, whom He has appointed heir of all things, through whom also He made the worlds (1:1-2).

This masterpiece of theology that we call the book of Hebrews opens with a declaration about the supremacy of Christ over all created beings and establishes His eternality by noting His presence and participation when the universe was created. Jesus' coming to Earth as the Son of God signaled the end of one age and the beginning of another. The age during which God spoke through the prophets to His people had ended, and the last days—in which Christ Himself is God's message to the world—had begun.

Biblically speaking, there is no question that we are in the last days. The next question is, How long will they last? If they began at the coming of Christ, we are well advanced in this era, and we must be in the last of the last days of the church age.

Israel is a nation again, and the world has largely turned against the Jewish people. And the removal of the church to allow for the rise of the man of sin must be near.

Are you ready?

DAY 351

ISRAEL, GOD'S TIMEPIECE

In Matthew 24:32-35, Jesus told Peter, James, John, and Andrew,

> Now learn this parable from the fig tree: When its branch has already become tender and puts forth leaves, you know that summer is near. So you also, when you see all these things, know that it is near—at the doors! Assuredly, I say to you, this generation will by no means pass away till all these things take place. Heaven and earth will pass away, but My words will by no means pass away.

In previous devotions, we established that Scripture uses a budding fig tree as an idiom for the rebirth of the nation of Israel. Here, the rebirth of Israel and the fulfillment of all things are said to occur within a single generation. The length of a generation is one of the more debated topics in Bible prophecy. Rather than enter the debate, we can agree that we are late in the generation that saw the rebirth of Israel.

In Daniel 9:24, we read the prophecy that "seventy weeks are determined for your people and for your holy city, to finish the transgression, to make an end of sins, to make reconciliation for iniquity, to bring in everlasting righteousness, to seal up vision and prophecy, and to anoint the Most Holy."

Daniel 9 then divides the 70 weeks into segments of 7, 62, and 1. The 7 weeks refer to the time to rebuild the temple, walls, and houses of Jerusalem. When you add the 62 weeks, you arrive at the day Jesus rode into Jerusalem on a donkey. After that comes a span of time, or the church age, and then the seventieth week will happen.

The rebirth of Israel set the prophetic clock in motion, and we are fast moving toward the arrival of the seventieth week. That means time is short, and God is preparing to bring about the great tribulation. Be sure to tell others how they can escape the wrath that will soon come upon the whole world!

DAY 352

THE JEWS AND THE NEW COVENANT

While there are many reasons to reject the entirely unbiblical teaching of replacement theology, one of the most significant is that it teaches something about God's nature and character that is not true.

For context, let's read Jeremiah 24:6-7:

> I will set My eyes on them for good, and I will bring them back to this land; I will build them and not pull them down, and I will plant them and not pluck them up. Then I will give them a heart to know Me, that I am the Lord; and they shall be My people, and I will be their God, for they shall return to Me with their whole heart.

To deny that the modern nation of Israel is a fulfillment of God's promises to regather His people from around the world is to deny God's very nature and character. It would be like saying that God has promised us "temporary" eternal life.

In Romans 11:1, Paul proclaimed, "Has God cast away His people? Certainly not! For I also am an Israelite, of the seed of Abraham, of the tribe of Benjamin." Paul's point was that if God had cast off His people, then why were some of them getting saved? Paul pointed to himself as an example. Does it make any sense for God to cast you off, then save you? Certainly not!

First Corinthians 11:25 says, "In the same manner [Jesus] also took the cup after supper, saying, 'This cup is the new covenant in My blood. This do, as often as you drink it, in remembrance of Me.'" The old covenant was a blood covenant, but the blood of bulls and goats could never take away sins. Hebrews says better blood was required for that to happen. So through the Jews, God sent His Son into the world to shed His better blood (Hebrews 12:24) on behalf of sinners.

The old covenant highlighted the sinfulness of all people, and the new covenant made possible what the old could not do: save people's souls through the blood of Christ.

DAY 353

THE LIGHT OF THE WORLD

In Genesis 1, we read the creation narrative, and verse 2 says, "The earth was without form, and void; and darkness was on the face of the deep." In this setting, the first thing God spoke into existence was the adversary of darkness, which is light: "Then God said, 'Let there be light'; and there was light" (verse 3).

This is a great reminder for all of us that our lives were "without form, and void" until the Light of the world, in the person of Jesus Christ, came into our lives. Where the darkness of unrighteousness once ruled, the light of Christ now reigns. The impure wisdom of the world that once guided us has been replaced by the pure wisdom from above, which now directs our path.

In Matthew 5:14-16, Jesus tells us how this change should affect us. We have been given a responsibility:

> You are the light of the world. A city that is set on a hill cannot be hidden. Nor do they light a lamp and put it under a basket, but on a lampstand, and it gives light to all who are in the house. Let your light so shine before men, that they may see your good works and glorify your Father in heaven.

Jesus is no longer physically present in this world, and He has commissioned us, as His friends, to take up the role as truth bearers and proclaimers of righteousness who walk in the pure wisdom of the Word.

The pictures of a light on a hill and on a lampstand in a home give us the scope of our responsibility to be light. In the world and at home, truth is to reign in our lives, and it is not to be hidden or covered in any circumstance.

DAY 354

THE HOLY ONE OF ISRAEL

In Romans 15:4, Paul communicated this important truth to us: "Whatever things were written before were written for our learning, that we through the patience and comfort of the Scriptures might have hope."

Here, Paul is referring to the Old Testament. That's where God gave His people many details about the coming Holy One of Israel. He did this to give them an immoveable hope even in the times when hope was a rare and precious commodity. In this way, God's Word brought patience and comfort.

The wonderful messianic title the Holy One of Israel is rich with reminders about His character, including the fact that the Lord is the same yesterday, today, and forever. That means He is still the Holy One of Israel, and thus, there must exist an ongoing relationship with the Jews, or Israel. As Paul said in Romans 9:1-5,

> I tell the truth in Christ, I am not lying, my conscience also bearing me witness in the Holy Spirit, that I have great sorrow and continual grief in my heart. For I could wish that I myself were accursed from Christ for my brethren, my countrymen according to the flesh, who are Israelites, to whom pertain the adoption, the glory, the covenants, the giving of the law, the service of God, and the promises; of whom are the fathers and from whom, according to the flesh, Christ came, who is over all, the eternally blessed God. Amen.

If God has cast off Israel, then Paul wrote those words in the flesh and not the Spirit. But the Holy One of Israel is still the Holy One of Israel. He is also the head of the church. Oh, that we would have a passion to see our friends, neighbors, and even enemies come to the light and thus know the truth.

We would do well to pray that God break our hearts for the lost to the degree that we would do anything to reach them with the truth.

DAY 355

LIVING PROOF

One of the primary arguments atheists give for denying God exists is a supposed lack of evidence. Yet the Bible tells us there is evidence all around us, and there is ample evidence within its pages to tell us there is someone who dwells outside of time who is all-powerful and can answer the big questions of life.

Philosophers pose four kinds of questions regarding life that they say demand an answer: origin, meaning, morality, and destiny: Where did we come from? What is the purpose of life? Is there a single moral standard for all people? What happens after we die? The Bible answers these questions not with theories and speculations, but with empirical evidence and facts that can be observed by anyone at any given point in history.

Romans 1:20 says, "Since the creation of the world His invisible attributes are clearly seen, being understood by the things that are made, even His eternal power and Godhead, so that they are without excuse."

The truth is that on the elusive matter of origin, evolutionary biologists admit they cannot explain, with facts and observable evidence, how life occurred. Yet these facts are clearly presented in Genesis and are consistent with what we observe in our world today. There is a night-day cycle that repeats itself every 24 hours; there are still two great lights in the sky, one lesser and one greater (the moon and the sun); the animal kingdom is still procreating "after its kind"; the seas are still divided from the dry land; and contrary to what we hear today, there are still two genders, male and female. All that is recorded for us in the first two chapters of Genesis and is consistent with what we see today.

Many people today make the demand that God show Himself and prove His existence, saying that only then will they believe. That demand has already been met—God came in human flesh and offered Himself as living proof of the existence of a God capable of creating all things.

DAY 356

JESUS IS THE MESSIAH

The leading Jews of Jesus' day—the scribes and Pharisees—were constantly questioning Jesus about His right to do the things He did, and by what power. He said His authority came from

> the Father Himself, who sent Me, [and] has testified of Me. You have neither heard His voice at any time, nor seen His form. But you do not have His word abiding in you, because whom He sent, Him you do not believe. You search the Scriptures, for in them you think you have eternal life; and these are they which testify of Me. But you are not willing to come to Me that you may have life (John 5:37-40).

The truth is that whether you search the Old Testament or the New, you are going to find empirical evidence that Jesus is the Christ, the Son of the living God. He was born of a virgin (Isaiah 7:14) in Bethlehem (Micah 5:2), called out of Egypt (Hosea 11:1), despised and rejected by men (Isaiah 53:3), and rode into Jerusalem on a donkey (Zechariah 9:9). His hands and feet were pierced, and His garments were divided by those who cast lots for them (Psalm 22:16-18). He was killed for the sake of others (Daniel 9:26), buried among the rich at His death (Isaiah 53:9), and His death led to the justification of others (Isaiah 53:11). The list of prophecies that were written hundreds of years before they were fulfilled goes on and on.

Nicodemus, whom Jesus referred to as "the teacher of Israel" (John 3:10), recognized that Jesus was no ordinary man: "There was a man of the Pharisees named Nicodemus, a ruler of the Jews. This man came to Jesus by night and said to Him, 'Rabbi, we know that You are a teacher come from God; for no one can do these signs that You do unless God is with him'" (John 3:1-2).

Jesus, through countless miracles and more, proved beyond question that He was and is the Messiah of Israel, the Savior of the world.

DAY 357

MIRACULOUSLY PRESERVED

The dangers of adding to, disparaging, or denying the Word of God as truth are many, and thus undermining Scripture is a favored tactic of our adversary, the devil. He is still using this tactic today, and sadly, one way we see this manifest is in the teachings of pastors who classify the Old Testament as "old news" instead of as the very foundation of the "good news" of Jesus Christ.

Romans 15:4 tells us that "whatever things were written before were written for our learning, that we through the patience and comfort of the Scriptures might have hope." The things "written before" are what we find recorded in the Old Testament. Paul said that in them we find comfort and hope—two things that are exclusive to knowing Jesus Christ.

Without a study of the Old Testament, we would not have the comfort of knowing that Jesus Christ is undeniably the Messiah. We would not know of the evidence that points to this: He was born of a virgin, in Bethlehem, from the tribe of Judah, called out of Egypt, only to be despised and rejected, beaten with stripes, and remained silent before His oppressors before He was killed among the wicked, then buried among the rich.

Prophetically, we would not know of God's promise to regather the children of Israel into the land of promise. We would not know of God's declaration that He would revitalize the long-barren land. We would not know that Israel will stand alone against the world, or that a coalition of nations will come out of the north to attack Israel, only to meet their demise on the mountains of Israel. Without the Old Testament, we would not know many of the characteristics of the man we call the Antichrist, or that he will make a covenant with Israel for seven years and break it at the halfway point.

God has miraculously preserved His unchanging Word so that we can know it is as relevant today as when it was written.

DAY 358

THE SIGNS OF HIS COMING

In Matthew 24, the disciples asked Jesus about the signs of His coming and the end of the age. Within His answer, Jesus said, "Of that day and hour no one knows" (verse 36). Yet even though the day and hour are unknowable, Jesus described, in direct and implied ways, the many signs that will indicate His return is near. The fact we will know when the day is near is the reason Hebrews 10:24-25 can tell us,

> Let us consider one another in order to stir up love and good works, not forsaking the assembling of ourselves together, as is the manner of some, but exhorting one another, and so much the more as you see the Day approaching.

"The Day" here is the Day of the Lord, also known as the great tribulation or the seventieth week of Daniel. It is possible for us to see the signs of the coming tribulation without infringing on the unknown day and hour.

For example, we would expect to see technology capable of monitoring global commerce. We would expect to see a polarized world in which people are willing to use violence to further or defend their agenda and aspirations. We would expect to see globalism on the rise and a communistic mentality becoming more widespread among people.

We would also expect to see apostasy on the rise in the church and lawlessness abounding in the world. And in light of what is now present and visible, we can know that Jesus' coming for the church, which will allow the lawless one to be revealed, is closer than the tribulation that follows it.

As Romans 13:12 says, "The night is far spent, the day is at hand. Therefore let us cast off the works of darkness, and let us put on the armor of light."

Even so, come, Lord Jesus!

DAY 359

JACOB'S TROUBLE

Zechariah 12:1-3 reveals this about the end times:

> Thus says the LORD, who stretches out the heavens, lays the foundation of the earth, and forms the spirit of man within him: "Behold, I will make Jerusalem a cup of drunkenness to all the surrounding peoples, when they lay siege against Judah and Jerusalem. And it shall happen in that day that I will make Jerusalem a very heavy stone for all peoples; all who would heave it away will surely be cut in pieces, though all nations of the earth are gathered against it."

Zechariah chapters 12–14 refer to the time of Jacob's trouble, when God finalizes His discipline of Israel. Obviously, Israel has to exist and be in possession of Jerusalem for the city to become a "very heavy stone for all peoples" and for all the nations of the earth to gather against it.

As the world moves in that direction, we need to recognize that the end purpose of the time of Jacob's trouble is the salvation of the Jews: "I will return again to My place till they acknowledge their offense. Then they will seek My face; in their affliction they will earnestly seek Me" (Hosea 5:15).

After the seal, trumpet, and bowl judgments, followed by the return of Christ with the church (Revelation 19:11-16), the salvation of the Jews will take place: "I will pour on the house of David and on the inhabitants of Jerusalem the Spirit of grace and supplication; then they will look on Me whom they pierced. Yes, they will mourn for Him as one mourns for his only son, and grieve for Him as one grieves for a firstborn" (Zechariah 12:10).

Many Jews have yet to turn to Yeshua. But October 7, 2023, brought about an interest in spiritual things in Israel. Someday, the people will see that the Holy One of Israel is indeed Jesus of Nazareth, the One whom they pierced.

DAY 360

WORDS AND THOUGHTS MATTER

At a time when it seems that for many, acceptance and tolerance have replaced reverence and holiness, we need to remember what the Word of God has to say about such things: "Let no corrupt word proceed out of your mouth, but what is good for necessary edification, that it may impart grace to the hearers" (Ephesians 4:29).

Note that speaking and hearing are both mentioned in this passage about the words that come from our mouths. The things that are said and heard by the body of Christ are to be absent of corruption. The word "corrupt" in this passage means "rotten, morally worthless, putrefied, or unfit for use." This last definition tells us there are things that should not come from our mouths or enter our ears, for they are unfit to say or hear.

While it is true there are some words we hear that are outside of our control, that is not what this verse is talking about. Paul is addressing things within our control—things that are not fit for us to say or hear, or to engage in.

In Psalm 19:14, David wrote, "Let the words of my mouth and the meditation of my heart be acceptable in Your sight, O Lord, my strength and my Redeemer."

While many would argue today that cuss words or dirty jokes are just words, King David clearly stated that our words are to be of an acceptable nature to the Lord. This is important because it highlights the fact that the words that exit our mouths come from the heart.

In Philippians 4:8, we are told, "Brethren, whatever things are true, whatever things are noble, whatever things are just, whatever things are pure, whatever things are lovely, whatever things are of good report, if there is any virtue and if there is anything praiseworthy—meditate on these things."

Meditating on these things will have a definite impact on what comes from our mouths!

DAY 361

RIGHTEOUS INDIGNATION

Today, lies are promoted and protected as truth, fictional ideas are presented as fact, and good and evil have exchanged definitions. There is much that happens that can give us reason to be frustrated or angry. Which is why it is so important for us to heed the instructions in James 1:19-20: "My beloved brethren, let every man be swift to hear, slow to speak, slow to wrath; for the wrath of man does not produce the righteousness of God."

Our wrath does not always manifest God's righteousness. Often, it manifests our flesh. There are times when righteous anger is justified, as when Jesus overturned the tables of the money changers and merchandisers. But we also have to remember what He was so angry about.

> Jesus went into the temple of God and drove out all those who bought and sold in the temple, and overturned the tables of the money changers and the seats of those who sold doves. And He said to them, "It is written, 'My house shall be called a house of prayer,' but you have made it a 'den of thieves'" (Matthew 21:12-13).

Jesus wasn't angry over Roman taxation. He said, "Render therefore to Caesar the things that are Caesar's, and to God the things that are God's" (Matthew 22:21). Jesus did not rage over Judas's betrayal; He called him friend even though He said he was a devil. What Jesus did become angry about was the way His Father was misrepresented to the world, and the turning of the Father's house into a den of thieves.

Yes, our world is a mess. Yes, it is upsetting, and yes, the world hates us and says all manner of evil against us falsely for His name's sake. However, it is His name and His church and His Word that should be our primary concern.

As Paul said, there are times to be angry, but in those times, we should not sin (Ephesians 4:26). Jesus showed righteous anger for the right reasons, and so should we.

DAY 362

PERFECT PEACE

Many people today have a negative perception of Christianity. In their minds, they see it as a list of "thou shalt nots," and therefore, restrictive to pursuing their desired behaviors. Peter even made this observation about how others view us as followers of Christ: "In regard to these, they think it strange that you do not run with them in the same flood of dissipation, speaking evil of you" (1 Peter 4:4).

The word "dissipation" means "unsavedness." In other words, the world thinks it is strange when we don't do what they do, and as a result, they will call us evil. Think about how this applies today. For example, a pro-life group is viewed as a threat to women's health when the pro-choice crowd is actually the guilty party with regard to that accusation. And those who believe in the sanctity of marriage according to the biblical definition of marriage are viewed as bigots and haters.

We are viewed by many as narrow-minded fools bound by the contents of an allegedly fictional book authored by a nonexistent God. But the opposite is true: We are not bound; we are free indeed. And the Bible is the supreme source of truth from the one true God.

Isaiah 26:3 affirms the freedom we know: "You will keep him in perfect peace, whose mind is stayed on You, because he trusts in You." Philippians 4:6-7 does as well: "Be anxious for nothing, but in everything by prayer and supplication, with thanksgiving, let your requests be made known to God; and the peace of God, which surpasses all understanding, will guard your hearts and minds through Christ Jesus."

The world may view us as living under the bondage of rules and restrictions, but the truth is that we are the freest people on Earth. We are free from living in opposition to God, and from living under the anxieties created by the perilous times in which we now live. We are so free from these things that as a result, we experience a peace that the world cannot understand.

DAY 363

DO NOT BE WISE IN YOUR OWN OPINION

Today, many world leaders operate under delusion instead of reality. Thankfully, we have a source of wisdom that can help keep us from falling prey to their opinions. "When Jesus had ended these sayings…the people were astonished at His teaching, for He taught them as one having authority, and not as the scribes" (Matthew 7:28-29).

Here, the word "sayings" refers to what Jesus taught in the Sermon on the Mount. His teachings were different from that of the scribes because He spoke with authority, not simply repeating what others had already said about the Scriptures, which was the method of the scribes.

This is what we are dealing with today—the repeating of narratives based on what a few supposedly great minds think about how the world should function. The problem is the source of their "wisdom." As James 3:13-17 points out:

> Who is wise and understanding among you? Let him show by good conduct that his works are done in the meekness of wisdom. But if you have bitter envy and self-seeking in your hearts, do not boast and lie against the truth. This wisdom does not descend from above, but is earthly, sensual, demonic. For where envy and self-seeking exist, confusion and every evil thing are there. But the wisdom that is from above is first pure, then peaceable, gentle, willing to yield, full of mercy and good fruits, without partiality and without hypocrisy.

Our world is filled with delusional thinking because so many people have no fear of the Lord. Thus, their wisdom is earthly, sensual, and demonic. In contrast, our wisdom as believers "is from above"—from the One who truly does know everything.

"Do you see a man wise in his own eyes? There is more hope for a fool than for him" (Proverbs 26:12).

DAY 364

OUR GOOD, GOOD FATHER

All through the Bible, we can learn about the character and attributes of God by observing His interactions with Israel. Consider the parallels between Israel and the prodigal son. After falling on hard times, the son finally came to his senses—as the Jews will someday—and this happened:

> He arose and came to his father. But when he was still a great way off, his father saw him and had compassion, and ran and fell on his neck and kissed him. And the son said to him, "Father, I have sinned against heaven and in your sight, and am no longer worthy to be called your son." But the father said to his servants, "Bring out the best robe and put it on him, and put a ring on his hand and sandals on his feet. And bring the fatted calf here and kill it, and let us eat and be merry; for this my son was dead and is alive again; he was lost and is found." And they began to be merry (Luke 15:20-24).

Like the returning prodigal, Israel is spiritually "still a great way off." Yet God has brought His people back to their land, and the land has flourished for them and is now teeming with life! Not because of them, but because of Him.

This is one of the few things that both Israel and the church will be present to witness as God fulfills His promises to His chosen people. We have been watching the Jews return to their covenanted homeland over the past 120-plus years after having been scattered among the nations for nearly two millennia. Yet in spite of their prodigal son-like rebellion, God has thrown them a welcome-home party and, figuratively speaking, killed the fatted calf.

How so? Israel enjoys a booming economy, a powerful military, unparalleled technology, and cutting-edge medical advances that have benefited people all over the world.

DAY 365

COME LET US WORSHIP AND BOW DOWN

Life is full of choices, some more significant than others, but all of us make choices every day. We choose what to eat, where to vacation, and what career path to take. We choose where to live and what activities to participate in. Some choices have a short-term impact, while others are more long-term, perhaps even a lifetime.

Joshua 24:15 speaks to one of the most important choices of all:

> Choose for yourselves this day whom you will serve, whether the gods which your fathers served that were on the other side of the River, or the gods of the Amorites, in whose land you dwell. But as for me and my house, we will serve the LORD.

Jesus said in Matthew 12:30 that a person is either for Him or against Him. Similarly, Joshua's statement tells us that we are either serving God or serving other gods. These choices are distinct from all others because of their significance. They aren't like choosing a meal or where to vacation. Rather, they involve choosing where we will spend eternity.

When we've made that most important of all choices to be for the Lord, that affects all the other choices we make every day, including the choice to worship God in spirit and truth.

The Greek word for "worship" literally means "to kiss the hand." The idea conveyed here is the acknowledgment of the superiority of another. It is not the act of kissing the hand itself that carries the full meaning, but rather, the posture necessary to do so. The word also means "to prostrate in homage or submission." Oftentimes when we hear the term *worship*, we think of singing songs in church before a sermon. But the true meaning of worship is to live prostrated before and in submission to God—a choice we must make every day.

NOTES

1. Danny McLoughlin, "32 Bible Statistics [2023]," WordsRated, February 2, 2022, https://wordsrated.com/bible-sales-statistics/.
2. "Religion," https://www.dictionary.com/browse/religion.
3. Karl Marx, 1843, as cited in "Introduction," *A Contribution to the Critique of Hegel's Philosophy of Right*, trans. A. Jolin and J. O'Malley, ed. J. O'Malley (Cambridge: Cambridge University Press, 1970).
4. This statement is widely attributed to J. Vernon McGee, but its original source is unknown.
5. "State of American Theology," Lifeway Research, 2022.
6. This quote is widely attributed to Abraham Lincoln, but its original source is unknown.
7. "What percentage of Christians believe in the rapture event?," Quora, https://www.quora.com/What-percentage-of-Christians-believe-in-the-Rapture-event.
8. Jim Cymbala, "Catching Fire," sermonindex.net, https://www.sermonindex.net/modules/newbb/viewtopic.php?topic_id=50748&forum=45.
9. "Religiously Unaffiliated," Pew Research Center, December 18, 2012, https://www.pewresearch.org/religion/2012/12/18/global-religious-landscape-unaffiliated/.
10. This quote is widely attributed to Corrie ten Boom, but the source in which it appears is unknown.
11. "Religion," Oxford Languages, https://www.google.com/url?sa=t&source=web&rct=j&opi=89978449&url=https://languages.oup.com/google-dictionary-en&ved=2ahUKEwj8jvPHqvaNAxU3l4kEHfNpD30QvecEegQIGhAJ&usg=AOvVaw3kNBXVjbAIAFeyFQVCJmJF.
12. "The contents of Magna Carta, *UK Parliament*, https://www.parliament.uk/about/living-heritage/evolutionofparliament/originsofparliament/birthofparliament/overview/magnacarta/magnacartaclauses/.

AMIR TSARFATI AND BARRY STAGNER

BIBLE PROPHECY: The ESSENTIALS

ANSWERS TO YOUR MOST COMMON QUESTIONS

AMIR TSARFATI & BARRY STAGNER

In *Bible Prophecy: The Essentials*, Amir and Barry team up to answer 70 of their most commonly asked questions, which focus on seven foundational themes of Bible prophecy: Israel, the church, the rapture, the tribulation, the millennium, the Great White Throne judgment, and heaven.

ALSO BY BARRY STAGNER

THE TIME OF THE SIGNS

Foreword by Amir Tsarfati

A Chronology of Earth's Final Events

BARRY STAGNER

Bestselling Coauthor of *Bible Prophecy: The Essentials*

When the disciples asked Jesus how to anticipate His return, He gave a remarkably detailed answer. As you study the signs Jesus pointed to, you'll see amazing evidence that we are living in the very time of these signs—and gain a clear understanding of what will happen, and when.

ALSO BY AMIR TSARFATI

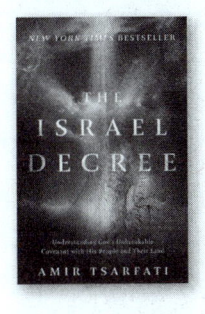

A *New York Times* bestseller, *The Israel Decree* traces the legal and prophetic history of present-day Israel, showing its connection to the ancient nation, and equips all Christians to understand Israel's significance today and embrace their role in God's unfolding plan.

While the book of Ezekiel was written to the Jews, its prophetic words reveal a strong message of hope for all believers. Discover the peace of knowing that in all situations, God is truly Lord over all.

This companion workbook to *Exploring Ezekiel* invites you to explore the themes of God's authority and faithfulness in greater detail and equips you to remain faithful until the end.

Bestselling author Amir Tsarfati reveals how Daniel's prophecies—and his unwavering faith amid a contentious culture—provide vital insights for living out these last days with hope and wisdom.

The *Discovering Daniel Workbook* will help you apply the remarkable insights of Daniel to your daily life, emboldening you to live with hope and confidence.

Amir Tsarfati, with Dr. Rick Yohn, examines what Revelation makes known about the end times and beyond. Guided by accessible teaching that lets Scripture speak for itself, you'll see what lies ahead for every person in the end times—either in heaven or on earth. Are *you* ready?

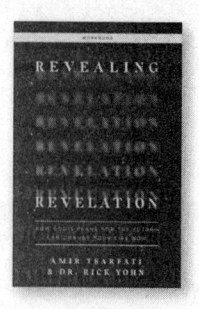

This companion workbook to *Revealing Revelation*—the product of many years of careful research—offers you a clear and exciting overview of God's perfect plan for the future. Inside you'll find principles from the Bible that equip you to better interpret the end-times signs, as well as insights about how Bible prophecy is relevant to your life today.

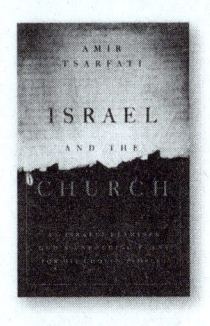

In *Israel and the Church*, bestselling author and native Israeli Amir Tsarfati helps readers recognize the distinct contemporary and future roles of both the Jewish people and the church, and how together they reveal the character of God and His perfect plan of salvation.

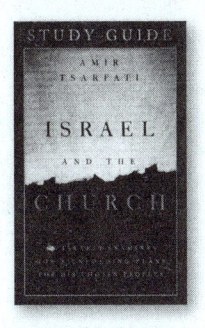

To fully grasp what God has in store for the future, it's vital to understand His promises to Israel. The *Israel and the Church Study Guide* will help you do exactly that, equipping you to explore the Bible's many revelations about what is yet to come.

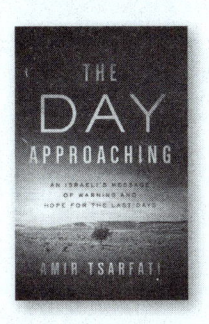

As a native Israeli of Jewish roots, Amir Tsarfati provides a distinct perspective that weaves biblical history, current events, and Bible prophecy together to shine light on the mysteries about the end times. In *The Day Approaching*, he points to the scriptural evidence that the return of the Lord is imminent.

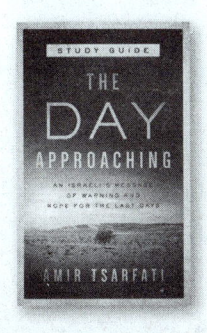

Jesus Himself revealed the signs that will alert us to the nearness of His return. In *The Day Approaching Study Guide*, you'll have the opportunity to take an up-close look at what those signs are, as well as God's overarching plans for the future, and how those plans affect you today.

Bestselling author and native Israeli Amir Tsarfati provides clarity on what will happen during the tribulation and explains its place in God's timeline.

With this study guide companion to *Has the Tribulation Begun?*, bestselling author and prophecy expert Amir Tsarfati guides you through a biblical overview of the last days, with thought-provoking study and application questions.

AMIR TSARFATI AND STEVE YOHN

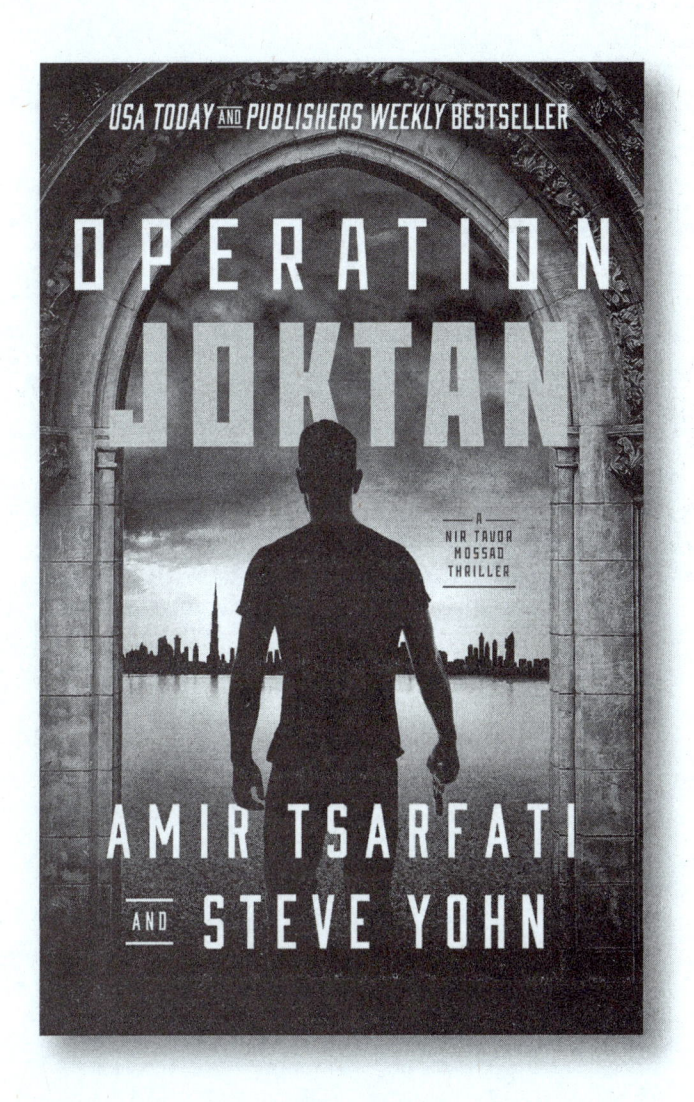

Book 1

In this first book in the Nir Tavor Mossad Thriller series, authors Amir Tsarfati and Steve Yohn draw on true events as well as tactical insights Amir learned from his time in the Israel Defense Forces. For believers in God's life-changing promises, *Operation Joktan* is a suspense-filled page-turner that illuminates the blessing Israel is to the world.

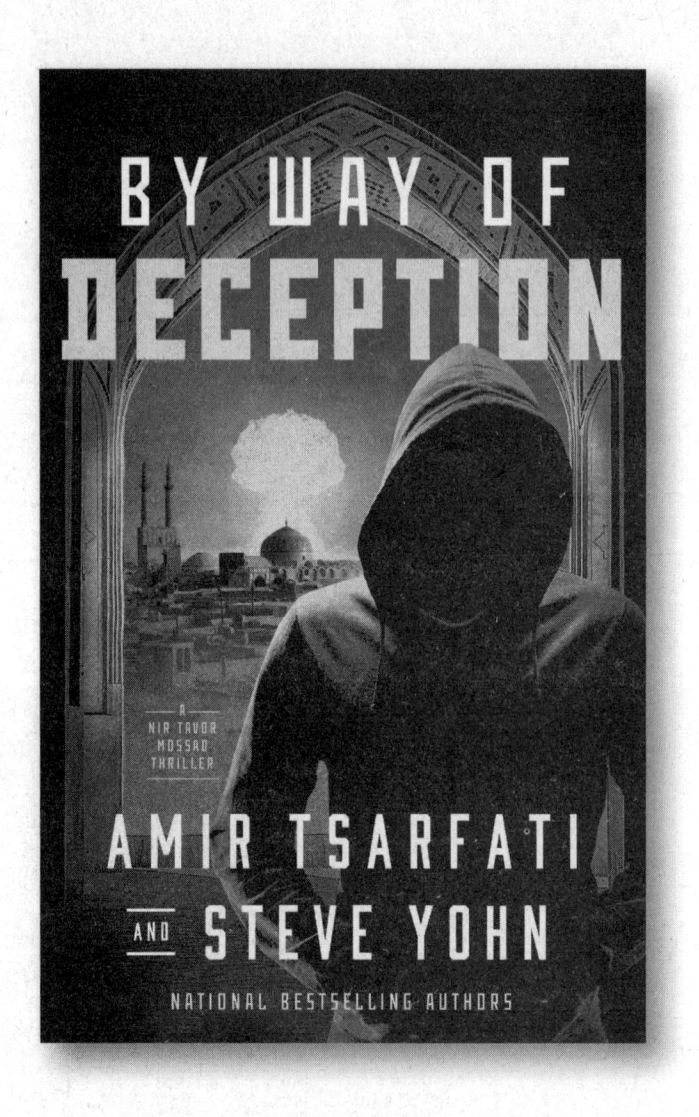

Book 2

Inspired by real events, authors Amir Tsarfati and Steve Yohn reteam for this suspenseful follow-up to the bestselling *Operation Joktan*. Filled with danger, romance, and international intrigue, this Nir Tavor thriller reveals breathtaking true insights into the lives and duties of Mossad agents—and delivers a story that will have you on the edge of your seat.

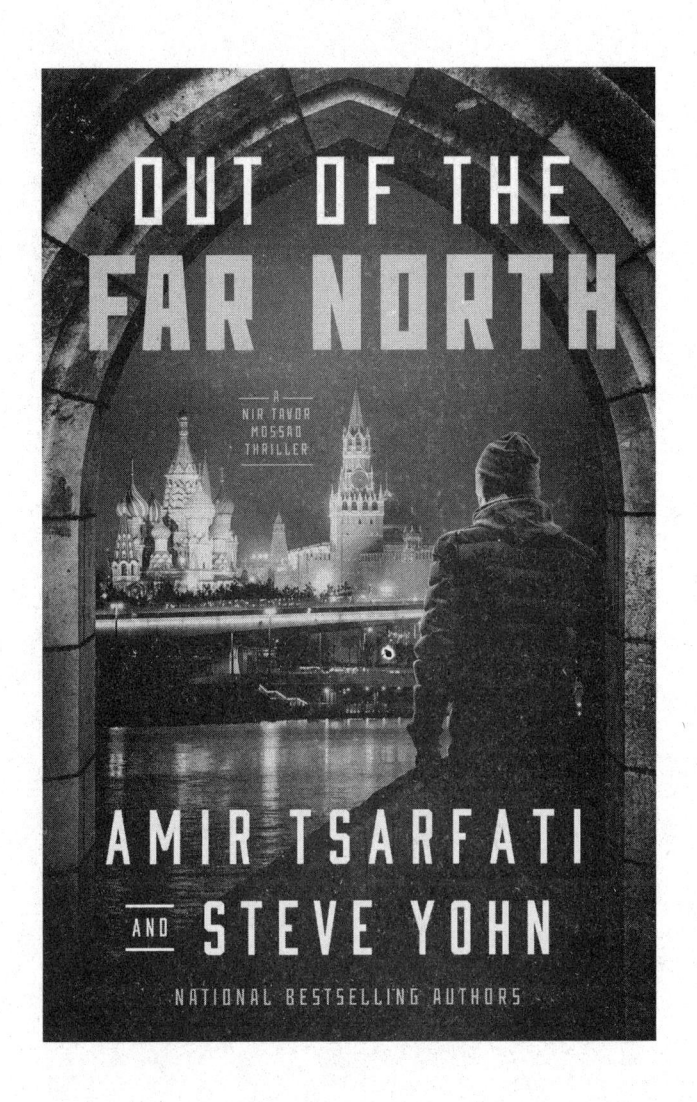

Book 3

Israel discovers that Russia is secretly planning an attack against it—but has no idea when and how. In the race to prevent a devastating conflict, will Mossad agents Nir Tavor and Nicole le Roux be able to outwit their enemies—or will their actions have catastrophic consequences?

Book 4

With Israel's energy future at stake and deadly adversaries uniting against the country, Nir and his team face their most dangerous battle for survival against forces determined to see the Jewish nation fall.

BEHOLD ISRAEL

Behold Israel is a nonprofit organization founded and led by native Israeli Amir Tsarfati. Its mission is to provide reliable and accurate reporting on developments in Israel and the surrounding region.

Through Behold Israel's website, free app, social media, and teachings in multiple languages, the ministry reaches communities worldwide.

Amir's on-location teachings explain Israel's central role in the Bible and present the truth about current events amidst global media bias against Israel.

FOLLOW US ON SOCIAL

@beholdisrael

BEHOLDISRAEL.ORG

To learn more about our Harvest Prophecy resources, please visit:

www.HarvestProphecyHQ.com

HARVEST PROPHECY
An Imprint of Harvest House Publishers